Eng...
Reading, Writing, and Interpreting Texts

English Studies

Reading, Writing, and Interpreting Texts

FIRST EDITION

Toby Fulwiler
William A. Stephany

McGraw Hill

Boston   Burr Ridge, IL   Dubuque, IA   Madison, WI   New York
San Francisco   St. Louis   Bangkok   Bogotá   Caracas   Kuala Lumpur
Lisbon   London   Madrid   Mexico City   Milan   Montreal   New Delhi
Santiago   Seoul   Singapore   Sydney   Taipei   Toronto

McGraw-Hill Higher Education

*A Division of The **McGraw-Hill** Companies*

ENGLISH STUDIES: READING, WRITING, AND INTERPRETING TEXTS
Published by McGraw-Hill, an imprint of The McGraw-Hill Companies, Inc. 1221 Avenue of the Americas, New York, NY, 10020. Copyright © 2002 by The McGraw-Hill Companies, Inc. All rights reserved. No part of this publication may be reproduced or distributed in any form or by any means, or stored in a database or retrieval system, without the prior written consent of The McGraw-Hill Companies, Inc., including, but not limited to, in any network or other electronic storage or transmission, or broadcast for distance learning.

Some ancillaries, including electronic and print components, may not be available to customers outside the United States.

This book is printed on acid-free paper.

1 2 3 4 5 6 7 8 9 0 FGR/FGR 0 9 8 7 6 5 4 3 2 1

ISBN   0-07-244442-8

Editorial director: *Phillip A. Butcher*
Executive editor: *Sarah Touborg*
Editorial assistant: *Anne Stameshkin*
Senior marketing manager: *David Patterson*
Associate project manager: *Catherine R. Schultz*
Production supervisor: *Gina Hangos*
Senior designer: *Jenny El-Shamy*
Photo research coordinator: *David A. Tietz*
Cover design: *Jamie O'Neal*
Interior design: *Artemio Ortiz*
Typeface: *10/12 Palatino*
Compositor: *Electronic Publishing Services Inc., NY*
Printer: *Quebecor World Fairfield Inc.*

Library of Congress Cataloging-in-Publication Data

Fulwiler, Toby 1942–
    English studies: reading, writing, and interpreting texts / Toby Fulwiler, William A. Stephany.—1st ed.
        p. cm.
    Includes bibliographical references and index.
    ISBN 0-07-244442-8 (acid-free paper)
    1.English philology—Study and teaching. 2. English literature—History and criticism—Theory, etc. 3. English language—Rhetoric—Study and teaching. 4. Reading (Higher education) I. Stephany, William A. II. Title.

PE65 F85 2002
808—dc21
                                        2001051414

www.mhhe.com

To all of our students, past and present, at the University of Vermont who make English Studies the exciting place it is today.

Acknowledgements

The authors wish to thank the many people who helped write this book. Heading the list are our students at the University of Vermont whose writing and insights informed virtually every chapter in this book. Our McGraw-Hill editors, Sarah Touborg and Anne Stameshkin, provided encouragement, guidance, and critical suggestions throughout the two years it has taken to write and revise this text.

We would also like to thank the following reviewers for their contributions to the development of this book:

Robert Blake, Elon College
Alan Brown, University of West Alabama
Gina Claywell, Murray State University
Alys Culhane, Plymouth State College
Andrea DeFusco, Boston College
Richard Dietrich, University of South Florida
Gaye Elder, Abraham Baldwin Agricultural College
Christine Flanagan, Camden County College
Philip K. Jason, United States Naval Academy
Homer Kemp, Tennessee Technological University
Beth Kemper, Campbellsville University
Nancy McCabe, Presbyterian College
Richard McLamore, McMurry Univeristy
Robert S. Newman, State University of New York at Buffalo
Angela M. Salas, Adrian College
Margaret Waguespack, Amarillo College
Margaret Whitt, University of Denver

Contents

PREFACE   xiii

INTRODUCTION   TOBY FULWILER & WILLIAM A. STEPHANY   1

The Way You're Supposed to Read   2
Reading to Understand   3
The Field of English Studies   4

Part I
READING AS A WRITER

Chapter 1 Exploring with Journals **Toby Fulwiler**   13

Academic Journals   13
Personal Journals   14
Writing about Reading   15
Asking and Answering Questions   16
Seeing   17
Connecting and Extending   18
Surprising Yourself   18
Conversing   19
Suggestions for Journal Writing   19

Chapter 2 Exploring Fiction **Ghita Orth & Allen Shepherd**   21

Once upon a time...   21
The Nature of Fiction   21
Character   23
Plot   24
Point of View   25
Setting   27
Symbolism   28
Style   29
Theme   30

    Reading a Story   31
        Tea Leaves (Janet Burroway)   31
    What Makes Good Fiction Good?   34
    Works Cited   36

Chapter 3 Exploring Poetry **Sidney Poger**   38

        Coda (David Huddle)   38
    The Nature of Poetry   41
    The Techniques of Poetry   43
        Rhythm and Meter   43
        Rhyme   45
        Alliteration   46
        Imagery   47
        Comparison   47
        Diction   48
        Structure   49
        Point of View   50
    Responding to Poetry   52
    Works Cited   52

Chapter 4 Exploring Drama **James Howe**   54

    Drama as Performance   54
    Reading Drama   56
    Writing About Drama   57
        Writing about Character   57
    Examples of Character Interpretation   58
        Writing About Language   59
        Dramatic Conventions   61
    Metadrama   62
    Television and Film   64

Chapter 5 Exploring the Essay **Mary Jane Dickerson & Richard Sweterlitsch**   65

    The Essay as Conversation   66
    Conversations with the Self   66
    Conversations with Others   68
    Voices That Shape the Essay   70
        Voices of Meditation   71
        Voices of Response   73
        Voices of Dissent   74
        Voices of Explanation   75
        Voices of Storytelling   76
        Other Voices   78
    Finding Your Own Voice   78

Contents

Chapter 6 Exploring Visual Texts **Tom Simone** 80

Visual Texts 80
Narrative Film as an Extension of Literature 82
Beginning to Read a Visual Text 83
George Lucas's Star Wars 84
Mise en Scéne 85
The Single Shot 85
Theme, Image, and Symbol 86
Analyzing a Visual Text 88
Suggested Further Readings 89

Part II
READING AS EXPLORATION

Chapter 7 Why Study Literary Theory? **Lisa Schnell** 99

The English Major as Anthropologist? 99
Expanding Our Field of View 101
The Pleasure of the Text 103
The Moral Conversation 104
　Two Questions for Student Writing 106
Brief Annotated Bibilography 106

Chapter 8 Feminist Readings, Feminist Writing **Mary Louise Kete** 108

The Short Answer 108
The Long Answer 110
Suggested Further Readings 116

Chapter 9 Expanding the Canon: A Multicultural Perspective **Helen Scott** 117

Eurocentrism and the Canon 117
The "Culture Wars" 120
Postcolonial Literature 122
Towards a Global Culture 126
Works Cited 127
Recommended Reading 128

Chapter 10 A Reader's Response **Nancy Welch** 129

No Apology Necessary 129
Reader Response: An Overview 130
Reader Response in Action 134
So Where Does It All End? 136

Acknowledgment   137
Works Cited   137

Chapter 11 Reading Films as Acts of Reading **Andrew Barnaby**   **139**

Reading as a Writer, Writing as a Reader   139
Revisionary Reading and the Impulse to Film   141
A River Runs Through It   142
Listening and Seeing versus Reading   146
Final Thoughts   148
   Questions to Ask When Comparing Films to Books   148
Works Cited   149

Part III
WRITING AS A READER

Chapter 12 Writing Critical Essays **Sarah E. Turner**   **157**

Being Critical: Describe the Text   158
   My Life had stood-a Loaded Gun (Emily Dickinson)   159
Being Critical: Question the Text   159
Being Critical: "So What?"   161
Being Critical: Pulling It All Together   162
Establishing a Critical Dialogue   163
Suggestions for Writing Critical Essays   166
Works Cited   167

Chapter 13 Writing Personal Essays **Mary Jane Dickerson**   **168**

Creating a New Text   169
My Story   170
Personal Essays   171
   Autobiography   172
   Autobiographical Questionnaire   172
   Conversation   174
   Exploration   176
   Engaging the Creative Process   178
   Open-Ended   181
Works Cited   181

Chapter 14 Imaginative Writing and Risk Taking **William A. Stephany**   **183**

"Rules" for Risk Taking   184
   Read Carefully   185
   Maintain a Consistent Voice   185

Contents   **xi**

    Revise and Edit   186
  Creative Choices   186
    Imitation of Form: Close Parody   186
    More General Parodies   188
    Imitation of Modern Literary or Cultural Forms   189
    Changing the Form   190
    Rewriting the Ending   191
    Creating Dialogues   192
    Some Final Examples   192
  The Experimental Tradition   193
  Works Cited   194
    That Time of Year Thou Mayst In Me Behold (William Shakespeare)   187

Chapter 15 Writing with Research **Richard Sweterlitsch**   195

  Getting Started   197
  Gathering Information First-Hand   198
  Seeking Second-Hand Sources   202
  Pulling the Paper Together   204
  Giving Credit   206
  Published Works Cited   208

Chapter 16 A Web of One's Own **Katherine Anne Hoffman**   209

  Research   210
  Evaluating Internet Sources   212
  Writing and Composing   215
  Publishing   216

Chapter 17 Examining the Essay Examination **Tony Magistrale**   219

  Writing Under Pressure   220
  Preliminary Steps and a Checklist of Practical Advice   220
  Types of Information Requests   221
  Planning   222
  Structuring Essay Answers   225
  The Take-Home Examination   228
    Using Class Notes and Journals   229
    Revising and Editing   229
  Beginning at the End: Ending at the Beginning   229

APPENDIX MLA DOCUMENTATION GUIDELINES   231
  GLOSSARY   255
  INDEX   259
  MISSION STATEMENT McGraw-Hill English   267
  CONTRIBUTORS   269

Preface

We wrote English Studies to introduce approaches we consider basic to study in contemporary Departments of English. Students taking their first college course in English will find this book worthwhile. English majors will find it essential.

The field of English Studies is broad, diverse, and ever more complicated. It encompasses the creation, history, interpretation, and appreciation of the best writing in the English-speaking world. And the study of English also includes the writing we do ourselves as we attempt to compose, revise, edit, and craft our own language to understand meaning for ourselves and communicate it with others. Therefore, this text approaches English studies from three distinct, but interlocking perspectives. The first section, "Reading as a Writer" looks at the traditional literary genres of poetry, fiction, drama and essay to which we add film and visual media. The second section, "Reading as Exploration," examines several of the prevailing critical approaches that influence how we read, see, and perceive the meaning of texts. Finally, the third section, "Writing as a Reader," explores what might be called "student genres," those forms in which students are expected to express their ideas about the varied texts they read and interpret.

English Studies addresses the conventions of literary and visual media from the viewpoint of students who not only study texts created by others, but who compose texts themselves. We believe that the more students write about literary texts, the better they will understand and appreciate them. Conversely, the more they read for both enjoyment and critical consciousness, the better they will write.

How to Read this Book

We believe this book works well when read cover to cover. At the same time, we also believe it can be read selectively, in bits and pieces, as interest or assignments demand. To this end, each chapter is self-contained and does not depend on reading other chapters for complete comprehension. However, for students who are writing papers in specific courses, the most profitable way to read might be to mix and match chapters from parts One, Two, and Three as particular assignments demand. For example, were you interested in writing a critical essay about poetry from a feminist perspective, you might read Chapters 3 ("Exploring Poetry"), 8 ("Feminist Readings"), and 12 ("Writing Critical Essays"). If, instead, you wanted to write a parody about a film you had seen, you might read Chapter 6 ("Exploring Visual Texts") along with Chapter 14 ("Imaginative Writing and Risk Taking").

A few more suggestions: For a more complete understanding of why we put this book together as we did, the "Introduction" should help. For a quick overview of the contents of each section, read the Section Introductions. For an especially engaging overview to the difficult theoretical topics covered in Section Two, be sure to read Chapter 7, "Why Study Literary Theory." Finally, you may notice that the opening chapter in the book, "Exploring Journals," is technically out of place, as it belongs more properly among the student genres in Section Three. It is so placed because we believe that the personal, informal writing you do for yourself in a journal enhances your understanding of any and all the other topics and chapters covered in the text, regardless of instructor writing assignments.

INTRODUCTION

Toby Fulwiler and William A. Stephany

If you like to read and write, find these activities easy, and do them well, you'll have a good time in college English classes. As Chris, a sophomore in one of our classes, wrote in his journal: "When I'm in the right mood, and have the right book, it goes down like cream. In 11th grade, my English teacher told us to pretend to be the characters in the book. I made it through one of Russell Baker's stories being a paper boy." However, for many students, not all reading "goes down like cream." Bill, a freshman, explained his attitude this way: "I've never liked reading, especially textbook reading. I don't think I've ever read a book for pleasure except when I was younger.... If I read a book I like, I don't mind reading at all, but I guess that's kind of silly because nobody likes to read a book he doesn't like." Meanwhile, Julie, another sophomore, told us: "As far back as I can remember, I have always preferred reading to writing. I think it's because I always found reading easy—I could always sit down and just read for hours (if a book was interesting) without even being told."

When we asked students in this same class about writing, we found mixed opinions as well. Hollis, a junior, told us what many of our students said: "I like to write, but it's very difficult for me unless I like what I am writing about." Peter, a freshman, said he enjoyed writing except in the "college application mode. You know, 'What was your most rewarding nonacademic activity?' or 'Write an essay telling us something about yourself.' That's the kind of writing I can't deal with." Students usually like to write about subjects they choose and in forms with which they are familiar. No surprises here.

In other words, if you are like some of our students, you bring with you mixed emotions toward reading and writing about various kinds of literature. While most of you have positive experiences reading and writing in private, many of you have some negative experiences when one or the other is assigned in school. In the rest of this essay, we'd like to look more closely at reading and then at writing, and see if we can't make a sort of peace between our private needs as readers and writers and the more public demands of the academic community.

THE WAY YOU'RE SUPPOSED TO READ

The way you're *supposed* to read stories, poems, or plays in order to comprehend them fully—as you need to do in order to write essays and examinations about them or discuss them in class—goes something like this: You sit at your desk, text in front of you, notebook open, pen poised. As you read, you mark important passages in the text; you summarize main ideas and trace recurrent themes in your notebook. You look up in a dictionary, encyclopedia, or glossary all words, names, and ideas you do not understand. And if you are reading a novel or poem or play, you pay particular attention to certain technical elements of the text.

Susan, a seasoned student of literary study, describes the *shoulds* of literary reading this way: "I have learned that there are a lot of things to look for when I read. For example, who is narrating? Does the narrator change? What is the author's style? What is the point of view from which the story is told? When I read, however, I don't always like to look for these things. I just like to read for the sake of reading. I don't like to read into stories as much as my former professors have done." While Susan clearly knows *how* she's supposed to read and *what* she's supposed to look for, a part of her rebels and wants to read more intuitively or impressionistically, with less deliberately analytical attention than some of her teachers have insisted on.

College students are not alone in rebelling against the kind of academic toughness that good reading is supposed to entail. In fact, one of the contributing authors in this volume confessed in his journal:

> When I read strictly for myself, late at night in bed or through sunglasses on the beach, I violate most of the rules I learned about how to read well. When an image or incident triggers a memory, I let myself daydream and wander off with it. When I don't know what a word means, I skip it. When I find the plot slow moving, I skim until things pick up again. When I'm not in the mood for one book, I start another, and again another. Right now I'm reading about seven books, three magazines, and a couple of catalogues. I no longer consider it a moral obligation to start a book at the beginning, to avoid peeking at the end, or to finish it once started.
>
> To remember something that strikes me as especially interesting, I write a note in the margin, dog-ear a page, or sometimes read the passage out loud to my wife. But I seldom trace plot, character, theme, or symbol methodically from page to page, beginning to end. Often I am confident that I understand the meaning of what I've read—but am not always sure that I could write a coherent essay about it.

Don't misunderstand—we're not making fun of either approach to reading, the rigorously academic or the casually private. It is not our purpose in this book to give you either negative lessons or simplistic formulas about reading literature. We think that serious reading in the academic community is, in many important ways, quite compatible with private enjoyment—but some adjustments may be useful. Reading itself is a complex intellectual activity, governed by conventions but not reducible to foolproof rules. We read, in other words, as members of one or several communities with certain assumptions and expectations that inevitably influence our reading. We do this—consciously or unconsciously—whether we read on the beach or in the classroom.

READING TO UNDERSTAND

The authors of this book no longer believe that we, or anybody else for that matter, will ever perfectly understand the central meaning of the literature we read or the films we watch, no matter how well we prepare ourselves. Each reader brings to any reading a background unique socially, economically, religiously, politically, esthetically, and intellectually. In other words, our personal history, even our present mood, influences our responses, and so makes each reading to some significant extent our own.

A few simple examples will show what we mean. Last semester, when one of our classes read John Steinbeck's novel about dispossessed farmers, *The Grapes of Wrath,* one student saw reflected in the plight of Steinbeck's Okies her own family's difficulties holding onto their Vermont dairy farm. Another student, a practicing Christian, found meaning in the parallels and dissonances between the lives of several characters and the biblical accounts of Jesus's life. Which reading was "correct"? Both? Neither? An obviously unfair question. As these readers were responding to the words of *The Grapes of Wrath,* they were collaborating with Steinbeck in the creation of a text. We believe that in a very real sense any text is created anew—written if you like—by the reader.

Not only does each reader bring something different to a work, but each rereading is different. The second time around, we build on that initial reading, noticing things that escaped us earlier, seeing indications of what is to come, finding patterns impossible to discern the first time. Too, we have become different readers than we were before, and if months or years have passed, we may have changed so significantly that the work itself no longer is the same. In fact, when we reread, we usually find it easier to follow the rules of good reading because we know so much better what the work is about.

It is not restating the obvious to suggest that we read anything better when it is already familiar to us. Consequently, we cannot make sense of any text—literary, scientific, or otherwise—if we don't already know what most of the words, concepts, and formulas mean. Any literature is approachable only because it builds on what we already know. We can understand older characters such as Falstaff, Lady Macbeth, and King Lear because they have traits we have seen in people we already know. We understand younger characters such as Oliver Twist, Holden Caulfield, and Caddy Compson because we have felt some of what they feel. The trick for an author is to give us enough of what we already understand in order to lead us where we have no firsthand knowledge—be it medieval England, Victorian London, Pencey Prep, or a shabby household in Mississippi.

So, in a very real sense, when we read a poem, play, short story, or Web page—or watch a film—a part of what we read we already know. From that vantage of familiarity we view the rest, the unknown. Ideally, we can engage the piece on a personal, as well as an academic, level and so make it *our own*. If we cannot do this, cannot identify with the narrator, or some character or character trait, or some aspect of the situation, we may have difficulty enjoying the work or understanding it well enough to profit from it.

THE FIELD OF ENGLISH STUDIES

What constitutes "English" as a field of academic study has evolved and expanded in remarkable ways in recent years. Throughout the early decades of the twentieth century, as the name might imply, English departments taught English literature. By the middle of the twentieth century, English literature had often been renamed "British" literature, acknowledging the centrality to this tradition of texts by Irish writers, many of whom defined themselves in opposition to England and so would not wish to be considered "English." And by then, departments had also expanded to include programs in American literature (almost always), composition (especially at state colleges and universities), the structure and history of the English language (frequently), and (more rarely) history of ideas and history of criticism. But since the 1970s—and especially in the last two decades of the twentieth century—the field of English has embraced new ideas about what constitutes the literary canon, new definitions about the nature of texts, increased attention to the production as well as the consumption of texts, and a new focus on literary theory. Is it any wonder that students declaring English as a major are sometimes confused about just *what* comprises this field of concentration?

Depending on the college or university, your English department might include any number of what appear to be subdisciplines so that "English" has become an increasingly complicated major. For openers, the very notion of what constitutes a shared literary history has been brought into question. The old consensus—that we study the most important texts of the British and American traditions—has been undermined by the realization that those texts were, demographically speaking, suspiciously similar to each other: virtually all by white male writers who shared similar educational, social, and economic advantages. The old assumption that these texts had "stood the test of time," that they constituted the best of what "our" culture had produced, obscured the reality that the selection process inescapably mirrored the tastes, the cultural assumptions, the prior academic training of the white, male, financially secure professors who did the selecting. While their motives may not have been intentionally exclusionary, large groups of people—and their literary traditions—were in fact excluded from this list: women writers, nonwhite writers, writers from

England's former colonies, gay and lesbian writers, writers whose works are translated into English and not just from the languages of Western Europe. At present, writers from these disparate traditions have been added to general survey courses, and new courses have been developed to help define their alternative literary histories. In the process, we have come to a more complete sense of what constitutes *our* shared literary heritage, especially as it reflects and helps create a pluralistic culture such as that of North America.

In addition to the traditional literary *genres* of poetry, fiction, drama, and (more recently) nonfiction essays, English departments now often provide a home to the study of various aspects of contemporary culture including film, folklore, literary theory, and a wide variety of visual and electronic texts—in fact, any kind of "cultural product," not just those that emerge from "high culture," has become fair game as the notion of "text" has expanded to include any kind of communication or product that's open to verbal interpretation. True, in many institutions some of these subjects are taught in other departments—communication arts, film, theater, television, popular culture, ethnic and feminist studies, and so on—but it is no longer surprising to encounter any of them in a contemporary English department.

Throughout most of the past century the field of writing was divided between first-year composition for relatively inexperienced writers and far more specialized courses in imaginative writing—usually limited-enrollment classes in poetry and fiction writing. Today, writing courses include everything from creative writing to business and technical writing, from professional journalism to personal journal writing, from research writing to creative nonfiction, from literary analysis to memoir and autobiography.

English departments also increasingly encourage a multitude of theoretical approaches to and practical strategies for reading and writing literature (or for producing and interpreting signs). The sciences have long recognized that in an experimental setting, the questions asked and the processes used in large measure presuppose and restrict the conclusions you're able to draw about the material being studied. It's taken us a bit longer, but English studies has been coming to similar conclusions. The same text yields vastly different readings depending on whether the questions asked carry with them the attitudes of formalism or of deconstruction or of feminism or of psychological criticism. None of these and none of the other theoretical stances will provide the "right" way to read, but good readers are likely to recognize that the more strategies they become familiar with, the more complex will be the range of questions they can ask of, and the possible responses they can hope to receive from, a text.

This all means that English departments nowadays tend to be exciting, demanding, complex, and sometimes chaotic places in which to spend your intellectual energies. With their wide range of interests and interpretive strategies, they can sometimes feel more like an interdisciplinary program than a single discipline. True, in strong English departments, hard conceptual work is a given, but for those who like reading and writing and language and cultural analysis, our work is an ongoing intellectual pleasure. English majors often have a ball with their work.

English Studies is also extremely practical. English majors sometimes feel anxiety about justifying their choice to relatives, to friends, and others who ask: "But what can you do with it?" Because there's no profession (other than teaching) attached to the major, pursuing these interests can look (or feel) self-indulgent. But in truth, the study of English may be one of the best majors to equip people to cope with, understand, interpret, and critique a world in which information and communication change in ever-accelerating cycles. Language and story and promotion and visual data have become like the air we breathe, the media through which we navigate every day, as invisible to us as water is to the fish who daily swim in it. People who remain ignorant or unaware of this environment are easy prey to manipulation by language and by image: by ads, by political rhetoric, by mass media, by canned and commercial entertainment—prey not just to people and institutions with sinister intent, but prey to flabby thinking as well. As George Orwell argued half a century ago in "Politics and the English Language," sloppy writing is almost always a function of sloppy thinking, but without having oneself developed the habits of good writing and critical skills, it is often difficult to identify what's "wrong" with language or with a visual image or with an institution, all of which can coat prefabricated fluff with a veneer of self-importance. In other words, because English Studies examines the broadest range of human culture, it may be the most empowering of all academic disciplines, the one most likely to help you control language and image, rather than being their victim.

But English Studies is practical in a more down-to-earth way as well. English majors find ready employment not only in the expected fields of teaching, writing, editing, and publishing, but in every possible field, including scientific, technical, social, legal, and commercial enterprises in need of perceptive generalists to interpret the current culture and anticipate future trends. The intense focus on language skills—reading, writing, speaking, and listening—as well as on critical and creative thinking prove to be exactly the foundation on which many employers are looking to build as they develop future leaders.

This text has been co-written by a team of English instructors who have spent the past several years examining the central core of contemporary English Studies and, for purposes of this text, breaking it into three broad areas: The first section, "Reading as a Writer," examines approaches to most of the textual genres you're likely to encounter in any English Studies program: poetry, fiction, drama, the essay, and film. The second section, "Reading as Exploration," explains the role of theory as well as three approaches through which you're likely to examine the central texts of English Studies, namely postcolonial, feminist, and reader-response perspectives. The third section, "Writing as a Reader," suggests strategies for handling a wide variety of writing assignments you will undertake on your way to graduation, including critical, personal, and imaginative writing; researching; testing; and electronic publishing.

PART ONE

Reading as a Writer

Everyone who reads this book is a writer. Everyone who wrote this book is a reader. Of course. We have found that when you *read as a writer,* your relationship to the text changes. What do we mean *read as a writer?* Well, first, understand that you, we, and people like Flannery O'Connor don't come from three different planets. We all struggle to get control of an idea, to find the words that belong to that idea, and then to present that idea in those words intelligibly and, we hope, with a little grace. Those stories, poems, and plays in magazines and textbooks were written by human beings just like us. You've probably written a story or two, maybe some poetry, certainly a lot of papers. So have we. Realizing that published words were written by men and women pretty much like yourself may not be a great revelation, but it can change the way you read, the attention you pay to words and works, and, in turn, the way you actually write. Here's what we mean:

Humanity The visitor to William Faulkner's home in Oxford, Mississippi, will find on the desk in his study a blue and white plastic Vick's inhaler. The author of "Barn Burning" and *The Sound and the Fury* sometimes suffered from nasal congestion. To read as a writer, it helps to know that even the greatest authors are mortal—that they catch cold and that they were once students and apprentices as we are now.

Comparing notes, the authors of this volume find themselves well aware of their own failings and imperfections as writers. We know too well that nothing we write is ever perfect—yet we do write books and articles and get them published. So too, we reason, must the great writers often feel about the limits of their own powers. And this realization—like the Vick's inhaler—helps reduce those giants to human size. If you've ever seen an author's early manuscript drafts, you know of the professional's willingness to revise and edit. As a student of literature, eventually you come to understand that any text is a "made" object, that it didn't spring full-blown from the mind of God or the muse of poetry. There was never any inevitability about it. It was probably sweated over, rewritten, and discussed just as your best writing is, and the printed version we study may be the third or the thirtieth rewrite.

Questions   As writers ourselves, we've become aware that almost all written works originate as responses to certain questions or problems. Behind virtually everything we write is a question: Behind a shopping list is the question "What do we need at the store?" Behind a letter home is the question "How are you?" or "How am I?" Behind a laboratory report is the question "What happened?" Sometimes, of course, the piece of writing doesn't answer the question well, or tries to answer a group of questions all at once, or asks still more questions. However, looked at this way, most pieces of writing make more sense and seem more approachable and understandable.

Answers   When we write something ourselves, we struggle to answer a question or solve a problem. Of course, it doèsn't always work out the way we intend. But watching ourselves work helps us to understand the efforts of other writers. We've also learned where many of those structured answers come from—the writing itself. We've come to realize that the very act of composing is an answer-creating, problem-solving activity. Writers often discover their answers in the very process of asking their questions. More than one novelist has told about characters "taking over" and creating a new direction for the second half of a book.

How does this help you as a reader? It lets you know that if you want to figure out a particularly puzzling part of what you're reading, you too should write and see what solutions you discover. As readers, we are still writers. We can use writing to solve reading problems. Our experience as writers also tells us that there is usually more than one answer to any given question. The story that ends one way might have ended differently had the author been in another mood, place, or time. The modern sonnet might have been done in free verse. Hamlet might have survived Act V. Realizing this, the reader-as-writer knows that the author has made choices, that these choices produce certain effects, and that other choices might have been made and would have produced different effects.

Seeing Words   The writer's struggle to compose is frequently a struggle to find the right words. Sometimes they come, and just as often they don't. Consider the genius of those who bat better than .500. As a writer, you can appreciate the way a word just fits, seems to be the only word that will do. Sometimes when you recognize one of these words on the page, you get the feeling that you know how pleased the author must have been to find it. Walt Whitman's description of the live oak "solitary in a wide flat space, *uttering* joyous leaves all its life" and Emily Dickinson's "certain *slant* of light, winter afternoons" induce a little shiver of rightness. You'll have your own favorites, of course. When you read with an awareness of how you and other writers select words, you'll understand better the writer's craft.

Hearing Rhythms   In our own struggle to construct sentences and paragraphs that sound fluid to the ear, we appreciate better the same struggle in the writers we read. We notice constructions that work, that have a particular balance, that are deliberately parallel (as we are making this one), that see long sentences set off by short ones. As writers ourselves, we marvel at the apparent ease with which a Henry James or a Toni Morrison pulls these off. Of course, we never know for sure whether they rolled easily off the author's pen or whether he or she struggled as we so often do.

Tracing Themes   In our own writing, we search for just the right pattern or repetition or other signal to keep readers clearly on the track. We may rearrange sections to make this happen and feel good when it works out, especially in longer pieces in which holding parts together is especially difficult. Then when we become readers, we look harder to see how other authors accomplish the same thing. Sometimes, of course, the search is made more difficult because the theme is subtly embedded in the text, as it is in a James Joyce short story, for instance, where little seems to happen. So we learn to reread such texts to discover what else is there.

Understanding Metaphor and Symbol   If you've ever tried to use figurative language to express your meaning, you probably stand in awe of the great masters of imaginative literature. The judicious but occasionally outrageous use of metaphor and symbol is often what sets the great writers apart: Ezra Pound's likening of faces in a subway crowd to "petals on a wet, black bough;" Wordsworth's image of "life's star," the soul, "trailing clouds of glory."

Sometimes, too, great metaphors become great symbols, like Keats's "Grecian Urn," Thoreau's "Walden Pond," Melville's "Moby Dick," or Plath's "Bell Jar." As a writer reading, you can watch how any particular effect is created. Think of alternatives. Look for continuity and extension—how long can she get away with that? Where will she bring it in again? Of course, literary critics train themselves to look for these features. But when you come at the problem of creating workable metaphor and symbol as a writer yourself, you read with more empathy and understanding.

Noticing Starts, Stops, Transitions, and Conventions   The writer as reader is far more likely to notice how other writers handle even the elementary problems of composition. If you always have trouble with first lines in whatever you write, you're more likely to notice how published authors start their pieces. You may read with awe a line like "Call me Ishmael," and at other times wonder, "Why did he start there?" You dig deeper into the work and begin to second-guess the author. You might notice how a key word at the end of one paragraph prepares you for what is coming in the next (or deliberately does not). You see this because you too work hard at transitions. And even the smaller matters, such as how white space allows the writer a sharp break in continuity, how semicolons function in certain situations, how good titles set up reader expectations (or the effects of sentence fragments such as this one). Readers who are also writers observe these and many other composition tricks because they are thinking about how they too might use them in their own writing.

Rereading and Rewriting We've discovered that when writing something fairly long and complicated, we need to reread our work to know where it has been and where it needs to go next. If we have that problem *as writers,* is it any wonder that we also have it as readers? Many lengthy and complex works need more than one reading—or viewing—to make complete sense. The first time through is often full of surprises—turns of plot, quirks of character, evolution of theme—so that it often takes a further experience with the text to arrive at a satisfying meaning. In other words, we're so busy experiencing that we're unable to reflect on or interpret that experience. A second reading or viewing of a complex text gives us a chance to put things together: to ask more questions and find more answers; to hear rhythms, watch words, and trace themes; to better understand the metaphor and symbol we encounter; and to match beginning with end, end with beginning. So, just as we revise our own writing to make it whole, we reread books and re-see films to understand what makes them whole too.

Preparing to Read Your reading and rereading of a given text will yield even greater understanding if you know the conventions of the genre to which it belongs. So, while on the one hand, each creative work is one of a kind, on the other hand, each is also related to others that have similar characteristics. Put simply, plays are commonly constructed with acts, scenes, and settings; novels with settings, characters, and narrators; poems with any or all of these, along with rhymes and stanzas; and so on. Each of the genres explored in the following chapters has its own unique conventions as well as conventions shared among other genres. The more you know about how each genre works, the more you'll understand other genres as well.

First things first: The chapter that begins this book describes the single activity we believe will be most helpful in making sense of the chapters that follow as well as the many texts undergraduates must read on their way toward a degree in English. In Chapter 1, "Keeping a Journal," Toby Fulwiler examines how informal journal writing helps writers and readers make sense of and extend their understanding of virtually every text they encounter or create. Readers are invited to use their journals to respond to readings, ask and answer questions, pose and solve problems, and see the world anew through their own language.

In Chapter 2, "Exploring Fiction," Ghita Orth and Alan Shepherd examine the genre of novels, novellas, and short stories—all those imaginative worlds that authors create to explore deeply truthful things. The chapter explains and illustrates the particular conventions that make fiction work: character, plot, point of view, setting, symbol, style, and theme.

In Chapter 3, "Exploring Poetry," Sidney Poger opens with an in-depth look at the revision of a single poem, examining how the changing of single words made major changes in the meaning of the poem. The chapter pays particular attention to the defining characteristics of poems, including rhyme, meter, imagery, diction, structure, and point of view.

In Chapter 4, "Exploring Drama," James Howe looks at plays primarily in terms of performance. The chapter takes a close look at the characters, structure, and language that define drama, along with the practical limitations imposed by the conventions of live performance.

In Chapter 5, "Exploring the Essay," Mary Jane Dickerson and Richard Sweterlitsch consider short works of nonfiction in terms of authenticity and voice. The premise behind this chapter is that the essay is the literary medium closest to an author's self and, therefore, most likely to reveal the writer's biases, values, and beliefs.

In Chapter 6, "Exploring Visual Texts," Tom Simone acknowledges that many influential literary experiences in the twentieth and twenty-first centuries are visual in nature. This chapter examines the media of film and video in literary terms, including theme, image, and symbol, but also in cinematic terms that include, shots, angle, and sequence.

CHAPTER 1

Exploring with Journals

Toby Fulwiler

Journals allow people to talk to themselves without feeling silly. And it's a lot more than that as well. The journal is a place to catch and record my thoughts, but also a place to develop and push them to more interesting places. It acts as a mirror for my ideas. Whenever I write about anything, quite simply, I learn more about it. For me and for many other writers, the most important reason to write in the first place is for ourselves, for what happens in our own minds when we make concrete our otherwise scattered and fragmentary thought.

Finding words, generating sentences, constructing paragraphs is our way of finding, generating, and constructing the meaning of our world. In other words, one of the most powerful reasons for writing is not to convey a message to someone else, but to find out for ourselves that we have a message to convey. Above all else, journals are think books. When people write to themselves in journals, diaries, and notebooks, they concentrate on personal meaning more than carefulness, correctness, or audience reaction.

ACADEMIC JOURNALS

Journals written for college classes differ from private diaries written solely for the writer's self. While historically the two terms—*journal* and *diary*—have been used interchangeably, I'd suggest making a useful distinction between them: Diaries are personal notebooks that contain private thoughts, memories, feelings, and dreams—things of importance to the writer and nobody else. Journals—at least in an academic context—have a more limited focus; they center more on the point where writers' personal lives meet their intellectual and social lives. For example, if an English teacher has asked you to keep a journal, it is probably with the hope that you will use it to locate, collect, and make sense of your thoughts about the content of the class: about your reactions to the novels, poems, essays, films you are studying; about your role in class discussions; about your candid reactions to particular lectures or discussions; about first ideas for writing assignments and, later, about thoughts on revising those assignments; about connections between ideas in this course and other courses; and about personal connections you make between your academic study and the rest of your life—whatever they may be.

At this point, it might also help to distinguish journals from class notebooks. Unlike diaries, class notebooks contain almost nothing at all that is private, being filled as they are with other people's ideas: lecture and discussion notes, copied quotations, next week's assignments, and so on. Class notebooks are especially useful to help you pass examinations, but seldom contain notes of value once the course is over.

Think of your journal as a cross between a diary (subjective) and a class notebook (objective): In the journal you write about the object of study from your own personal perspective, and you write primarily to yourself. Here's how I might diagram that difference on a continuum from private to public:

Diary	*Journal*	*Class Notebook*
(private)	(personal)	(impersonal)

The key difference between a diary kept exclusively for yourself and a journal assigned for a class is obvious: Your professor will probably look at your journal (or samples from your journal) from time to time. She or he may want to look through it to see what you are thinking about William Shakespeare, Herman Melville, or Virginia Woolf. If your teacher wants to look at your journal, chances are good that it is not to grade it in any conventional sense, but to see how you are thinking about ideas in the course. I cannot, of course, guarantee that your teacher will look at it this way. That is simply how most of the English teachers I know, including the authors of this book, use journals. Check with your own instructor to be sure. Students commonly have questions about journals; they wonder about the mix of public and private expected in an assigned journal. In fact, one student, Missy, described her concern this way:

> 9/3 For three years now I've kept a journal on my own—a personal one, that I sort of talk to when I'm troubled or angry and confused about things. It's like talking to a friend who just listens with great patience and never argues with me. But now I'm supposed to keep one for my English class and I'm not sure how that will work—I don't see how I can write personal things in a book that my professor is going to read. How can a journal be both personal and kept for a class at the same time?

Good questions. In the rest of this chapter, I will try to lay out the territory of the journal to suggest what it might look like, how it might work, and what you might put in it.

PERSONAL JOURNALS

Maybe your instructor has not asked you to keep a journal—or has made it a recommendation and intends to do nothing specifically or formally with it in class.

In either case, the journal is a good project to assign yourself. Few students would elect to write other academic assignments on their own—what, are they crazy? Can you imagine writing research papers or critical essays without being required to? However, many people do elect to keep journals because they are useful for both intellectual and emotional reasons—and they are easy to keep.

For that reason, journals have a long and respected literary history, although historically, writers made little distinction between notebooks they called "journals" versus those they called "diaries." Some authors even became famous because of these personal notebooks: Samuel Pepys, for instance, kept what he called a *Diary* (what I'd call a journal) that remains one of the liveliest accounts of daily life in seventeenth-century London in existence; James Boswell's eighteenth-century *London Journal* is as famous as anything else he wrote. Some journals, such as those by William Byrd and William Bradford in the seventeenth century, are especially useful for their historical information about the settlement of colonial America—as were the journals of nineteenth-century American explorers Lewis and Clark.

Published journals, diaries, and letters provide crucial insights into the personalities of complex writers and thinkers. For example, as a teacher of nineteenth-century American literature, I know the centrality of journals to the lives of writers such as Ralph Waldo Emerson, Henry David Thoreau, and Margaret Fuller. Their journals contain nearly all the germinal ideas and language for later well-known published essays. *Walden* (1854), considered one of the great works of nineteenth-century literature, not only draws on the daily journal Thoreau kept during his stay at Walden Pond, but the published form of *Walden* is structured in a journal-like form, taking readers chronologically through the cycle of the seasons.

Journals are worth your while, as they have been to published writers, because writing in them helps you sort out your own ideas about the meaning of life—not to mention sorting out your ideas about school, assigned readings, and provocative lectures—which in turn gives you more confidence speaking up during class discussions, taking exams, or writing papers. Journals help thinkers, writers, and students because writing about ideas helps you both understand and remember them better. Journal writing lets you try out and play with ideas before you finish a paper and turn it in for grading.

For some time now, I have asked students in my various literature and composition classes to keep journals to help them understand the authors, ideas, and contexts of those courses. Students often tell me that journals are the best writing assignment I give: The frequent writing, both in class and out, allows all of us time to find and share insights about the readings. Students seem to like the noncompetitive climate fostered by the mutual sharing of journal entries in class and the more candid relationship to me, their instructor, that journal writing promotes.

Writing about Reading

Perhaps the best advice about a keeping a journal for an English class is the simplest: Write a little about everything you read. Keep your journal with your books, and every time you read a chapter, story, article, or poem, catch your reaction in writing, even for just five minutes. Don't try to sound profound. Don't worry about your spelling or punctuation. Instead, write in your own informal talky voice and try to pin down what about the text annoys or delights you, or makes you curious or confused. If you have time, reflect more deeply about your reaction and perhaps copy down the more interesting lines from the piece. In the following entry, Kate responds to her first reading of Natalie Goldberg's *Writing Down the Bones:*

> [1/28] I've just finished the first few chapters of *Writing Down the Bones*. Goldberg motivated me to jump straight to the computer and try some of her exercises, like writing without stopping for ten minutes and writing for another ten minutes with the screen turned off. It was the first time I can remember writing without worrying about commas and spelling. I just wrote, like she suggested, and it really felt liberating. I think freewriting is a great way to let go of the structure that encloses my life.

Here, the text prompts Kate to try out a writing exercise that leads her to an insight about the way she too rigidly structures her life.

In another entry, this time in response to reading an E.B. White essay, Kate writes:

> [2/9] "Farewell, My Lovely" is a good example of displaying research in a personal way. White's description of the Model T Ford and its influence on American life also includes his personal memories with the car—how it wouldn't start, sometimes wouldn't stop, and was always contrary in some peculiar way. He makes the car sound alive, almost like a playful mischievous horse, as he describes the way it sometimes moved of its own free will once it started up—"I can still feel my old Ford nuzzling me at the curb, as though looking for an apple in my pocket" (25). It caused him all sorts of trouble, but he still misses it. That's the way I'd like to write, using my own past experiences to reflect on what I'm reading and thinking today.

Asking and Answering Questions

Throughout the course of our normal day, we run a lot of questions and problems through our heads, most having to do with things that bother us personally, some having to do with what we are studying. Keeping a journal provides a place to collect these questions (both personal and academic), to articulate them precisely, and with luck, to lead to answers. Recording such questions provides you with a focus for your reading and something to talk with teacher or classmates about. In the following example, Marcia generates several questions from her reading of Henry David Thoreau's *Walden:*

> [4/13] I was rather confused at the beginning of this chapter. What is the deal with the conversation between the Hermit and Henry? … What really caught my attention was the specific description of the fight between the black and the red ants. Is Thoreau trying to compare the world of ants to the world of people?

As Marcia wonders about what she reads, she increases her chances of finding answers to her own questions—which she seems to do in commenting on the black and red ants. Journals are a good place to guess and try out hypotheses and see how much sense they make to you. For example, Trey switches directions mid-writing as new thoughts emerge in analyzing a short story by Edgar Allan Poe and he answers his own question:

> [2/7] The first thing that struck me about "The Black Cat" was Poe's opening paragraph. Poe has this quirk about telling us that what he is about to say is so horrible it's extremely hard to believe. Well, I think it's unnecessary because we already know it didn't happen. So we're going to believe just the same without the opening paragraph…. Wait a minute! I take back what I just wrote. I think that first paragraph does a lot. It explains the narrator's feelings *now* so when we go back in time we understand and identify with narrator far better.

Seeing

When you write about what you look at, be it text or object, you see more and more carefully. It happens to the biologist in the field, the chemist in the laboratory, or the scholar in the study. The act of writing focuses your attention more sharply, pushes you to find words for what you see, and guarantees a record to help you remember later. The journal, of course, is the perfect place to catch such close observations. In the following entry, Richard examines closely the first page in the Edgar Allan Poe story, "The Fall of the House of Usher":

> [3/15] The mood of the entire first paragraph is such that we feel the impending doom of this guy's situation. Even in the first sentences he seems to be buried, in a sense, in his own living tomb—dark, dreary, soundless, the clouds hanging over him "oppressively." His first glance at the house of Usher leaves such a sense of horror, with its bleak walls and eye-like windows … What stood out to me most though was his personification of the house … Roderick Usher pretty much mirrors the house, and all those descriptive words about the house hold true for Roderick as well.

By writing out both paraphrases and direct quotations of what he found on the page, Richard "sees" that page better. Even if he never rereads this entry, writing it out has increased his chances of understanding and remembering that

Poe passage for a long time to come. A good exercise? Write all you can in your journal about what you find on the first page of a novel, story, or essay. It's a good way to train yourself to read closely.

Connecting and Extending

One of the best things you can do with journal writing is look for connections to other ideas, themes, and authors studied in the same course. In the following example, David reacts—tongue slightly in cheek—to a specific line in Walt Whitman's "Song of Myself" by comparing him thematically to Emerson, whom we had studied some weeks before:

```
[11/5] Now here is a good one: "Divine am I inside and
out, and I make holy whatever I touch." How about a foot-
note there? Haven't I heard that "we are all divine" spiel
somewhere before?! Hey, Walt, didn't I see you at last
month's Harvard Divinity School graduation when Emerson
gave that wild speech? This guy moves himself right in
with the transcendentalists, doesn't he?
```

The connection here is a good one, of course, since Whitman was, in fact, heavily indebted to Emerson for his central ideas, including the divinity of all people. When I read David's journal entry, I laughed and enjoyed David's sassy irreverent tone ("Hey, Walt") because it was clear he knew what he was writing about.

Another kind of connection occurs when you use your journal to comment on your other classes. Sometimes you will see parallels between what you're reading in an English class and what's going on in a history, philosophy, religion, or art history class you are enrolled in at the same time. When you find such intersections, capture them in your journal.

Surprising Yourself

One of my favorite journal assignments to my literature students, whether reading fiction, drama, or poetry asks, "Write about the passage you do not understand." Responses to this prompt often lead to better understanding of the confusing passage, often surprising the writer with a key insight. Look at Bobby's entry as she tries to make sense out of Emily Dickinson's poem "I Heard a Fly Buzz When I Died":

```
[4/6] Boy, I was on the wrong track with Emily Dickinson!
Completely! I read too fast the first time—I felt rushed
and summarized her—how ridiculous! I hardly even read this
fly poem on page 111. But now, slowing down and reading
it literally really seems to help.
    OK, so in this poem nothing seems to happen. But that's
the point! Nothing happens in the sense that she doesn't
find enlightenment as expected. You know she is rather
anxious for this but it doesn't happen. I cannot believe
how much there is in this little poem … She ends her poem
```

> pessimistically, yet began it optimistically, looking forward to some kind of enlightenment or salvation, but finds, instead, only the buzzing of a fly—and what do flies do? Feed on dead things!

Bobby proved to be an especially prolific writer, her journal approached 100 pages by semester's end. Because she made journal writing part of her regular study routine, she increased her chances of generating insights useful in both writing papers and taking examinations.

Conversing

If you are asked to keep a journal by an instructor, chances are she will look at it occasionally to see your concerns and to see whether or not the course is making sense to you. You can use the journal to create a dialogue between you and your instructor about things that concern you but that you haven't time to talk about in person.

Sometimes students give me suggestions in their journals—about my assignments. For example, one time Bill wrote to me:

> [4/26] Before starting to write on Moby Dick, I would like to make a special request ... that you maybe give a second thought to assigning a 500-page book like *Moby Dick* in the last few weeks of classes.

In truth, next time I assigned *Moby Dick*, a staple in my nineteenth-century American novel course, I moved it forward two weeks in the schedule. Of course, journals are not letters; they are written primarily to oneself, not one's instructor. But in the somewhat artificial learning environment called school, journals may accomplish some of the expressive communication between teachers and student usually reserved for media such as letters, e-mail, or oral conferences or the more informal one of talk.

SUGGESTIONS FOR JOURNAL WRITING

Let me conclude with a few suggestions for keeping a journal. Keep in mind that a journal is, fundamentally, a collection of your thoughts captured at different moments in time. Remember, too, that a teacher who requires a journal may want it to be done in a particular way. If not, here are some suggestions that may work well:

1. **Divide a small loose-leaf notebook into several sections.** Use one section to collect your reading notes; use another to write whatever else you are thinking about the course, reactions to class discussions, and the like; use yet another section for personal ideas, reflections, or feelings that have nothing to do with the course. If you like, make other sections for things such as scrapbook clippings, observations about other classes, and any other categories of ideas you want to keep track of or wrestle with.

2. **Write often, regularly, and at length.** I intend to write every day, but often that doesn't work out: Sometimes I skip a day; other days I write more than once. But the habit of regular writing increases my chances of finding and developing ideas. Sometimes I think I have a lot to say and nothing much comes out; sometimes I start strictly from habit and surprise myself by finding a good idea. Ernest Hemingway disciplined himself to write daily, regardless of inspiration, for essentially the same reason: the habit of writing increases your chances of finding new thought.
3. **Write in your most natural voice.** The journal is a place to relax and concentrate on the what and why of ideas, not a place to worry about reader's reactions to your thought. There's a good reason for this: The degree to which you worry about matters of form, grammar, mechanics, or style is the degree to which you subtract energy from the content of your idea. Worry about nice-looking, organized language when you write the final drafts of formal papers; focus on your most honest thoughts—which usually means writing in your most informal voice—when you write in a journal.
4. **Write double entries.** A wonderful idea borrowed from science writers is the double-entry notebook. It works like this: write only on the right-hand pages of your journal; keep the left page blank. Periodically—once or twice a week—return to earlier entries and comment on what you wrote there, expanding, modifying, arguing as it suits you. In other words, on left-hand pages adjacent to right-hand entries, write about your former writing and develop a dialogue with your past self.
5. **Index your journal.** At the end of the semester, put in page numbers, titles for each entry, a table of contents, and write an introduction. This will make your journal a more finished (for this period of your life), organized document to share with a professor or simply for you to find sometime later in your life. But the real purpose of indexing is once again for yourself. The act of reviewing entries, fashioning titles, and organizing the journal takes you once again through nineteenth-century American literature, etc., only now from more distance. Rereading and re-seeing your journal in this fashion is one of the best synthesizing activities you can do.
6. **Explore formal writing assignments.** If you keep a journal faithfully and record thoughts about your readings and class discussions, you'll find in the journal entries the seeds (connections, questions, answers) for both more personal and analytical papers due in your course. You can also rehearse ideas for formal papers by talking with yourself about whether this or that idea should be abandoned or advanced.

One final note: Journal writing is essentially whatever you make it. Of all the modes of writing described in this book, this one gives you greatest freedom to make it what you want. If you are studying literature, you will probably write a lot about your reading; if you are studying composition or creative writing, your topics will be unlimited. In any case, the journal is your territory—explore it, map its boundaries, and cultivate it well.

CHAPTER 2

Exploring Fiction

Ghita Orth and Allen Shepherd

ONCE UPON A TIME ...

We all love stories. A tale told around a fire at the mouth of a cave captivated the human spirit at the very beginnings of language. People are no different today. Each year thousands of stories are produced for film, stage, and television. Millions of parents all over the globe still enchant their children with "Once upon a time" tales.

If stories are so basic to human nature, why do we have to study them? And just what do we mean when we say we "study" a story?

We study or analyze any work of literature to understand it better—what it says and how it says it; to discover how the piece is put together and to grasp the relationship of the parts to the whole; to see the work in the contexts of history, gender, culture; to understand why the story affects readers as it does; and in a very real way, to participate in the creative process of making a piece of fiction. The active reader often has a conversation with the text and, through that text, with the author. The reader asks questions of the text and then looks for the answers the text may give. For example, how will the heroine escape from captivity? What does the author mean by "goodness"? What is the effect of telling this story in the present tense? Through this sort of conversation, the reader in fact helps to create the text.

THE NATURE OF FICTION

Fiction today is surely the most familiar and accessible of literary forms. Like other art forms, it is also ultimately mysterious, but from the "once upon a time" of childhood, we do *know* about fiction and almost instinctively understand what makes a good story. As you no doubt remember from your own childhood experiences, kids have very distinct preferences and strong biases in bedtime reading. A mother who tries to substitute *The Cat in the Hat*, which she likes, for *Where the Wild Things Are,* her child's favorite, may get into serious trouble. Similarly a father who tries inventing stories will soon learn about desirable characters, acceptable plots, and feasible kinds of conflict. From our preschool years, we are familiar with many aspects of fiction.

Given greater experience and sophistication, our tastes change. We appreciate more of the art of fiction and, more prosaically, we are prepared to investigate just how a piece of fiction—whether short story or novella or novel—actually works. We know well enough the rewards of reading fiction, that it enlarges our knowledge, our experience, our understanding, and range of feeling.

There are of course many different kinds of fiction, about whose relative merits readers are likely to disagree. One of us, for example, has always liked mystery stories, but he doesn't any longer much care for science fiction or fantasy. He still enjoys Ian Fleming, creator of James Bond, and thinks no one is a better companion for a long plane trip than John Grisham. At the end of this chapter we will take up the surprisingly involved question of what it is that makes good fiction good. For the moment it's enough to recognize that whether it is categorized as "quality lit" or "pop" or "escapist" writing, fiction offers many and various rewards.

The ideal reader, by Henry James's definition, is the one on whom nothing is lost. That kind of perfection is a tall order indeed; we aspire to be attentive, intelligent, and responsible, but of course don't always succeed.

To examine how fiction works, we ought to have a demonstration story. Barry Hannah begins one of his better known stories, "Love Too Long," with these lines:

> My head's burning off and I got a heart about to bust out of my ribs. All I can do is move from chair to chair with my cigarette. I wear shades. I can't read a magazine. Some days I take my binoculars and look out in the air. They laid me off. I can't find work. My wife's got a job and she takes flying lessons. When she comes over the house in her airplane, I'm afraid she'll screw up and crash. (9)

By the end of the first paragraph, Hannah has got the reader wondering who this man is and just what's wrong. Clearly the man is desperate, going to pieces, and somehow his wife is involved. She has a job and he hasn't. She's taking flying lessons and he's stuck in the house. From the last sentence, we may wonder whether he is afraid of her or afraid *for* her. Probably both. In any event, Hannah has set the hook in the reader—we've got to read on and find out.

What leads most readers to want to read on are *characters* and *plot*. We become interested in characters, the people in fiction, particularly when they are introduced as vividly as in Hannah's story, and we want to know what is going to happen, the significant order of what happens being the plot. In one paragraph, of course, plot doesn't develop very significantly, but already there is enough evidence to distinguish between *story* and plot. Story is simply what happens. Plot is likely to involve causation—why things happen as they do.

Thus it seems from the first paragraph that the narrator's desperation is in part attributable to his wife, to her employment and her zooming around overhead. He is also developing, it would appear, a heightened sense of his own insignificance. "I got to be a man," he says shortly (9).

Character

Traditionally, character has been regarded as the most important component of fiction. How does a writer go about developing a character in fiction? What we first respond to in Hannah's story is the character's *speech*—the words themselves, the rhythm of the sentences, the state of mind they reveal. The *language* is vivid, colloquial, exclamatory. The *rhythms* are broken, staccato. The disjointed sentences seem to burst forth. We can't presume too much at the outset, but our man's mental state is both complex and recognizable. He is hurt and confused and angry and self-condemnatory. Speech, then, set down as either monologue or dialogue, is a principal means of characterization. We do want to know what people sound like.

Physical description is another effective means of character development. Explicit self-description would probably be awkward to incorporate into a monologue such as "Love Too Long." We do, however, get a few evocative visual details. We see our unhappy husband wearing sunglasses (in the house), probably to hide behind; smoking a cigarette or even a succession of them; perched anxiously on one chair, and then moving to another; with the binoculars perhaps hanging on a strap around his neck; and with unread magazines forming a base for the surrounding clutter.

Given the descriptive details of the story's opening, we are reminded of nothing so much as the last survivor in a fortified post anticipating yet another, this time irresistible, assault. Later in the story Hannah writes a scene of confrontation between our narrator and a (of course) superior antagonist. Hannah writes: "He [the antagonist] was a huge person, looked something like a statue of some notable gentleman in ancient history. I couldn't do anything to bring him down. He took all my blows without batting an eye" (15). Here by inference we see the narrator—his self-image. Again he is looking up, without the protective distancing effect of binoculars or even sunglasses this time, and the enemy is overwhelming, invulnerable, and dismissive. Our narrator, inferentially self-described, is small, unimpressive, and ineffectual.

We have also encountered in this single paragraph two other techniques of characterization: portrayal through *action* and through *gesture.* We have seen that the narrator cannot be still, cannot rest, cannot stop thinking; that he is driven, obsessed. His looking up into the sky with his binoculars is a *gesture* that suggests the answers—peace, ease, happiness—reside with his wife, who may appear at any moment. All along, of course, we have been privy to his thoughts and feeling. The character's *thoughts*—their content, coherence, and sequence—represent a basic element of characterization, as we come to know his world from the inside.

Plot

Plot, the order of events in a story, is usually considered, along with characterization, as among the most significant elements of fiction. Good writers don't need plots that are dramatic or violent or even entertaining to gain and hold our interest. Events at a quiet family party will do perfectly well, and did for James Joyce in his story "Clay." Joyce's story, the account of an elderly spinster's visit to a family for whom she once worked, impresses some readers as a rather stale slice of life, in which the innocuous word "nice" dominates, and whose action barely skirts the inconsequential. Other readers discover in "Clay" a succession of carefully understated scenes that poignantly portray the barrenness, lovelessness, disorder, and loss that Joyce represents as the essence of his protagonist's experience. The subtle plot leads to no significant changes in the lives of any of the characters; indeed, Joyce's principal point is that they are all trapped. Maria, the protagonist, is not a very perceptive woman, and thus the *epiphany*, or flash of intuitive understanding, is reserved for another character, who now sees her painful plight differently. He does not, however, recognize that his own situation is scarcely preferable.

Seldom is plot the most significant component of a story. However, the art of storytelling involves the creation of an entire world, and significant events, dramatic or not, are evidence of a world in motion. Events may cause people to change, and most fiction is dynamic, is about change.

What makes a plot move, what glues the events together, is a kind of tension called *conflict*. Sometimes this struggle of opposing forces is resolved, providing a certain satisfaction for the reader. The tension induced by the conflict is eased and some sort of balance and order restored. The point at which one opposing force overcomes the other and the conflict is resolved is the *climax*. Not uncommonly, however, fiction is open-ended, without definitive resolution. The narrator of "Love Too Long" never does achieve dependable understanding, let alone a happy ending. "I'm going to die from love" are his last words.

One of the opposing forces involved in conflict is likely to be the central character. The other force, or forces, which may be essentially external or essentially internal, include

1. Another character or group of characters.
2. The forces of nature or the power of the universe.
3. Society or culture.
4. An aspect of the character's own personality or value system.

Given that Hannah's narrator seems somewhat paranoid, we may conclude that his own personality is a significant source of conflict; certainly other characters stand in his way, literally or metaphorically, and his joblessness may reflect social adversity. We may even detect Nature's opposition when the narrator tells us that he is light and nimble and good at elevated construction work, "but the sun always made me sick up there ..." (10).

Point of View

One of the crucial decisions a writer makes is which *point of view* to use in telling a story. You may have been taught that there are only two options: "first person" and "third person." Fiction writers have created several kinds of first-person narrators. The narrator may, for example, be recounting his or her own story. Think of Holden Caulfield, of *The Catcher in the Rye.* Or the first-person narrator may be recounting events that she or he has heard of but not actually participated in or witnessed. Often a first-person narrator looks back, telling of past events. If so, the narrative will be cast in the past tense. A narrator who recounts events *long* past can be called a *retrospective narrator.* But perhaps the events are still going on; if so, the narrative will be cast in the present tense. Remember how Hannah's story begins? ("My head's burning off and I got a heart about to bust out of my ribs.") He's telling us about it as it's (still) going on.

Critics commonly believe that the use of the first-person narrator creates a sense of immediacy or authenticity, of a story being conveyed directly. The first-person narrator may see and know only what is humanly possible. Such a narrator, that is, cannot read other characters' minds or know what is happening a mile away. He or she may speculate endlessly, as Hannah's protagonist does, but cannot be sure of anything and may be deceived. For the writer and for the reader as well, this mode of narration has the advantage of consistent focus, keyed to a single individual's experience. Hannah's use of the first-person point of view enables us in some measure to share our narrator's perspective, to wonder with him, to endure his distress.

But how does a writer influence the ways we respond to or judge such a narrator? In "Love Too Long," for example, does Hannah make us think the narrator really knows what he's talking about, that he is a man whose experience and intelligence and perceptiveness we can depend on? The answer seems to be yes, with some qualifications: Although there are a good many things the narrator does not fully understand, he *knows* that he does not understand.

First-person narrators lacking self-knowledge may be unreliable witnesses to their own lives. Such an *unreliable narrator* may be blinded by the limitations of personality or by youth and innocence. One such naïve narrator is Huckleberry Finn. Huck greatly admires some poetry that Mark Twain clearly thinks is terrible. The poet, Huck tells us, kept a scrapbook and "used to paste obituaries and accidents and cases of patient suffering in it ... and write poetry after them out of her own head. It was very good poetry." After quoting an awful poem, Huck says of the poet, Emmeline Grangerford, "She didn't ever have to stop to think," which pretty well nails down the point (88). Here is the third stanza of that poem, "Ode to Stephen Dowling Bots, Dec'd [Deceased]":

> No whooping-cough did rack his frame,
>   Nor measles drear, with spots;
> Not these impaired the sacred name
>   Of Stephen Dowling Bots.

In employing an unreliable narrator, Twain is really communicating with us over the narrator's head, using a variety of irony known as *ironic point of view*. That is, we and the author know and understand things that this first-person narrator does not.

At this point we should acknowledge that occasionally a second-person narrator may be encountered, as in Jay McInerney's contemporary novel, *Bright Lights, Big City,* in which the reader is enlisted as both protagonist and narrator. Thus the novel's first sentence: "You are not the kind of guy who would be at a place like this at this time of the morning" (1). This "you" clearly isn't an example of direct address *to* a reader, as in *The Catcher in the Rye* when Holden tells us, "… the jerk noticed her and said hello. You should've seen the way they said hello" (48).

The much more common alternative to first-person narration, however, is third person, in which the anonymous narrative voice has one degree or another of omniscience. Thus, for example, in eighteenth- and nineteenth-century novels a common technique is *total omniscience,* in which the story is told as if it were seen through the eyes of God. The totally omniscient narrator, if so inclined, may perform as a mind reader. For instance, this is how Arnold Bennett's *The Old Wives' Tale* begins:

> Those two girls, Constance and Sophia Baines, paid no heed to the manifold interest of their situation, of which, indeed, they had never been conscious. They were, for example, established almost precisely on the fifty-third parallel of latitude (3).

Here is a narrator who knows with remarkable exactness both where on the map the girls live and what it is they have never known about their own situation. That is to say, the narrator knows what's inside and what's outside, what exists and what doesn't.

This sort of omniscient narrator will on occasion even address the reader, as in this passage from Henry James's *The American:* "The gentleman in whom we are interested understood no French, but I have said he was intelligent, and here is a good chance to prove it" (5). James's omniscient narrator uses the first person "I," but, unlike Hannah's "I," is not a character in the story. Instead, he or she appears to be the author's representative or persona.

Such direct address to the reader by a first-person narrator who is not a character is commonplace in nineteenth-century fiction. In much modern fiction, however, the author consciously chooses *limited omniscience*. Thus, for instance, a writer will use a narrator who is not a character, but then restrict that narrator's presentation to what is perceived by just one of the characters. Look at how William Faulkner begins his short story "Barn Burning":

> The store in which the Justice of the Peace's Court was sitting smelled of cheese. The boy, crouched on his nail keg at the back of the crowded room, knew he smelled cheese, and more; from where he sat he could see the ranked shelves close-packed with the solid, squat, dynamic shapes of tin cans … (3).

Chapter 2   Exploring Fiction

Note that Faulkner focuses on what the boy smells, where he sits, what he can see. Critics today favor the term *focalization* to describe this use of a character's perspective. The boy's is the *central consciousness* in the story.

The writer may maintain the perspective of a single character throughout a work or may shift focalization from one character to another. Although a short story writer usually adheres throughout to a single consistent focus of narration, a novelist has the option of employing a number of different points of view. Thus, for instance, Faulkner's *The Sound and the Fury,* in which the story is told in three successive first-person accounts by Benjy, Quentin, and Jason Compson, followed by a final third-person section that operates primarily as a commentary on the preceding three. *Why* a fiction writer chooses the point(s) of view he or she does is always a useful question to consider, for, as Henry James noted, point of view is that technical aspect that leads the reader most directly into the central interpretive questions posed by a piece of fiction. For example, pondering point of view in fiction may lead to our determining whose story it is, which character's experience is central. And this in turn helps us decide what the story is about.

Setting

To simplify and clarify discussions of fiction—how it gets written as well as how it gets read—we are in the habit of partitioning character from plot and plot from thematic concerns, when, as we well know, everything is going on simultaneously and is related to everything else. So it is with *setting,* usually defined as where the story takes place, the background against which the action of narrative occurs. Fair enough, particularly if we add *atmosphere,* which implies mood or emotional aura. But look at the following paragraph, the first in James Joyce's often anthologized story "Araby," which exemplifies how a writer begins establishing setting and atmosphere, but which also contains significant intimations of character and theme:

> North Richmond Street, being blind [dead-end], was a quiet street except at the hour when the Christian Brothers' School let the boys free. An uninhabited house of two storeys stood at the blind end, detached from its neighbors in a square ground. The other houses of the street, conscious of decent lives within them, gazed at one another with brown imperturbable faces. (33)

Curiously enough, it is only with the first sentence of the next paragraph that we can tell what the point of view is to be—"The former tenant of our house, a priest, had died in the back drawing-room." As "our house" suggests, the speaker is a first person narrator—an adult recalling his childhood, we subsequently learn.

What can we say of setting and atmosphere as conveyed in this first paragraph? As Joyce scholars invariable remark, the setting is autobiographically derived, Joyce having lived at 17 North Richmond Street and having attended the Christian Brothers' School. It is then, in all likelihood, an authentic re-creation, although such authenticity is unlikely to affect our pleasure one way or another. The child who is about to appear will play out several scenes of a deeply felt adolescent drama within the round of these imperturbable brown faces, as if to a maddeningly unresponsive audience, the houses personifying the decent, unimaginative, God-fearing dullness of their adult inhabitants.

Setting continues to be one of the most significant components of the story. Because "Araby" recounts the classic adolescent experience of isolation, alienation, and unrequited love, it seems wholly appropriate that the setting is developed from the beginning as if it were a series of staged scenes from a play in which the narrator fruitlessly aspired to play an heroic role. But at the end he is framed by another drearily anti-romantic theatrical set: "I found myself in a big hall girdled at half its height by a gallery. Nearly all the stalls were closed and the greater part of the hall was in darkness" (40).

Symbolism

Of all the components of fiction the one that often seems to produce the most involved interpretive questions is *symbolism*. For openers, we should consider what symbols are, how they are identified, and what significance they have. A *symbol* is a concrete object, action, setting, character, or image pattern that suggests more than its literal meaning; it functions as itself, but implies additional significances.

Thus a flag, the Skull and Crossbones, is a concrete object that stands for piracy. Symbols are often said to be of three types, two of which are the *universal* and the *particular*. An example of the universal symbol is the long journey that suggests the course of human life. A symbol of more limited application is the bull, which may be understood to represent a rising and active stock market. Less common is a *nonce* symbol, one that is invented for a specific purpose and that is peculiar to the work of an individual writer. Thus, for example, Melville's great white whale Moby Dick takes on symbolic significance only in the context of his novel.

Flannery O'Connor was once asked at what stage of her writing she "put in the symbols." It is an entertaining notion—O'Connor slipping in a symbol every three or four pages—but of course that's not what happens. Symbols are fundamental and functional; they are organically related to all the other components we have been concerned with. It's also true that much first-rate fiction has no symbolic content at all. To assume then, as some people do, that the symbol is hiding there somewhere and can be hunted down is a serious interpretive misconception.

How do you recognize a symbol? Careful reading and common sense are the most important requirements. Only after you feel you fully understand the literal level of the story's meaning and yet sense a pattern of suggestive details, a dimension beyond the literal, will you wish to explore symbolic interpretation. Sometimes symbolic significance is readily accessible through speech, gesture, and action. In Hawthorne's tale "The Gray Champion" the scene is a public gathering in Boston at which frightened colonists face a show of military force ordered by the arrogant royal governor, who is contemplating further oppression. From out of the crowd appears a venerable man dressed in ancient clothes and possessed of great authority. He reproves the governor, foretells his downfall, and reassures the people. In this heroic champion, many readers presume, Hawthorne symbolizes the spirit of New England's liberty.

Or consider a one-page chapter, "The Pipe," in Melville's *Moby Dick*. Ahab, smoking his pipe, stands alone on deck, reflecting on the requirements and consequences of his single-minded determination to hunt and kill the white whale. He finds that he can no longer enjoy his pipe and throws it overboard. What Melville, himself a lifelong pipe smoker, may be suggesting in this apparently symbolic act is that Ahab is casting away his serenity, rejecting creature comforts, even denying a bit of his humanity in his quest to kill the whale.

Symbolism in fiction depends for its effectiveness on the reader's making the right associations, understanding the ways in which symbols may expand and deepen meaning. Symbols make good literary sense only when considered in the overall context provided by a piece of fiction. The original Greek word for symbol (*sumbolon*) denoted half of something broken in two. Symbols do not stand for other things, but are themselves part of a larger whole. As an interpreter of symbols in fiction, then, you are concerned with putting things together, with seeing the story in more than one dimension.

Style

An author's style has been described as the sum of all the choices made. For our purposes, we'll limit that to choices of words and sentence patterns. Words, of course, may be big or small, abstract or concrete, harsh or gentle, and more. Sentences may be short or long, simple or complex, direct or circuitous, and more. Here's an illustrative paragraph from *The Sun Also Rises* by Ernest Hemingway, a writer noted for his distinctive style:

> The taxi went up the hill, passed the lighted square, then on into the dark, still climbing, then leveled out onto a dark street behind St. Etienne du Mont, went smoothly down the asphalt, passed the trees and the standing bus at the Place de la Contrescarpe, then turned onto the cobbles of the Rue Mouffetard. There were lighted bars and late open shops on each side of the street. We were sitting apart and we jolted close together going down the old street. Brett's hat was off. Her head was back. I saw her face in the lights from the open shops, then it was dark, then I saw her face clearly as we came out on the Avenue des Gobelins. The street was torn up and men were working on the car-tracks by the light of acetylene flares. Brett's face was white and the long line of her neck showed in the bright light of the flares. The street was dark again and I kissed her. Our lips were tight together and then she turned away and pressed against the corner of the seat, as far away as she could get. Her head was down. (25)

Readers tend to have Hemingway's style pegged—simple words in short sentences. They seldom go beyond that. But look at what can happen when you do. Asked to write about the style of that passage, here's what one student wrote in her journal:

> The adjectives Hemingway employs have dark corrosive overtones (the word dark is repeated 4-5 times). The sentences which describe Brett are very short and simple while the sentences which tell the setting are very long and descriptively full of detail. Lots of the words have geometrical references (square, long line, car-tracks, etc.). The entire paragraph is styled to imply the heavy influence of modern technology and the post WWI industrial age. The adjectives used to describe people are mechanistic. Everything is in definite terms: dark/light, close together/far away as she could get—no variation and no real sympathy for the characters or the environment. Use of extremes. In the first sentence the taxi is the subject and as the sentence progresses the rhythm is long, up and down, etc., like the taxi ride itself. However, once the sentences deal with the interaction of Jake and Brett the sentences become quick and abrupt as if necessarily so for the action (Jake's kissing Brett) to occur in the first place. The paragraph is complete in itself; there is a setting, a rising, climax, & falling action, etc. The style of landscape mirrors what is going on in Jake's & Brett's emotions and relationships. Very visual paragraph. (Melissa Denick)

In her analysis Melissa comments on stylistic elements such as word choice and variation in sentence length. More important, though, she notices the effects of those choices. In other words, she shows us the power of an author's style to project meaning beyond itself—to illuminate characterization, conflict, theme.

Theme

The central or dominating ideas in a story we may call its *thematic concerns.* How do we go about formulating the thematic concerns of a piece of fiction? What do we look for? Themes in fiction are usually expressed through character, action, and image. Ask yourself what has happened to the principal character or characters. Have they made discoveries? What kinds of changes do you see in their circumstances? Important actions are not necessarily physical or dramatic. Some fiction is more cerebral, and the principal action is intellectual or emotional. Consider what kinds of *images* predominate in the story—images being the sensory content of the work, whatever appeals to the senses.

Let's try to apply these ideas to a formulation of the thematic concerns of "Love Too Long," to use the story for illustrative purposes one last time. At the end, the man's situation has not changed appreciably. The last line of the story, "I'm going to die from love," very much resembles the first, "My head's burning off and I got a heart about to bust out of my ribs." He has certainly gone through a lot of marital pain and suffering, much of it comically described, and has in the process achieved a greater measure of self-awareness. But this is not necessarily going to change his life. Some of the story's dominant images include the wife flying overhead, the huge person who looks like a statue, and a rotting croquet ball lost in the grass, one of the narrator's self-images.

As our consideration of this story would suggest, the meanings of good fiction are not reducible to simple, explicit statements, handy moral guides or codified popular wisdom. Serious fiction does not offer instruction in the same sense that an editorial or a sermon or a book review does. From this it does not follow, however, that statements articulating thematic concerns are of necessity vague, general, or abstract.

What in the end may be said of the subject of "Love Too Long" is that Hannah offers us the anatomy of a man whose life is overtly in crisis, whose response to the way things are appears to be compounded of surprise, outrage, and dismay, but who in fact has at some level anticipated much of what is going on, and more grimly, sees it as both inescapable and deserved.

As to the story's thematic concerns, we may conclude, as is evident in Hannah's treatment of the subject, that he finds this aspect of the human condition widespread, perhaps inescapable, that it is reason for sadness perhaps but also productive of much desperate comedy as well.

READING A STORY

As we've been suggesting, active readers have conversations with a text, and thus help create it. Now that we've talked about the elements of fiction that interest readers and draw them into the world of a story, we can demonstrate how that conversation operates and the rewards it can bring. The following, despite its brevity, is clearly a "story," one that can demonstrate the power of fiction to engage us. As we read it we can ask questions of Burroway's presentation of character, plot, point of view, setting, symbolism, and style and discover answers that can lead us to the story's thematic concerns.

Tea Leaves

Janet Burroway

He came from Harris and Wynton to put the new program on her pc. He was thin as a digit. His fingers on the keyboard had an octave span.

Shift Search, he said, Alt F3, Control, Enter.

The CEO had circulated an austerity memo on air-conditioning, and the sweat beaded out from under her bra. The name of her new nail lacquer was Rosy Refrain; it occurred to her that this was clever without exactly making sense.

Hit the Escape key. Look, all you have to do is this and this.

You go so fast, she said. Would you like some coffee?

He eyed her briefly. I don't drink coffee.

Tea?

What kind of tea?

There was Irish Breakfast in the lounge, she thought, and maybe Camomile. The hair at her nape was curling in the damp. She herself had brought the Lemon Zinger, she pointed out. This was a judicious guess.

I don't like it too strong, he said.

I can use one tea bag for both.

When she was halfway there he called, No sugar!

She brought the tea on a copper tray, which was the best she found in the kitchenette. There were chocolate mint Girl Scout cookies from Lily Ellis's daughter's troop.

He was into the Autoexec.bat, doing something complicated as Prokofiev.

I'm afraid your tea will get cold, she said. Please drink it. Please.

He didn't look up. Once I get the program set up it practically runs by itself, he said.

Although neither of the two people in this short story is given a name, each is presented as a distinct individual through the various means by which fiction writers delineate character. When we ask what the computer expert is like, for example, the story answers our question. We notice that he speaks mostly in brief, fragmented sentences, often solely in "computerese." We find that he works for a presumably large company, Harris and Wynton, and spends his days putting programs onto office computers. Although the story doesn't directly describe him or his actions, we realize that he's seated at a computer and that his attention is almost solely directed at its keyboard, which he manipulates with deftness and speed. He seems enclosed in the world of machines, with which he is proficient.

The woman in "Tea Leaves," the story tells us, also works in the corporate sector—in a company large enough to have a CEO, concerns about excessive electricity costs, and an employee lounge. And what is *she* like, we wonder. Again the story answers. When we listen to her speak, for example, we hear someone who, unlike the man, is interested in the person she is with, commenting on the speed at which he works, offering him refreshments, concerned that his tea will get cold. The narration also provides direct description of her, which makes her seem more three-dimensional than the disembodied man from Harris and Wynton. The woman we're shown is warm, with "sweat [beading] out from under her bra," and "the hair at her nape [is] curling in the damp." She has a bodily presence in the story, and both she and the reader are aware of her physicality.

The story, then, has introduced us to two quite different people sharing its office setting—a man whose concerns and responses are primarily mechanical and a woman who is more interested in the human being she is sitting with than in the program he is installing. This difference between them provides the story's source of tension, its potential conflict; the problematic interaction between the two characters moves the story's plot, however minimal, forward.

And where are readers to locate themselves in this conflict of interests—with which character is our allegiance to lie? The story's point of view answers our questions. Because Burroway has chosen limited omniscience, with the woman as the story's central consciousness, the reader is invited to align with this focal character as the story's protagonist. We recognize that we are glimpsing her perceptions of the man, as well as the man himself. For her, "keyboard" implies art rather than technology; she sees the computer expert as having a pianist's hands with "an octave span," and his running the "Autoexec.bat" as performing an intricate Prokofiev piano piece. His world means little to her unless perceived in her own terms.

The story's style—its selection and use of words—also makes clear the protagonist's responses to sensory experience, as in her thoughts about the name of her nail polish. To her, tea is not just tea, as it seems to be to the man; it is "Irish Breakfast," or "Camomile," or "Lemon Zinger." And to present it to him she chooses the "best" tray in the lounge and adds cookies. That she knows these are Girl Scout cookies, evidence of family in the life of one of her co-workers, is a detail with interesting implications. It suggests, as does her deferential attitude to the computer expert—until now a stranger to her—that she herself is single and that what we are witnessing, perhaps stereotypically, is her effort at attracting him.

Wondering how that attempt will fare and what we are to make of it brings us to questions about the story's thematic concerns. One wonders if the tea offering may not itself have symbolic suggestiveness, especially when the protagonist virtually begs the man to stop his work long enough to partake of what she has offered him: "Please drink it. Please." It comes as no surprise to the reader that "he didn't look up." His lack of interest in the tea—and by extension the woman who has tried to make it a bond of connection between them ("I can use one teabag for both")—is foreshadowed by his curt rejection of her earlier offer, "I don't drink coffee," and by his fussiness about what kind of tea he will drink, in precisely his own way—not strong, and without sugar. To use an ironically apt cliche, it is clear to the reader that this woman is not his cup of tea.

The story's plot, however, does not present any overt resolution of the conflict of personalities and concerns that we have witnessed. "Once I get the program set up it practically runs by itself," are the man's, and the story's, concluding words; the statement may mirror the woman's hope of what might happen once she has managed to "set up" some kind of human contact with him but also dash that hope in reinforcing his focus on the technological and the fact that, his computer skills no longer needed, these two are not likely to meet again. The story's tension remains unresolved.

Does the protagonist realize what has *not* occurred in this scene between her and the man and recognize his implicit rejection? Since the text doesn't really answer that question, this lack of resolution seems part of what the story is centrally "about." Burroway's title, "Tea Leaves," alludes to a fortuneteller's supposed ability to read the future in the dregs of a tea cup. The story's thematic focus, then, seems to be on the uncertainties of our attempts to read each other clearly, and the discrepancy between expectation and actuality that is at the heart of so much human interaction. This man is *not* a pianist; he is not susceptible to the woman's attempts to form even a minimal relationship with him, someone whom she has romanticized and thus misread. The essential divergence of these two characters' worlds is apparent to the reader, if not to the protagonist.

This may seem like a lot to say about such a very short story—are we misreading *it*, or reading *into* it, rather than just reading it? I think not; we have simply asked the kinds of questions we would ask of fiction of any length, and looked for the answers the story provides. We might even legitimately extend this conversation with the text further and see the story as suggesting a larger issue, that Burroway perceives the disconnection between aesthetic sensibility and the advances of technology as problematic. With a computer we need only do "this and this" to "hit the Escape key" and be home free. But until there is a program for "Autofictionreader.bat," we must develop and strengthen our own abilities to respond to the subtleties and implications of the storyteller's art, and thus draw conclusions that are more revelatory than the "judicious guess" of the protagonist of "Tea Leaves."

WHAT MAKES GOOD FICTION GOOD?

Well, it all depends. Judging fiction is not an arcane or elitist practice, limited to book reviewers and academics. We all do it; thus by the time you're fifty pages into a novel you've made a good many judgments. But what criteria do you apply? What follows is not an attempt to prescribe proper criteria; the selection process is inevitably subjective. The aim is rather to suggest a number of possibilities and then to invite you to formulate, as clearly as possible, your own bases of judgment. After all, you'll probably be reading a fair bit of fiction the rest of your life.

It is certainly true that as we grow older our ideas of what makes good fiction good change, often substantially and sometimes rapidly. Thus, for example, for many people, reading Jack Kerouac at age fifteen is very different from reading him at age twenty-one. At fifteen the visionary exuberance of *On the Road*, the Beat bible, with all its male camaraderie and cross-country travel, may seem wonderfully attractive, even intoxicating. At twenty-one, however, though it may still be fun to read, the novel may impress as juvenile, naive, repetitious, and insubstantial.

I am glad that I discovered one of Kerouac's mentors, Thomas Wolfe, when I was sixteen. Then I identified implicitly with Eugene Gant, Wolfe's autobiographical hero, and loved the rhetorical flights of *Look Homeward, Angel*. Less than five years later, however, as my surviving marginal notes testify, although I could remember why I had regarded Wolfe as Great American Novelist No. 1, I couldn't (or didn't) any longer respond to the novel's self-absorbed romanticism. Wolfe hadn't changed; I had.

Chapter 2 Exploring Fiction   **35**

Just last semester Rita, a student in Contemporary American Novel, explained that although it had come highly recommended, when she had first read Toni Morrison's *Song of Solomon,* she hadn't cared for it at all. Why was that? Because, she said, unconsciously she had still associated truth-telling, one of her most important criteria for good fiction, with conventional realism. What's true, in other words, she had thought, is what's usually thought of as real, and in *Song of Solomon* one principal character, Pilate, has no navel, some characters are said to fly, and many of them are, to say the least, profoundly eccentric.

Her recent reading, however, had been different, as she better understood what Morrison was doing and had changed her mind about the equivalence of truth-telling and conventional realism. What we see in *Song of Solomon,* she explained, particularly in its second part, is what's called magical realism, and the aim of the magical realist is, exactly, to enrich our idea of what is real by incorporating *all* dimensions of the imagination, particularly as expressed in myth, magic, and religion. This is not to argue that magical realism is intrinsically superior to conventional realism, just that Rita came to appreciate a new synthesis, that her bases of judgment have changed.

I recently conducted a survey in several literature courses, populated mostly by sophomores and juniors, asking what they believe makes good fiction good. Listed below are the eight most common responses, rank-ordered from the most to the least frequently encountered:

1. The lead character(s) should be compelling, interesting, believable, fully developed; they should be multidimensional and come alive.
2. The plot should be coherent, realistic, intriguing, and driven by a central (thematic) purpose.
3. The story should have emotional relevance; that is, the writer should treat people and situations I can understand, relate to, and care about.
4. The story should have an important underlying theme that speaks on a pressing issue or interesting topic.
5. The story should present a challenge; as one respondent observed, "I like having to dig for things in fiction."
6. The author should convey an in-depth knowledge of the subject matter.
7. The story should be written in plain English.
8. The story should be original in conception and execution.

How many of these criteria do you agree with, and does this ordering make sense to you?

There are probably as many reasons for taking pleasure from fiction as there are fiction readers. We find that in meeting fictional characters and living through their experiences with them we can increase our understanding of the real and various worlds in which we live, and of the complex people who inhabit those worlds with us. But there are those who are drawn to fiction designed to do just the opposite—to take us away from the circumstances of our lives.

The other day one of us found a glossy advertisement for Harlequin romance novels in her mailbox. "What's better," the ad asked, "on a day when your spirits need lifting than to pick up a book that transports you to a thrilling new world of romance and adventure?" Such books, as their publishers promise, are "uppers," instant tickets to fantasyland—easy to read, easy to write about, anything *but* subversive of a reader's peace.

So what can be learned from that kind of fiction? The plot events in escapist fiction, for example, are unrealistically dramatic, and what the ad calls "intriguing plot turns and strange twists of fate" occur in magical "exotic settings with romantic strangers." Such "strangers," the men and women who people Harlequin romances, are stereotypically perfect; readers are happy to identify with them as they "unravel the misunderstandings of hero and heroine." Note there are no *protagonists* here, central characters who may be less than attractive, admirable, or successful, but rather formulaic "heroes" and "heroines." The airbrushed illustrations of such characters in the Harlequin ad depict only the bold and the beautiful, and the (always heterosexual) couples are all Caucasian.

It's clear, then, that the purpose of these novels is to allow the reader to *be* an idealized heroic character who, despite "fighting against all odds," will "find your happy ending." No need when reading to consider the implications of unresolved conflicts or ambiguous conclusions; "endings" in such novels are always "happy", to reward the reader who has been living vicariously in their pages.

As the ad makes clear, there are no subtleties or complexities of plot, setting, character, or denouement for a reader of Harlequin romances to investigate. Nor are there resonant thematic concerns to discover; fiction of this kind tells us what we'd like to believe, providing "message" instead of meaning. It doesn't pretend that the clichés it often enacts—love conquers all, virtue is rewarded in the end, for instance—are true to our experience of the world because, as the ad makes clear, such truths aren't its concern. Nor need they be yours as a reader of escapist fiction, which, as the ad proudly declares, is a "a wonderful way to make your dreams come true." Reading, and writing about, the kinds of fiction we've been discussing in this chapter definitely won't make your dreams come true, but, like all good fiction, it may help you to understand them better.

WORKS CITED

Bennett, Arnold. *The Old Wives' Tale*. New York: Modern Library, n.d.

Brodkey, Harold. "About the End." *New Yorker,* March 17, 1993, 72.

Burroway, Janet. "Tea Leaves." *Micro Fiction: An Anthology of Really Short Stories,* ed. Jerome Stern. New York: W.W. Norton & Co., 1996, 114.

Faulkner, William. "Barn Burning." *Selected Stories of William Faulkner.* New York: Modern Library, 1962.

Hannah, Barry. "Love Too Long." *Airships.* New York: Delta, 1979.

Hemingway, Ernest. *The Sun Also Rises.* New York: Scribner's, 1970.

James, Henry. *The American.* Boston: Riverside-Houghton Mifflin, 1963.

———. "The Art of Fiction." *The Future of the Novel.* New York: Vintage-Random House, 1956.

Joyce, James. "Araby." *Dubliners.* New York: Modern Library, n.d.

McInerney, Jay. *Bright Lights, Big City.* New York: Vintage, 1984.

Salinger, J. D. *The Catcher in the Rye.* Boston: Little, Brown, 1951.

Twain, Mark. *The Adventures of Huckleberry Finn.* Boston: Riverside-Houghton Mifflin, 1958.

CHAPTER 3

Exploring Poetry

Sidney Poger

The word final, superior to all.
Walt Whitman

One of my colleagues, the poet David Huddle, has written a poem called "Coda," in which he tells of an incident his parents related to him during their twice-a-month phone calls:

Coda

David Huddle

Sons grown and gone, they adopt a mutt
that comes, stays ten years, and learns their ways.
On slow walks that good dog leads my parents
a hundred yards out of the gravel driveway
until a gunshot rips through one day's silence.
My mother and father break into a trot,
even though they are old now, too old to run like
this to the curve of the road and the sight
of fat old Daisy's neck a bloody spout,
one spent shell steps away, smoke still spooling,
the backs of two running boys, the one not
carrying the gun looking back and laughing.
They are not strong enough to lift the weight
of their dog. They turn back to the empty house.
Through the hundreds of miles between my house
and theirs, my daughters, my wife, and I
take turns talking with my parents in our
twice-a-month phone call. In our talk we try
to pretend it won't be long before our
visit next summer. I hardly hear how
their words sound; I've lost them and they've lost me,
this is just habit, blood, and memory.
They pause, then they tell us about Daisy,

> how she must have walked right up to those boys
> before they shot her down.... And yes, I am
> seeing just how it was. My mother's voice
> breaks. I am with you, I want to tell them,
> but I manage to say only that I see.

Huddle says that writing about poetry is, like writing poetry, an act of inquiry: In both processes you ask yourself questions and see what the answers might be. The difference is that when you are reading a poem, you have the answers the poet has found to his own questions. Since he has kindly allowed me to examine the various drafts he preserved while writing his poem, I will try to retrace the process Huddle went through, seeking the questions he might have asked to determine how he arrived at the words that make up his poem. As in the game of "Jeopardy," we have the answers; what are the questions?

When asking himself how to describe the distance between himself and his aging parents, Huddle's first answer was to measure the time it took to drive there:

ORIGINAL: It takes sixteen hours to drive from my house to theirs.

This is good poetic practice, measuring distance in terms of hours. Huddle then turned to the more usual measurement of distance by miles, probably figuring that the large number of miles would emphasize the separation, not the hours needed to get there:

REWRITE 1: It's more than eight hundred miles from my house to theirs.

Both measurements are played off against the speed with which the telephone covers the distance. Then, for one draft only, Huddle tries another statement:

REWRITE 2: There are hundreds of miles between my house and theirs.

Finally, he places the measurement, still in hundreds of miles, into an introductory dependent clause that contrasts with the telephone in the main clause:

REWRITE 3: Through the hundreds of miles between my house and theirs, my daughters, my wife, and I take turns talking with my parents in our twice-a-month phone call.

By answering one question, about how to measure the distance separating him from his parents, Huddle has answered a couple of others: contrast between distance and communication, between parents at one end and himself and wife and children at the other, between my house and theirs.

These revisions are clear and relatively easy to follow. The questions are direct and indicated by the answers. More difficult to trace are the revisions to the last line where his problem was how to make these lines sound right, how to make them fit. Huddle wants to tell his parents how he feels about the severe disruption of their lives, but finds it difficult to express his sympathy over the telephone. At first Huddle concludes the poem with how much he could sympathize with his parents' tragedy:

ORIGINAL: this seeing the one measure of my love.

Then he measures his distance from his parents through his extension or holding back of sympathy:

REWRITE 1: Always I can choose just to listen or to try to see it all, every choice a measure of love.

Then the choice becomes more specific:

REWRITE 2: Always I have a choice, accept the blur of facts or imagine it all, choosing to see a measure of love.

Huddle's next answer is in direct empathy with his mother's distress and then the distancing of the goodbye:

REWRITE 3: And yes, I am seeing everything. My mother's voice breaks off. I am with them! I am with them! We say goodbye. We say take it easy.

Apparently that conclusion, with its distancing through the easily repeated cliché of farewell, was not the answer. Still, Huddle struggled with his choice, with what he wants to say and what he can say:

REWRITE 4: My mother's voice breaks. I am with you, I want to tell them, but instead I murmur, *I see, I see.*

Huddle tried one more answer, by interposing the phone between himself and his parents, essentially comforting the phone and not them:

REWRITE 5: And yes, I am seeing just how it was. My mother's voice breaks. I am with you, I want to tell them, but I tell the thing in my hand that I see.

But this seems to be too much. David is not writing about how the telephone gets in the way, but how time and distance do. And so the telephone disappears, replaced by the strivings of the poet to say both what he feels as well as what he says to express those feelings. Although the meaning is the same as the phrase "measure of our love," the language changes, emphasizing not the amount of love but the speaker's difficulty in expressing the love:

REWRITE 6: And yes, I am seeing just how it was. My mother's voice breaks. I am with you, I want to tell them, but I manage to say only that I see.

    This process of writing poetry resembles, in many ways, what we do when we read poetry. Huddle has asked himself a series of questions that come under the general question, How can I communicate what I feel in words? The answers he finds, provisional and temporary as they may be, help him to ask further questions whose answers clarify even more what he wants to express. Reading the poem helps us to see what answers Huddle found. In asking ourselves what questions these answers were meant to satisfy, we duplicate Huddle's process of writing the poem. When we compare Huddle's answers with those we might have framed, we see how skillfully Huddle has proceeded, and we see whether these answers fit in with our experience.

Chapter 3 Exploring Poetry   **41**

This double process of exploration, of finding our way back through the answers the poet has provided to the questions the poem asked him, as well as to see how the answers fit in with our experience, is how poetry is read and written about. But if all this seems comprehensible and straightforward, what makes us so nervous when we are asked to consider a poem and write about it?

Poetry can be daunting. We don't read poems very often, we don't talk in this careful way in lines and revisions, and many students contend that nobody likes poetry anyway. But even those who twitch nervously before reading a poem admit that, since poetry is made up of words, and words communicate something, we should be able to discover how the poem works, write something about the poem, and find out what we think about it.

THE NATURE OF POETRY

Poetry insists on the word. With other forms, plot, character, and point of view are primary considerations. Because the poet uses fewer of them, words are central to the form. While many struggle to translate poetry from one language to another, poetry is, as Robert Frost has suggested, *what is lost in translation.* In other forms we want to know what happens next: Will the king regain his throne? Will the young lovers be united? Will the murderer be discovered? Poetry insists that we read not only to get to the end of the work, to find out what happens, but also to enjoy the language along the way.

But what exactly makes poetry different? Consider the following sentence: "So much depends upon a red wheelbarrow glazed with rainwater beside the white chickens." Now consider it as the poet arranges the words in a pattern on the page:

so much depends
upon

a red wheel
barrow

glazed with rain
water

beside the white
chickens.   (38–39)

William Carlos Williams

This new arrangement sets off the words so that each one becomes important, so that we read each word to see how it fits in with the others and what they all mean together. The four stanzas of Williams' poem present three sharply colored details of "red," "glazed," and "white," which fill our mind. These stanzas literally depend on the first, as they hang below it on the page, but that stanza depends on the details; "so much" is left ambiguous, in contrast to the concrete words of description, so that we can wonder about the difference between the sharply defined bits of the picture and the ambiguous things that depend on it. This poem is a paradigm, in which the images support the language. Rather than reading the sentence to get to the end to see if we understand it, we read and reread the poem to see the tensions and interactions of its parts.

Poetry sometimes repeats certain sounds for the fun of it, as in Edgar Allan Poe's description of the merry sound of silver bells:

> Hear the sledges with their bells—
> Silver bells!
> What a world of merriment their melody foretells!
> How they tinkle, tinkle, tinkle,
> In the icy air of night!
> While the stars that oversprinkle
> All the Heavens, seem to twinkle
> With a crystalline delight
>
> Edgar Allan Poe

Poe doesn't describe the shape or materials of which the bells were made but reproduces their sharp sounds and quick movements through the use of the sound of the letter *i* and the sounds of *m, n, r,* and *w*. This is fun to recite (find the entire poem and recite it out loud—all the different bells and their different sounds are treated in splendid fashion). The poem does not put forth meaning but mood and the pleasure of the different kinds of bells.

We should simultaneously consider *what* is communicated in a poem, as well as *how* it is communicated. It is the *how* that often makes us nervous. Surely such a small poem as "The Red Wheelbarrow," which takes up only eight lines, cannot have all those things in it that call for a school assignment. We feel the author could not have intended us to go over it so carefully, no matter what our instructor says, and even if we could, what we might find out is going to be thin indeed.

How do we deal with those particulars in order to find out not only how the poem works, but how it works in order to develop meaning? In response to this question, Richard, a student in my modern poetry class, wrote the following about Yeats's "The Song of the Happy Shepherd," which goes in part:

> But O, sick children of the world,
> Of all the many changing things
> In dreary dancing past us whirled,
> To the cracked tune that Chronos sings,
> Words alone are certain good.

Richard illustrates Yeats's theme through his own attention to words:

```
Against the backdrop of mortality painted throughout
the poem, Yeats uses a statement and its repetition to
```

assert the value and immortality of words. "Words alone are certain good." Even though the glory of "the kings of old time" is now but "idle words," they still exist even though the kings and the world they ruled are gone. This gives us the image of the all-powerful word that stands alone under its self-generating power. Even the "wandering earth," giving us the image of nature as directionless and chaotic, "may be only a sudden flaming word / In clanging space a moment heard / Troubling the endless reverie."

The image of "the word," according to Richard, seems to amount to a value that the poet associates with the worth of his work. The power of kings and even of the earth itself are mere words. In the confusion of dreams and the search for truth, Yeats seems to say that words, even by themselves, have enormous power. Of course, the repetition of this statement ("Words alone are certain good") adds to its force and establishes this idea as a main theme.

Good poems are often dense; they contain a great deal of matter to be tasted, chewed, and digested. Poetry often says complex things with a minimum of words because the author pays attention both to the words and to their patterns. The poet relies on both *denotation*, what the word means, and *connotation*, what the word suggests. English is particularly fortunate in having an enormously rich vocabulary, having borrowed words from more sources than any other language. It has a great storehouse of synonyms, words whose connotations suggest wholly different contexts. If someone asked, "Did you see the fire last night?" you might answer, "No, I saw a conflagration." Or a blaze or a bonfire. Each of these positive answers defines more carefully what the speaker wants to convey about what happened.

THE TECHNIQUES OF POETRY

A poem is so compressed that, if everything is considered that can be considered, you will never run out of things to write about. In all forms, good literature is not exhausted through any single interpretation. Each time you write, you support your own interpretation and marshal all the evidence you can to support it. Without finding out all you can, you cannot know what is relevant and make the strongest case for your own interpretation.

Rhythm and Meter

Among the important devices peculiar to poetry is rhythm, the rise and fall of stress. Meter is regularized rhythm, the way in which we measure and describe the rhythm. In English words of two or more syllables, we stress one of those syllables (*pen* cil, *tel* e phone, re *solve*). Poets often arrange these stresses in patterns of repetition, patterns with Greek names like "anapest" and "dactyl."

Samuel Taylor Coleridge demystifies these terms in his little poem "Metrical Feet: Lessons for a Boy" where the lines provide examples of the metrical feet they name:

> Trochee trips from long to short;
> From long to long in solemn sort
> Slow Spondee stalks; strong foot! yet ill able
> Ever to come up with Dactyl's trisyllable,
> Iambics march from short to long;
> With a leap and a bound the swift Anapests throng. (401)

A *foot* is the basic metrical unit, usually consisting of one stressed and one or two unstressed syllables, and a line consists of a series of these feet. George Herbert plays with a variety of these traditionally measured lines in the first stanza of his poem "Easter Wings":

> Lord, who createdst Man in wealth and store,
> Though foolishly he lost the same,
> Decaying more and more,
> Till he became
> Most poore.
> With thee
> O let me rise,
> As Larks, harmoniously
> And sing this day thy Victories.
> Then shall the fall further the flight in mee. (223)

This stanza goes from five to four to three to two to one foot per line and then back again in lines predominantly set in iambic feet. In this poem, Herbert represents a set of wings (turn the stanza on its side to see the wings) that settles to earth as it loses faith in God and then takes off again as it regains that faith, a movement represented as well by the shape of the poem.

In the last hundred years poets have relied less on meter—measurable rhythm—than on freer uses of rhythm. Thus meter has become more difficult to measure. What is most important is the way in which the rhythm is continued or broken or tampered with in order to emphasize certain words and ideas. Even more traditional poets alter an expected metrical pattern to emphasize specific words, as John Milton alters the expected iambic pentameter in his sonnet "On the Late Massacre in Piedmont":

> A̲ve̲nge, O Lord, thy s̲la̲ughtered sa̲ints, whose bo̲nes
>   Lie sca̲ttered on the A̲lpine mo̲untains co̲ld,
>   Ev'n the̲m who ke̲pt thy tru̲th so pu̲re of o̲ld
>   When a̲ll our fathers wo̲rshipped sto̲cks and sto̲nes,
> Forge̲t no̲t: in thy bo̲ok re̲cord their gro̲ans
>   Who were thy she̲ep, and in their ancient fold
>   Sla̲in by the blo̲ody Pi̲edmontese that ro̲lled
>   Mo̲ther with I̲nfant down the ro̲cks. Their mo̲ans

Chapter 3 Exploring Poetry

The vales re<u>d</u>oubled to the hills, and <u>they</u>
   To <u>H</u>eav'n.*

(98)

Through changes in the expected rhythm as well as through repetition of the long O sound, Milton emphasizes the idea of revenge, the slaughtering of the innocents, and the admonition "Forget not." Even the moans of the victims are doubled through their echoes from the hills, which are carried to the Lord, who will avenge their deaths. Similarly, Huddle emphasizes the opening words of his poem, "Sons grown and gone," in order to stress the idea of his parents being alone.

Rhyme

Modern poets also use repeated sounds in new as well as in old ways. Most of us recognize rhyme, the words in the middle or at the end of lines that repeat the last stressed vowel sounds, sometimes spelled differently but sounded the same, and any following letters (*moon, June, spittoon, honeymoon*). These are often arranged in patterns the listener recognizes and appreciates. Rhymes not only please us, they reinforce meaning through sound, driving deep into our consciousness. A rhyming couplet may call attention to itself in order to emphasize some conclusion. Shakespeare often does this in his curtain lines, as in Olivia's prayer at the end of Act I of *Twelfth Night*:

Fate, show thy force: ourselves we do not owe.
What is decreed must be, and be this so.

Poets now tend to use, more and more, *slant rhymes,* which may have the same vowel sound and different consonants (*break, strafe*), or the same consonant sounds with different vowels (*thing, slang*). Such rhymes call attention to themselves and to their lack of perfect fit. Dean, another student, discovered how different rhymes make different meanings in Yeats's "The Fisherman," which concludes:

A man who ... cried, Before I am old
I shall have written him one
Poem maybe as cold
And passionate as the dawn.

```
When [Yeats] mentions the reality of the world he uses
some rhymes that are not perfect, whereas when he is talk-
ing about the fisherman his rhymes are better. For exam-
ple when addressing the reality he rhymes "loved" and
"reproved," and "hate" and "seat." He seems to be stating
through these imperfect rhymes that reality is imperfect,
whereas when he talks about the fisherman he uses perfect
rhymes such as "still," "hill," "goes," "clothes."
```

[Underlining Indicates Emphasis. All emphases have not been indicated, only those most important]

Dean discovers Yeats's point that the world of imagination is more regular and more perfect than reality itself. If neither the fisherman nor his world survives, the world of imagination still springs from the devices of the poem.

Alliteration

One of the favorite devices of poets in English is the repetition of initial consonant sounds, or alliteration, as in "On the bald street breaks the blank day" from Tennyson's "In Memoriam." Alliteration is English's substitute for the wealth of rhymes in a language such as Italian, most of whose words end in a vowel. It is easy to find a rhyming word in Italian, much more difficult to do so in English, a language considered word rich but rhyme poor. Translators of Dante, for instance, have labored under the difficulty of reproducing Dante's interlocking rhyme scheme from *The Divine Comedy* in English. Readers like to hear these alliterations, which not only give pleasure and aid memory but also emphasize key words. Huddle uses alliteration in "Coda" to call attention to the line "one spent shell steps away, smoke still spooling." He repeats the initial *g* of *grown* five times in the first five lines. There is only one other initial *g* in the poem, on the word "gun" in line 12, as if the word "gunshot" marks a major turning point.

I asked my modern poetry students to explain what repeated sounds communicate to them. Tom wrote: "Repeated sounds and/or alliteration can help a poem to roll off the tongue in an expressive, sometimes pleasant way." Gail pointed out one use of rhyme and alliteration to underline Yeats's theme in "An Acre of Grass," that, as one grows older, he or she needs more passion to write poetry:

> Grant me an old man's frenzy,
> Myself must I remake
> Till I am Timon and Lear
> Or that William Blake
> Who beat upon the wall
> Till Truth obeyed his call ...

She finds the growing passion of the older man reflected in the growing number of musical devices:

```
The rhyme scheme of the poem reflects the growing energy
of the poem. The first two stanzas contain only final
rhyming couplets, but the last two stanzas each have two
sets of rhymes. The rhyme scheme gets more lively as the
speaker's "old man's frenzy" grows.
   Another element that reflects the growing energy of the
poem is the alliteration—it is used fairly sparingly in
the first two stanzas, and more than twice as often in the
last two stanzas. The effect of this is to increase the
tempo of the poem and imbue it with more energy.
```

While Mike suggested the example, "Melville meanders motionlessly on Mondays," Piper suggested that alliteration makes the poems smoother and more fun. "It also shows a concentration on word choice." This brings us around to the importance of the single word and its relation to other words.

Imagery

The poet also uses imagery, language that appeals directly to one of the five senses. Poets try to make readers see, hear, smell, taste, and feel what they are describing. The reader, because of his or her experience, can participate more fully in the experience of the poem. Kelly says that imagery works "because it allows your imagination to visualize what the words are saying." Keats is a master of imagery as he describes his desire for wine in "Ode to a Nightingale":

> O, for a draught of vintage! that hath been
> Cool'd a long age in the deep-delved earth,
> Tasting of Flora and the country green,
> Dance, and Provençal song, and sunburnt mirth!
> O for a beaker full of the warm South,
> Full of the true, the blushful Hippocrene,
> With beaded bubbles winking at the brim,
> And purple-stained mouth. (205)

One can see the "sunburnt mirth" of the peasant and the mouth of the glass stained with wine, hear the Provençal song, smell the mustiness of "deep-delved earth," taste flowers and meadows, and feel the coolness of the wine as well as the warmth of the country in which it was grown.

Piper writes admiringly of Wallace Stevens's "The Man on the Dump" which, she points out, claims "The dump is full/Of images." "Its visuals are so intense that it can almost appeal to the sense of smell. You can see the dump and almost smell "the wrapper on the can of pears."

Comparison

We might also notice that poetry contains frequent comparisons: The poet never seems to say anything straight. This is not done to bedevil the reader and provide subjects for papers, but because we only learn about something unfamiliar by comparing it to something familiar. If you taste venison for the first time and someone asks you what it tastes like, you might answer: like beef, but richer and gamier. Although this description is inadequate (another answer might be, go and try it for yourself), it shows how one person communicates with another through comparing the new with the old. These comparisons are called similes if they include the words "like" or "as" and metaphors if they omit them. If the poet says her boyfriend is like an oak, she does not mean that he is 30 feet tall and drops acorns. By mentioning the oak, she suggests qualities of steadfastness, size, protection, and beauty, which are not explicit parts of the comparison, but important in what she wants to convey. Sometimes the poet goes out of his or her way, as Emily Dickinson puts it, to "Tell all the Truth but tell it slant." Dickinson uses a metaphor to compare prose with poetry (which she calls "Possibility") to show the latter's larger vision:

> I dwell in Possibility—
> A fairer House than Prose—
> More numerous of Windows—
> Superior—for Doors—

When Robert Frost compares a woman to "A Silken Tent," he does not mention the woman, except in the opening words: "She is, as in a field, a silken tent." Frost's description of the tent, as standing on its own but gently bound to the earth, like the woman he is complimenting, through ties of love, makes the secondary or metaphoric meaning more important than the literal description of the tent.

Diction

The choice of particular words affects how we understand the poem. As my old Shakespeare professor used to say when discussing *King Lear:* "It is one thing to call a man a son of a bitch; it is another to call him son and heir to a bitch; and it is another thing entirely to call him son and heir to a mongrel bitch." Since a poem is made up of words, each of which must be paid attention to, one must consider the kinds of words selected, or the diction; when David Huddle called the dog his parents adopted "a mutt," he is suggesting that it is a dog adopted from the pound, not a pedigreed animal. Are the words difficult, unusual, or used in an unusual or formal way, as in the beginning of Milton's "Lycidas"?

> Yet once more, O ye laurels, and once more
> Ye myrtles brown, with ivy never sere,
> I come to pluck your berries harsh and crude,
> And with forced fingers rude
> Shatter your leaves before the mellowing year.   (142)

Are they short, common, and direct, as in Leigh Hunt's poem "Rondeau"?

> Jenny kissed me when we met,
> Jumping from the chair she sat in;
> Time, you thief, who love to get
> Sweets into your list, put that in:
> Say I'm weary, say I'm sad,
> Say that health and wealth have missed me,
> Say I'm growing old, but add,
> Jenny kissed me.   (763)

Are the words meant to resemble the rhythms of everyday speech, or are they meant to distance us from the everyday? Huddle begins his poem with such flat speech:

> Sons grown and gone, they adopt a mutt
> that comes, stays ten years, and learns their ways.

When Gail was writing about Wallace Stevens's "On the Manner of Addressing Clouds," she made some of her discoveries through an examination of diction:

```
The language of the poem, as in most of Stevens's work, is
opulent. He uses magnificent language to write about lan-
guage: "sustaining pomps," "exaltation without sound," "music
of meet resignation." Such gorgeous language is a way of cap-
turing the reader in a situation and making it seem beyond
the bounds of everyday experience. It is as though Stevens
strips away the plain layer of everyday existence to reveal
a sensuous world of sound and language.
```

Structure

Once you have determined the *diction* or choice of words and *tone of voice* or the speaker's attitude toward self, audience, and subject, you have to decide which words are emphasized. This is done not only through examining rhythm, rhyme, and sound, but also through examining how the unit of thought works. Is the unit of thought expressed, for example, in the line, in one of Whitman's lists in "Song of Myself":

> The carpenter dresses his plank, the tongue of his foreplane
> whistles its wild ascending lisp (41)

Or is it the couplet, as in A. E. Housman's "Terence, This Is Stupid Stuff":

> But oh, good Lord, the verse you make,
> It gives a chap the belly-ache. (209)

Or is it in the stanza, as when Andrew Marvell starts the first verse of "To His Coy Mistress" with a proposition:

> Had we but World enough, and Time,
> This coyness Lady were no crime

decides in the second stanza that we haven't:

> But at my back I alwaies hear
> Times winged Chariot hurrying near:

then comes to a conclusion in the third stanza:

> Now therefore ... (1090–91)

Is the thought expressed through direct comparison (metaphor or simile) or through an implied comparison, as when Ralph Waldo Emerson uses architectural terms in the second stanza of "The Snow Storm":*

> Come see the north wind's <u>masonry.</u>
> Out of an unseen <u>quarry</u> evermore
> Furnished with <u>tile,</u> the fierce <u>artificer</u>
> Curves his white <u>bastions</u> with projected <u>roof</u>
> Round every windward <u>stake,</u> or tree, or <u>door.</u> (42)

Are there forms that control the shape the thought takes, such as the octet and sestet of the Italian sonnet, in which the first eight lines present one thought and the last six present a response, or the three quatrains and a couplet of the English sonnet, which presents three parallel ideas and a summary couplet? Or are there fourteen-line poems that play off against the traditional forms? Huddle's "Coda" is made up of two such fourteen-line poems—are they matching poems, the first describing the event, the second the communication of the event? (Most of Huddle's other poems in the volume *Stopping By Home* are also fourteen lines long.) All these ways of presentation guide us to an understanding of the poem we could not have realized otherwise.

Point of View

The reader must determine who is speaking in a poem. It is never the writer, but some imaginary person (see Chapter 2, "Exploring Fiction"). Even if the poet wants to express some of his or her own values, one changes one's experiences in reconstructing them. We have to ask ourselves: Who is the imaginary speaker? Is he or she well educated? Old or young? Serious or frivolous? The point of view the poet chooses determines the diction, and the diction reveals the values of the speaker. The speaker may urge his dying father to struggle against the onset of death, as Dylan Thomas portrays in "Do not go gentle into that good night" (128), but the dying father may have wanted to say something completely different.

The poet may speak almost directly in his or her own voice; the speaker may be close to the poet but is a persona. When Milton addresses the reader to "[justify] God's ways to man" in *Paradise Lost*, he looks for God's reasons to an open-minded audience. When Pope "vindicates" God's ways, he explains to a more hostile audience what God intended. Neither of these voices indicates Milton's position as the great rebel nor Pope's role as a Catholic constrained by a Protestant majority. Huddle has parents who adopted a dog that was shot, and has a wife and two daughters, but the poem does not show his skill at volleyball, his beautiful reading voice, his life as a teacher. The poem shows him only in his role as husband and son, not in all of his complex life. "Persona" is the term that identifies the voice speaking a poem, to emphasize that it is a fiction, constructed for a rhetorical purpose by the real human poet.

*[Emphasis Added.]

While all forms of literature can use dialogue, there are poems that advance like drama through people speaking to each other, changing their minds as they talk out their different views, as Mary and Warren do in Robert Frost's "The Death of the Hired Man." Their two definitions of home are very different in spirit and expressed in different voices:

[WARREN] "Home is the place where, when you have to go there,
They have to take you in."
[MARY] "I should have called it
Something you somehow haven't to deserve." (20)

Neither definition is complete without taking the other into consideration, and by the end of the poem Warren has come to adopt Mary's view while she has made room for his. Robert Browning carries off perhaps the more difficult, and more showy, task, in his dramatic monologues, of suggesting the action with only one voice, which implies the reaction of that second person. In "My Last Duchess," we have the story of a failed marriage, negotiations for a second marriage, and hints of its possible difficulties, all represented through the welcoming voice of the Duke.

Poets change their voices from poem to poem. T. S. Eliot uses one questing voice in "Ash Wednesday," another in *Four Quartets,* a third narrative voice in "The Love Song of J. Alfred Prufrock." Eliot warned his reader not to mistake the voice in *The Waste Land* as his own when, in an early version, he titled his poem with a quote from Dickens: "He Do the Police in Different Voices."

Even though poetry may share the action and descriptions of narrative and drama, poetry has other resources. Poetry probably began as entertainment sung to a lyre, hence the term *lyric.* While the word "lyric" originally described singing, we now apply it generally to those poems, or parts of poems, whose personal melody impresses us above all else.

Some poems may be built on pure description. In "The Bells," Poe describes the sounds of various bells and their effects on the reader; there is no story, no narration, no dialogue, no action. The poem proceeds through the musical description of sound and rhythm. Another poem may deal with generalized topics, but without applicability to any specific person, as when Robert Herrick advises young girls to enjoy their beauty while they can in "Gather Ye Rosebuds While Ye May." Of course, you can use songs to persuade to action; after all, Herrick's is one of the most famous seduction poems in the language. But even though you may use this poem as a means to action, its main impulse is to sing something about our condition on earth.

Some call the lyric impulse, the impulse to sing, the purest strain of the poetic, most divorced from the forms of fiction and drama. Admittedly, the lyric voice is difficult to write about since it is allied with song, and music may rise beyond our powers of analysis. But poetry is made up of words, not notes. Former student Piper notes, "Words can become notes within the sound of the word. The lyric poem ... lulls or compels you to keep reading." With a careful examination of what you have read and an understanding of how the poem is put together, you will respond to poetry as it deserves to be responded to: as one of the most polished forms of art.

RESPONDING TO POETRY

I asked my students what they look for when they read a poem. Each of their responses was real and to the point. Sharon responded: "I look first to see what the meaning is. The first level meaning. If that's too difficult I look also primarily for the beauty of the words—phrases that jump out at you, unusual metaphors, or striking images." Teri emphasizes language: "When I read a poem for pleasure I look for colorful words and language, movement—sometimes a story." Debbie and Melissa agree on looking for "how it makes me feel." "Definitely the first and most important thing ... is its relevance to myself, life, experiences, etc.... If the poet is writing about something I have seen, felt, experienced, hoped to experience, it makes that poem more than just words." Richard also talks about relevance, but in different terms: "I look for a satisfying conclusion—does the poem 'click shut,' that is, is the ending strong enough to have an effect on me?"

These are general expectations, but when you study a poem in order to write a paper, the first question you might ask is: How does this poem work? You can begin to answer that question by considering the devices described here. Another approach is to ask the kinds of questions posed in Chapter 7, "On Not Being a Tourist, or Why It's Important to Study Literary Theory." But no matter what question you ask in a paper, part of its answer is another question: How does the poem mean what I think it means? Only as the answers to the second question affect the first should they be brought within the compass of the paper. Every teacher groans inwardly when he or she sees a paper that specifies details without discrimination: "The rhyme scheme is ABAB, there are a great number of words that start with 'g.'" Only if the rhyme or alliteration or rhythm affects the meaning should it be mentioned. Gail sums up the process: "I prefer poetry that uses concise, firm, concrete images that swoop down and surprise you into thinking."

WORKS CITED

Coleridge, Samuel Taylor. "Metrical Feet: Lessons for a Boy." *The Poems of Samuel Taylor Coleridge.* Ernest Hartley Coleridge. Oxford Standard Authors. New York: Oxford UP, 1960.

Dickinson, Emily. "I dwell in Possibility." *Final Harvest: Emily Dickinson's Poems.* Boston: Little Brown and Company, 1961.

Donne, John. *The Poems of John Donne.* Ed. Herbert Grierson. New York: Oxford University Press, 1951.

Emerson, Ralph Waldo. "The Snow Storm." *The Complete Works of Ralph Waldo Emerson Poems* vol. IX. Ed. E. W. Emerson. Boston: Houghton Mifflin, 1904.

Frost, Robert. "The Death of the Hired Man." *North of Boston.* New York: Holt, 1916.

Herbert, George. "Easter Wings." *Major Poets of the Earlier Seventeenth Century.* Ed. Barbara K. Lewalski et al. New York: Odyssey, 1973.

Hunt, Leigh. "Rondeau." *English Romantic Poetry and Prose.* Ed. Russell Noyes. New York: Oxford University Press, 1956,

Housman, A. E. "Terence, This Is Stupid Stuff." *English Poetry in Transition 1880–1920.* Ed. John M. Munro. New York: Pegasus, 1968.

Keats, John. "Ode to a Nightingale." *Selected Poems and Letters.* Ed. Douglas Bush. Boston: Houghton Mifflin, 1959.

Marvell, Andrew. "To His Coy Mistress." *Major Poets of the Earlier Seventeenth Century.* Ed. Barbara K. Lewalski et al. New York: Odyssey, 1973.

Milton, John. "On the Late Massacre in Piedmont." "Lycidas." *The Complete Poetical Works of John Milton.* Ed. Douglas Bush. Boston: Houghton Mifflin, 1965.

Poe, Edgar Allan. "The Bells." *Edgar Allan Poe: Poetry, Tales, and Selected Essays.* New York: The Library of America, 1996.

Shakespeare, William. *Twelfth Night.* New Haven: Yale University Press, 1954.

Thomas, Dylan. *The Collected Poems of Dylan Thomas.* New York: New Directions, 1953.

Whitman, Walt. "Song of Myself." *Leaves of Grass.* Ed. Scully Bradley et al. New York: Norton, 1973.

Williams, William Carlos. "The Red Wheelbarrow." *Selected Poems.* New York: New Directions, 1963.

Yeats, William Butler. "The Song of the Happy Shepherd." "The Fisherman." "An Acre of Grass." *The Collected Poems of W. B. Yeats.* New York: Macmillan, 1956.

CHAPTER 4

Exploring Drama: Reading Script into Play

James Howe

I had to grow into loving theater. I could always absorb poems and stories so that they became part of me, but plays seemed different—more public somehow—maybe because they're written to be performed. Fiction is meant to be read privately (even though it could be read aloud to listeners). But without stages and actors and actresses, there would be neither playwrights nor plays. Every printed version of a play is a script waiting to be enacted.

I had to learn to read plays that way—knowing that their final form occurs in the theater, not on the page. And I would suggest that we learn to write about them that way too. This chapter will explore what "that way" means for us, first as a theater audience, and then as readers and writers.

DRAMA AS PERFORMANCE

In performance, characters come to life. They occupy physical space, they move, and nearly always they speak. While reading fiction or poetry, we imagine; as an audience for a play, we see and hear.

In some ways, of course, a play is a lot like a novel or short story. Its *action* usually takes narrative form. Its *characters* do things and say things that are consistent with their roles, and these "things" in turn form the *plot,* including the *conflict* (usually between two or more characters, or between two elements within one character, or between characters and their environment, social or natural). The action of this conflict intensifies to a moment of emotional or intellectual *climax* (or both). At this climax, the two main conflicting elements confront each other most directly, so that we see their nature more clearly, and understand the fictional world more completely.

In writing about drama, therefore, we can usually write about its story. But we must do it differently than we do for other literary forms, and this difference has less to do with its content than with the nature of its presentation. For example, there is seldom a narrator, even implicitly, to tell the characters' story for them. (Plays that incorporate onstage narrators are usually seen as self-consciously "experimental" for doing so.) Therefore, once a performance (or a reading) begins, the *point of view* cannot be changed.

In addition, the plot needs to unfold more quickly than in a novel. The action is often telescoped into extremely concentrated form. In the medieval allegorical play "Everyman," the central character Everyman is confronted by the character Death on the last day of his life. In *Macbeth,* the main character changes from loyal subject to king-killer in the very first act; in *Othello,* the hero's rapturous love is transformed by Iago into murderous rage within the first two acts. Indeed, the word "dramatic" is often used in common speech as a synonym for "intense" or "concentrated" effect.

There is a practical reason for this: In the theater, we can only sit so long, and we can only pay attention so long. Unlike the process of reading, which we can do on our favorite couch, picking up our book and putting it down at leisure, in a theater we're stuck in a single seat for the whole two or three hours—longer in some other cultures or in some earlier periods of our own. We tend to get tired, and our attention starts to drift, so a play has to be forceful and quick moving, start to finish. It has to have drive.

Another difference between fiction and drama is that dramatic effects are *stage* effects. In novels we are often asked to imagine a particular scene as it might look if it were unfolding in real life. A play, however, is presented on a particular stage, and its visual effects depend on this stage—its size and shape, the nature of the scenery and costuming, even its placement in the theater. For example, in 1600 Shakespeare's stage thrust out into the middle of the audience, and was an open-air platform. No artificial lighting emphasized the separation between actors and audience; an actor literally stood in the middle of the audience, lit by the same daylight. Under such relatively intimate circumstances, the soliloquy—a character speaking his mind directly to the audience—seems more natural than it does in the conventional modern theater, where the stage area is more distinctly set off from the audience, and where artificial lights emphasize this separation by illuminating the players and leaving the audience in darkness.

For the sake of clarity about stage effects, let's take a closer look at Shakespeare's stage. It was essentially a bare stage. The few sets (there was virtually nothing we would call scenery) were symbolic rather than realistic. They represented generic places like a garden, a cave, a mountain, a throne, but not particular places, and they did not have the details usually associated with verisimilitude—the attempt to make the imagined seem "real." Indeed, this stage, like the classical Greek one, was essentially unlocalized; because it didn't represent a particular place, it could be any place, and any time as well.

The effectiveness of our reading of Shakespeare's plays depends on imagining their action on this stage. For example, in Shakespeare's *Henry The Fourth, Part One,* when Falstaff falls in battle "as if he were dead," it's helpful to imagine this act from the perspective of the audience at an actual performance.

As readers, we know from the stage direction that Falstaff is faking. From the perspective of an audience, though, we don't know about the stage direction; we only know what we see: that Falstaff "falls down *as if he were dead*." As the term implies, stage directions provide guidance about how the play should be staged, in this case directing the actor to pretend to die. If the actor does this well, as audience members (who don't get to read stage directions), we would believe that Falstaff is dead, so that when we read that Falstaff gets up again a little later, we should imagine as readers the surprise we would "really" experience in the theater. Further, if we see Falstaff as a character who is larger than life, perhaps embodying some basic quality that exceeds our normal human limits (like spontaneity or freedom from conventional codes of conduct), then the surprise may seem almost miraculous. We might even see his return to life as a kind of resurrection, a reaffirmation of the enduring power of a basic life principle.

In addition to the absence of a narrator, the compressed development of the plot, and the use of stage effects, a play's presentation differs in one other crucial way from fiction and poetry. The characters have great power simply because of the fact that actors physically act out their stories. Characters seem to exist directly before us in our own immediate field of experience. It is harder to diminish their presence by arguing, as we can with characters we imagine from reading a novel, that they are not lifelike. In fact, in "reality," when a person is suddenly run over by a truck—or when anything similarly outside our normal range of expectation occurs—we do not have the leisure to pretend that it isn't really happening. Quite to the contrary, we feel pain, we see blood, we hear sirens, and when we try to walk away, we find that our legs don't work. It may be preposterous, but it is also "real." When a play works, we often respond in a similar way to characters who are palpably before us in the theater.

READING DRAMA

Of course, in a literature class the script itself is all we have, so it's important to keep in mind that in a sense it only *seems* to be a text, that it is actually a play waiting to be acted. We will then be less likely to look for an authoritative (or even ironic) narrative voice and less likely to evaluate characters and events on the basis of their resemblance to "life." Instead, we will accept what the script gives us and try to imagine it as acted on a particular stage. We will read it as if we were directors planning a production. We will read it in the awareness that the play is partly our own creation, that we ourselves mediate between the script and the world (as represented by an audience). At the same time, though, we must imagine it as we would have it played onstage *to* ourselves as a part of that audience. By giving the script an interpretation and then imagining its effects onstage, we complete it and bring it to life. Indeed, if there is an authoritative point of view, it is ours. As imagined directors, we determine the perspective from which it will be staged, and as its imagined audience, we respond to it.

WRITING ABOUT DRAMA

When we write about a play, we present the results of our reading. Therefore, we may write about any of the stage conventions we just discussed and about how a particular play accommodates itself to them. In doing so, we might also have to study how these conventions were used in the past (for example, what kind of stage Shakespeare's theater had) in order to assess how a play's conventions might have worked during its own time. In literature courses, however, most of us will be writing most of the time about those elements of drama that are similar to fiction or poetry. We will be analyzing character, plot, tone (or atmosphere), and language, but always in the awareness that these elements are meant to happen on a stage. And whatever our topic, we will be discussing how it contributes to a final effect, or to an interpretation, of the full play (as we imagine it performed).

Writing about Character

Before our formal writing begins, we must choose a topic. We might decide to analyze the nature of a character (or some aspect of the plot or language), and we begin collecting information. In a play, most of this information consists of the character's speeches and the reactions of other characters—physical or verbal—to him or her, since there is no narrator to describe either the character or the actions. We study what the character says to figure out what kind of person he is. If, for example, we see that a character never tells a lie, has no sense of humor, never expresses any emotion, and is named Truth, we might think of her as allegorical rather than fully dimensioned and realistic. This is not good or bad; it is simply one dramatic genre rather than another.

In this way, a play teaches us how to see, teaches us what to expect. In this example, we might expect a lesson about truth and the way it operates in the world—but we might not expect our strongest emotions to be engaged. Truth is not like us, she does not suffer from pain and confusion and failure, nor feel pride and joy. We do, and we feel most sympathetic to characters who resemble us in these things. Therefore, we might analyze the idea Truth represents, and how clearly and forcefully she enacts that idea, but we probably would not evaluate her on the basis of whether or not she makes us cry. She seems better suited for other effects. An analysis of the main characters (or of any of the other major elements of a play), often shows us that play's *conventions*—the kind of effects it seems to pursue. This in turn will help us imagine how it might be presented on a stage.

And when we do imagine it onstage, we see at once how limited characters are. Because there is seldom any clear authorial voice, they can seldom act as their author's mouthpiece. When they step forward to tell us what they think, they speak merely in their own persons; their understanding is limited (as ours is) by temperament and by their ability to understand. When Othello asks us to think of him as "one that lov'd not wisely but too well," for example, we must reserve judgment. We know that he's just killed the woman he loves, and then found out that his suspicions about her were wrong. We know that, under the circumstances, he may be slightly unhinged, may be trying desperately not to lose his noble self-image. Sometimes a character deceives himself; sometimes, he may actually be lying. Whatever is happening, we usually have to figure it out for ourselves.

EXAMPLES OF CHARACTER INTERPRETATION

In Shakespeare's *The Taming of the Shrew,* Kate is the shrew; she feels mistreated by her family and by society. She beats up her sister, yells at her father, and breaks a lute over the head of a tutor. Meanwhile Petruchio, who is looking for a wealthy wife, sees that she is not yet spoken for and admires her spirit. Clearly, however, his wooing is going to be a challenge. Kate is extremely suspicious and has no reason to trust her new suitor. So he develops a plan of attack, and it is so successful that many people think he's a bully.

One of my students, Laurie, found this idea interesting, and decided to test it by studying his character. However, she does not take even his most obvious speeches at face value. Rather, she uses them to assess his degree of self-awareness. Petruchio, she writes,

```
… proceeds to outline his plan of attack, telling us he
is going to put on an act, put on false appearances, to tame
her:
```

Say that she rail, why then I'll tell her plain
She sings as sweetly as a nightingale.   (2.1.170–171)

```
He shows us that he is aware [enough] of fronts and plans
to use one himself.
```

Laurie looks below the surface of her character's speech. She is interested in Petruchio's plan to deceive Kate, but she is even more interested in how this plan implies that he is self-aware, thus possibly not self-deceiving, possibly even admirable. The rest of her essay tests this hypothesis against Petruchio's acts and other speeches.

Another problem, however, is that our way of seeing a character is probably only one of many plausible ways. This is true because we must figure everything out for ourselves and every reader "sees" a little differently from every other reader. Thus, while discussing the personality of Kate in the same play, another student, Hilary, focuses on how Kate responds to Petruchio's apparent bullying when he demands that Kate agree with whatever he says, no matter how wrong:

```
Kate's first act of acquiescence, some might call it sub-
mission, comes when she says, "But sun it is not, when you
say it is not; / And the moon changes even as your mind.
```

Chapter 4 Exploring Drama: Reading Script into Play

> / What you will have it nam'd, even that it is, / And so it shall be so for Katherine" (4.5.19–22). Now we see her hesitancy has been replaced by a more mature and self-aware assurance. In learning the rules of the game from Petruchio, she has become comfortable within the boundaries it has created, and she is able to lay down her guard and not feel the fool because of it. It is to a new level of understanding that Petruchio has led her and not as some might think into a role of submission [italics added].

Rebecca, a third student, exemplifies the cause of this problem, the fact that different readers see differently. She comes to a conclusion very similar to Hilary's, but she gets there from a quite different set of observations:

> Although she [Kate] originally is violent and rude, she is also interesting and human. In contrast, at the end of the play, she seems artificial and shallow. This drastic change in behavior leads us to believe that she may be pretending.

Therefore,

> she is not tamed; she is taught, taught how to play Petruchio's game.

Hilary too interpreted Kate as pretending at the end of the play, but because she seemed truly at "a new level of understanding," not because she seemed "artificial and shallow."

WRITING ABOUT LANGUAGE

As we have seen, the language of the characters is all we have to study in a play, and it can be studied in ways other than in its relation to character. Just as with a study of the characters, however, we must imagine it as it would be presented in the theater—as we might hear it spoken. We must ask ourselves questions such as, How might this particular character, with this particular temperament, speak this line? How must he or she feel like to say this? And therefore, what might the inflection of this line be? What might the voice sound like here? To answer these questions, you'll need to pay attention to the details of the passage you're analyzing, but also to the play as a whole, since that will provide the broader understanding of character and of the play's conflicts and thematic concerns that will help you understand the significance of this passage.

Let's look closely at the specific language of the following dialogue from the opening moments of Lorraine Hansberry's *A Raisin in the Sun*. The play is set in an apartment in an African-American section of Chicago in the 1950s. Ruth is a mother, Travis, her 10- or 11-year-old son:

RUTH: Sit down and have your breakfast, Travis.

TRAVIS: Mama, this is Friday. *[Gleefully]* Check coming tomorrow, huh?
RUTH: You get your mind off money and eat your breakfast.
TRAVIS: *[Eating]* This is the morning we supposed to bring fifty cents to school.
RUTH: Well, I ain't got no fifty cents this morning.
TRAVIS: Teacher says we have to.
RUTH: I don't care what teacher say. I ain't got it. Eat your breakfast, Travis.
TRAVIS: I *am* eating.
RUTH: Hush up, now, and just eat!
[The boy gives her an exasperated look for her lack of understanding, and eats grudgingly]
TRAVIS: You think Grandmama would have it?
RUTH: No! And I want you to stop asking your grandmother for money, you hear me?
TRAVIS: *[Outraged]* Gaaaleee! I don't ask her, she just gimme it sometimes!
RUTH: Travis Willard Younger—I got too much on me this morning to be—
TRAVIS: Maybe Daddy—
RUTH: *Travis!*
[The boy hushes abruptly. They are both quiet and tense for several seconds]
TRAVIS: *[Presently]* Could I maybe go carry some groceries in front of the supermarket for a little while after school then?
RUTH: Just hush, I said. *[Travis jabs his spoon into his cereal bowl viciously, and rests his head in anger upon his fists]* If you through eating, you can get up over there and make up your bed.

The first thing we might notice about this dialogue is the enormous range of emotions that Travis goes through in such a short period of time—maybe a minute of stage time. His first words are spoken "gleefully," but Ruth seems hostile to everything he says, and his emotional reactions go into a downward spiral, from exasperated, to grudging, to outraged, to anger. Ruth's speeches seem to consist of nothing but orders and put-downs. In these few short speeches, she issues ten separate commands; she denies or negates what he says five times; and she resorts to guilt, talking about how much she's "got on her" this morning. Twice she resorts to naked power, calling him by all three names—Travis Willard Younger—and then cutting him off in mid-sentence with *"Travis!"*—leaving it to the actress to find the tone of voice that would convey the printed italics and the exclamation point. And she seems insensitive to the embarrassment he fears at not having the fifty cents he'll be asked to produce.

This probably isn't their normal relationship. Travis seems too spontaneous at the start of this passage and too resourceful at the end, in suggesting that he could hustle some work at the supermarket, to be a habitually abused child. So we're left wondering what could have caused such an apparently abnormal outburst of hostility from a normally supportive mother. The rest of the play will help to explain why she reacts this way, but we might take note of what exactly in Travis's words seem to prompt her reaction, since they turn out to be thematically central. The first is that Travis's first two speeches both concern money, the mysterious check that's coming tomorrow and the fifty cents he needs for school. His words seem to touch Ruth's submerged anxiety about money, and she lashes out. The second cause of her hostility seems to be his mention of other family members who might give him the money he needs—these are the times she uses his name as a weapon. As it turns out, the family is in a financial dilemma that centers on another mother-son relationship, that between Grandmama and Daddy; the two figures who are really in the background of this dialogue between Ruth and her son. The language in the dialogue, which at first glance might just seem interestingly true to life, turns out to be a subtle introduction of the main themes of a play that will turn on questions of the value of money, maternal love, and the anger and frustration of children.

DRAMATIC CONVENTIONS

Sometimes, a play behaves unpredictably, in ways that seem to subvert the expectations of some of the conventions we have been discussing—and sometimes with powerful effect. Although our seats are physically fixed in a particular place in the theater, and even though there is seldom a narrator to manipulate our reaction to the play, the playwright *can* change our perspective, by encouraging one set of expectations, and then violating them. For example, in *Merchant of Venice* Shakespeare seems to be writing a conventionally moral play about the values of Christian love and mercy, contrasted with the Jew Shylock's miserliness and desire for revenge. But when the Christians defeat Shylock at the climax of the play, they seem as merciless and vengeful as they had accused him of being. Indeed, the villain seems to become their victim. The expected roles of the conflicting characters are reversed, the expected conventional value system is subverted, and for almost four centuries now the play has remained a puzzle.

Why might a playwright do such a thing?

We have seen how the performance aspect of drama engages complex theatrical conventions. The ending of *Merchant of Venice* requires us to reconsider the implications of some of these conventions. Having been drawn into the story, our emotions are engaged. If it works, although we know the play is make believe, we "believe in" it—its setting, its characters, its plot—as if it were reality itself. If we are puzzled by the play, we will feel this puzzlement personally and actively try to resolve it. In essence, by making us think harder, the playwright asks us to see more!

In the case of *The Merchant of Venice,* Shakespeare (writing for a largely Christian audience) creates Christian characters with whom we are likely to associate ourselves, whatever our religious beliefs, because they seem motivated by positive qualities such as mercy and love. We cheer for Portia as she defeats the enemy. Then we see that in winning, she and the other Christians show not mercy or love, but delight in vengeance. And we in the audience are forced to question our own virtue—we have caught ourselves cheering the vengeful Christians on! Suddenly the issues of the play become personal. We ourselves are implicated in the hypocrisy of the Venetians. We must reexamine ourselves in the light of our reaction to the play. In other words, because we are puzzled, we turn inward. As a result, the play strikes us more forcefully—and more meaningfully—than most "conventional" plays. Some of the most provocative student essays will address a question such as, How does this play make me feel? and then analyze the play to answer the follow-up question, How did it get me to feel that way?

METADRAMA

Metadrama is a term that has been used by literary scholars to discuss plays (or parts of plays) that seem self-consciously to refer to the conventions of drama itself. In a similar way, people speak of fiction that is self-referential about the process of writing fiction as Metafiction; of history that explores problems inherent in writing history as Metahistory. But this self-referential quality seems more pervasive in drama than in other forms of writing, perhaps because of the very nature of the stage: Flesh-and-blood humans are really acting in our presence. And that word "acting" sums up the ambiguity. You and I act every minute of our real lives, but we use the word in an entirely different sense when we speak about the behavior of "actors" on a stage. The phenomenon has been recognized at least since the fifth century B.C.E. when Aristotle began his definition of tragedy by calling it "an imitation of an action."

In its extreme form, playwrights can call into question the most basic conventions of the genre. Luigi Pirandello, for example, creates six characters whose script involves their search for an author and a story so that they can have roles to play. This is important to them because without a role, a character has no identity. In *Six Characters in Search of an Author* there is nothing for us to pretend to believe in. We are forced to see such characters to be pure artifice, lacking even the "reality" of conventional dramatic pretense, a situation we have to pay attention to because they themselves insist upon it in their speeches. Yet gradually we perceive that in their search for identity on stage, they are not so different from us in our own lives. And when we see this analogy we may ask, Who in fact are *we*? What identity have we that we can count on? Are we waiting for someone to write a script for us?

Metadrama is powerful because it draws so directly on the essential nature of the theater. It refers explicitly to itself as an illusion whose reality is *only* apparent, and insists that its power—the power of theater—is drawn from this fact. Because it is not real, we give it license to portray our frailties more strongly, more appallingly than we would normally allow even our friends to do. And because it is not real, we feel we need not take it too seriously. We need not construct our normal defense mechanisms against it. We need not deny its truth. And paradoxically, because it is not real, its power can be even greater than most of our encounters with the normal world.

Even when this quality is not written into the script, actors and actresses often emphasize the metadramatic nature of theater. They often find their masks

Chapter 4 Exploring Drama: Reading Script into Play

and costumes to be strangely liberating. In their apparent anonymity, behind an assumed role, they can "act out" human impulses and qualities that in normal life must be suppressed, or at least restrained. There is always a tension between the actor's need to hide his "real" identity in order to play a role, and the freedom he feels to express himself through the role. All of us feel jealousy, for example, but few of us would give it the full expression we might sometimes wish. What an opportunity the role of Othello gives us! Metadrama merely makes this theatrical truth explicit.

Perhaps in recognition of this aspect of the stage, many playwrights build the tension between acting and being, between the normal limits of acceptable behavior and the gargantuan dimensions of secret desire, into the characters in their scripts. For example, Shakespeare's King Richard III gloats about his ability to fool the other characters. Quite explicitly, he is a character who "acts"— who does onstage in his role what an actor does: He pretends to be different than he is. However, he does so in order to achieve his true desire: to be king. Part of his power is that by acting, he can "stage" the full monstrousness of his desire, and we can marvel at his skill in doing it. Such characters enact the dual quality of our nature too.

One of my students was interested in discovering why, although Richard is a villain, we like him in the early parts of the play. In trying to figure this out, Tammy becomes conscious of Richard as a character who acts, and how this influences her feelings:

> When Shakespeare attaches us to a devious character he enables us to take a journey to the darker side of nature. While doing this, he also sees how far he can push our sense of morality. His method of doing so is to worsen the character's behavior by degrees until finally we can like him no more.

Tammy then focuses on a particular event from early in the play by way of example:

> The scene I'm referring to is usually called "the seduction of Anne," but I think it would be safe to call it the "seduction of the audience" as well. What's so incredible about this scene is that the audience doesn't really expect him [Richard] to succeed, but he does. He is an even better con-artist than we had thought he'd be … We can't help but admire the wordplay and manipulation on Richard's part …

Later in the play, as Richard's villainy gets worse and worse, Tammy doesn't justify her turning against him from the moral point of view, which would run the risk of imposing her own standards of morality on Shakespeare. Instead, she justifies *her* change by noticing a change in him:

> At this point there's no hope for liking Richard. If *he* can't live with his conscience, how can *we*? [italics added]

Then Tammy moves toward her conclusion, continuing to draw on her self-consciousness about being part of an audience. By the final act,

```
Without the shows to suspend our moral judgment we can no
longer like him, and therefore we have no hero to like in
this play. We also feel guilty for ever having liked him,
and even worse, being his accomplice by liking his tricks
well enough to enjoy his successes.
```

This consideration of audience response, allows Tammy to show *how it feels in the audience* to watch a play that, from an intellectual point of view, teaches a simple lesson about conventional morality. This approach also allows her to identify the source of the play's power, and then analyze the way it realizes that power—the way it draws us in and can then force us to second-guess ourselves.

TELEVISION AND FILM

Part of the power of a play is our awareness that it is a performance (if we are seeing it) or that it is meant to be performed (if we are reading it), even though it pretends to enact reality. As readers of a play, in particular, in imagining its performance, we readers complete the script; we give it a self-consistent interpretation of how it might be staged and what it might mean. Perhaps comparison with the visual media of television and film will help clarify this aspect of drama. While they are similar to drama in many respects, they are not live performances, but are interpreted for us by the camera—an intermediary eye that oversees and, to some extent, interprets what we see. The camera can zoom in to a close-up—of a facial expression, a bleeding wound—and it can zoom out, to a panorama of a whole field of battle with a cast of thousands and can show "real" clouds rolling in from the horizon. This intermediary role of the camera serves as an analogue to the narrative voice in fiction: It can underline a particular perspective or emphasis by the angle of its shooting. In a sense, the camera's perspective is more dictatorial than the authorial voice of fiction or the director's perspective in the theater. While reading a play, we can stop to think. In the theater, we can move our attention from one character or part of the stage to another. But in film and television, we see nothing at all except what the camera shows us.

In visual media, as in drama, we can discuss the nature of the scenery and other visual effects; as in drama and fiction, we can discuss the elements of conventional storytelling (character, plot, language); and as in fiction, we can discuss point of view—that is, how the camera is manipulated to achieve different effects. (To be sure, to do this last thing well requires a kind of technical knowledge entirely different from that required in the analysis of a play.) And at last, in writing about television and film, as in writing about any literary form, the most important element is the writer's clear awareness of his or her own responses, and his or her sensitivity to the artist behind the words and images. We must always be asking: *What* does the work get me to *feel?* and *How* does it get me to feel *that way?* and *Why?* (For more information on responding to visual media, see Chapter 6.)

CHAPTER 5

Exploring the Essay

Mary Jane Dickerson and Richard Sweterlitsch

Historically, the essay finds its roots in classical literature, where it developed as epistles (letters), commentaries, or, simply, histories. In later literatures, the essay appeared as treatises, tracts, discourses, and themes. It was not until the sixteenth century that the French writer Michel Montaigne proposed "essay" as a name for the form.

In following centuries, novelists and poets often wrote lengthy essays as prefaces to their published fictions and poems; political firebrands found the genre congenial to their efforts of persuading the masses to action; journalists wrote extended analyses of news events, often inserting their own experienced judgment. Today, the essay is an extremely malleable genre, yet the ancient discourses of Plato and the modern essays of Joan Didion have much in common and may be studied critically for their aesthetic qualities as well as for their rhetorical value.

The artistry in an essay may be enjoyed with the same appreciation for language, imagery, figure of speech, structure, rhythm, and sound that we learn to value in poetry, drama, and fiction. We invite you to use whatever you have learned about these genres and apply it whenever appropriate to the essay.

As with all literary genres, essays can be discussed in terms of form, theme, language, symbol, and so on; however, our focus for this chapter is on the essayist's voice—the personal presence of the author in the essay. Of all literary genres, the voice you find in an essay is most likely closest to the author's self. That is, while all writers adopt a stance of one kind or another in whatever form they write, odds are that the stance of an author in essay mode is closest, in a literal sense, to what he or she believes, experiences, and values in person. There are, of course, many exceptions, such as the satirical stance of a Jonathan Swift ("A Modest Proposal") or Margaret Atwood ("The Female Body") or the comic stances of a James Thurber or Dave Barry (virtually everything each has published). But, a great many authors select the essay mode precisely because it lets them speak most directly as themselves.

When we read an essay, we enter into dialogue with this authorial voice—more often, more directly, more intensely—than in the more fictive genres. The voice we read, witness, and hear in an essay is, commonly, the author's own—

or, perhaps, one of an author's several voices, each expressed in a form or style most appropriate for the essay occasion. Let's look more closely at what we mean by both terms, *essay* and *voice*.

THE ESSAY AS CONVERSATION

> They are young welterweight boxers so evenly matched they might be twins—though one has a redhead's pallor and the other is a dusky-skinned Hispanic. Circling each other in the ring, they try jabs, tentative left hooks, right crosses that dissolve in midair or turn into harmless slaps.

With these opening words to her essay "On Boxing," Joyce Carol Oates places us ringside in what she calls "the drama of life in the flesh." We are hooked, leaning toward the ring to see what happens next.

For those of us living in New England, Donald Hall is our own witness to certain seasonal truths in his essay "Winter":

> In New Hampshire we know ourselves by winter—in snow, in cold, in darkness. For some of us the first true snow begins it; for others winter begins with the first bruising assault of zero weather; there is yet another sort, light-lovers, for whom winter begins with dark's onset in mid-August.

Essays such as these tell us from their very beginning that something is about to happen. They also show us how two different voices re-create parts of their lives and worlds for our understanding and pleasure. As we read, we connect our lives to the essayists' words, images, and ideas. When we respond to them with our own words, we link ourselves with their voices. And, if we decide to write essays of our own, we can re-create place or season or occasion to extend its meaning to others who read and hear our voices.

The essay is a way of keeping in touch with others and with the boundless stretches of the human imagination as it engages the here and now. The verb "to essay"—from which the noun "essay" comes—even means to test, to explore an idea, to observe and then reflect on what you see. What's more, the essay offers us a readily available way to answer back to what's going on around us if we decide to give in to the urge to write.

It's no wonder, then, that reading and writing essays are crucial in American education because, for both students and teachers, these are ways of acquiring new visions and of adding our insights to the store of knowledge. The essay has long been a most democratic and inclusive literary form, one that has always attracted writers when they want to speak directly to us in their own voices.

CONVERSATIONS WITH THE SELF

The act of writing an essay sets conversations into motion: a more intimate conversation between writer and reader, and a larger social conversation that takes place between self and society. For example, as we read and respond to "Winter," Hall shares with us his tough but clear-eyed love and respect for New England weather; we, in turn, as readers extend this dialogue to recall how our own place and seasons have altered and shaped our ways of living. Our conversation with Hall widens to take in people from his past and present—his grandparents, his mother and her sisters as children, and a "we" that includes his wife and sometimes his children. In the course of this extended conversation, we may also evoke family and friends in remembering our own wintry seasons, past and present.

Likewise, Oates's descriptions of one fight calls up for her the scene of many others that she has watched, particularly the ones that she most associates with her father's love for boxing. Our own knowledge of Americans' fascination with sports enters into her elevation of boxing into "one of those legendary magical spaces." While reading and responding to Oates as she tells us what goes on in the boxing ring, we cement our own relationships to the sports-minded culture we live in.

Whether we are the author or the reader, the essay allows us to talk with ourselves as well as to the world. Consider the personal reflection that lies at the heart of Maureen Turley's essay "Women's Studies: My Right to an Education." As a sophomore at the University of Vermont, Turley explores memories and experiences evoked by dialogues with her parents and teachers and with writers she has been studying in a literature survey course. These help her reflect on the detail and shape of her whole educational process:

> It seems my education has always been strictly divided into male and female subjects. I remember in high school telling my mother that I might be interested in being a veterinarian. She frowned at this and told me I wouldn't really like being around sick animals.... While my parents and teachers forgave my incompetence in mathematics, they supported and encouraged my interest in literature.

Through her dialogue with books she has read, this essayist explores how her education has shaped her self-image.

> I remember reading Whitman's *Leaves of Grass,* where the poet encouraged that the truth for all men was to see a part of himself in every profession, as male and female, black and white. It strikes me this feeling of infinitude is predominantly a male feeling, especially regarding professions. During our education, women are largely absent or viewed in traditional roles such as teachers and nurses. We grow up thinking we cannot be writers, lawyers, doctors, or politicians. Unlike Whitman, most women have a much harder time feeling multitudinous.

Essays encourage writers to make connections by responding to the words of others and by engaging in conversation with the self.

A distinctive quality of the essay is the way the voice of the essayist is quickly identified with the speaking voice. A writer of essays appears to communicate directly with readers. For example, many American readers know Donald Hall as a poet who speaks in many voices decidedly not his own. He assumes or takes on in his poetry the voice of an Arctic explorer or of an early American farmer. Yet, it's the voice of Donald Hall that re-creates in his essays what it's like to go through the rigors of a New Hampshire winter or to carry on a lifelong love affair with baseball. The same is true of Joyce Carol Oates, who also writes novels and short stories. But when she's writing about boxing, she's Joyce Carol Oates, a resident of Princeton, New Jersey, not a fictive voice speaking in a novel set in the late nineteenth century in a house high above the banks of the Hudson River.

Straight speaking—sounding the way others expect us to sound—is a mark of the essay. Artists who excel in other genres, as Hall and Oates do, also enjoy essays because they are able to address us in a more straightforward manner, as themselves, as if we are equals with whom they wish to start and carry on conversations.

In contrast, poetry, drama, and fiction encourage authors to create a fictive voice that keeps plot, character, and image in the realm of the imagined even when their work is based on actual experience. The voice of the novelist or the poet is metaphorical in a way the essayist's voice never is. Dickens says this is the world *as if I were* David Copperfield; Frost says this is the world *as if I were* a swinger of birches. But Katherine Anne Porter says in her essay "St. Augustine and the Bullfight": "I intend to write something about my life, here and now, and so far as I am able without one touch of fiction, and to hope to keep it as shapeless and unforeseen as the events of life itself from day to day." In other words, she will write about this world as she has seen it and lived it.

Here again is the voice of Maureen Turley speaking to us from her experience as a contemporary college student. Hers is no imaginary voice either; since what she has to say matters deeply, she puts herself on the line.

> The problem with including women writers in undergraduate English courses is that the professor wants to communicate cultural assumptions about society and about the human condition through writers in different eras. Since women writers often depart from those assumptions to provide insights about how the other half of the human race survives, they don't portray the true emotional and intellectual climate of an age. They don't represent the recognized interpretation of an era in their works. So the educational system either distorts women so they fit the norm or omits them entirely. In anthologies, women writers exist only in the briefest of excerpts and their contributions lose value and importance. While Woolf's contributions are presented cosmetically, Dickinson is regarded as being totally cloistered from the real world.

There is concern and anger in Turley's voice, and her straightforward honesty gives power to her ideas. Her urgent voice brings her essay to life.

CONVERSATIONS WITH OTHERS

We have spoken of the ever-present, straightforward voice of the author, but we recognize, too, that an essay may freely incorporate other genres and other voices within its text. In doing so, authors establish a dialogue with other essayists or sometimes with their own other voices. For example, in her essay "In Search of Our Mothers' Gardens," Alice Walker includes a poem that is a tribute to her own mother as a powerful way to end her essay about creative black women: "This poem is not enough, but it is something, for the woman who literally covered the holes in our walls with sunflowers." Here Alice Walker poet joins Alice Walker essayist.

In a more general sense, authors may write in response to newspaper articles they have read, or movies or boxing matches they have seen. They draw the voices, visions, and experiences of others into their essays, thus establishing a conversation. In this way, too, the essay becomes what we call an intertextual genre, or a kind of collaborative effort. But the collaboration does not end there. Writers write for readers. When we read an essay, we not only hear the voice of the author and overhear the ongoing dialogue the writer carries on with the self and with others past and present, but we also enter the language of the essay, adding our voices as readers thinking and maybe even writing in response. We become part of the dialogue set into motion by the essayist.

Some essayists incorporate into their work the process of dialogue with other voices, which becomes, in turn, part of the dialogue the essayist is carrying on with the reader of the moment. Such intertextual freedom and collaboration is what Ursula Le Guin describes as happening to her essay "The Fisherwoman's Daughter." In tracing its origins as a speech given several times at colleges around the country to its publication in the *New York Times Book Review,* and finally to its present form in her book *Dancing at the Edge of the World,* she notes that her essay is "a collaboration, which is what I saw myself doing as I pieced together the works and words of so many other writers—ancestors, strangers, friends."

If essays allow for such communities of writers, we add to this a community of readers. As we speak to you in this chapter about the essay, we address you as unnamed college students enrolled in literature courses on unfamiliar campuses. But as we speak, we also conjure up students whose names and faces we do know because we talk to them each day about the literature we are reading and writing about. Sprinkled throughout our conversation with you are the voices of many published writers but also essays written by our students. Our voice is deliberately and consciously speculative as much as an actual conversation is apt to be, because we are exploring a literary genre that resists easy categorizing and defining. Instead, it's as if the essay as a genre insists on remaining in the process of becoming much like a writer who is speaking, whose voice we hear and respond to as we read and write.

Many essays originate as lectures or speeches. This public speech connection with the essay helps to account for its relatively short prose form and its relatively plain language—a kind of literary lecture taken in at a sitting. Reading an essay is witnessing verbal performance, much as one experiences at a lecture.

In "Why I Write" Joan Didion reemphasizes the power of speech and the importance of this sound as it resonates from the printed page:

> Of course I stole the title for this talk from George Orwell. One reason I stole it was that I like the sound of the words: *Why I Write.* There you have three short unambiguous words that share a sound, and the sound they share is this:
> *I*
> *I*
> *I*

What alerts us to this verbal performance is Didion's very casual use of the ordinary and everyday phrase "of course." We're immediately within the range of her speaking voice, marked as well by her reference to her writing as a "talk." Note her repetitious use of the words "sound" and "I." They affect us as readers and remind us that her essay is "I," Joan Didion, sounding herself. Later in the same essay, she writes: "In many ways writing is the act of saying *I,* of imposing oneself upon other people, of saying *listen to me, see it my way, change your mind.*" Through the words she uses, by her conscious arrangement of them on the page, with her allusion to Orwell's essay, we find ourselves, as we read, in the presence of Didion's verbal performance.

The contemporary American essay is firmly rooted in the eighteenth-century writings of Benjamin Franklin, Thomas Jefferson, and Tom Paine as well as the nineteenth-century forms of Ralph Waldo Emerson, Margaret Fuller, and Henry David Thoreau. By the end of the twentieth century, the essay had emerged as one of the most vital and varied forms of American literature, with practitioners such as Tom Wolfe, Joan Didion, Tim O'Brian, and Maxine Hong Kingston writing in forms variously called literary journalism or creative nonfiction, some of which blur the lines between fiction and nonfiction, between what is imagined and what is real.

It is appropriate that all of us share in the study of the literary form that is most available for our own continued self-education—in and beyond the college and university. As Elizabeth Hardwick says in her introduction to the first volume of the *Best American Essays* series, the essay is "not a closed shop"; it's open to all of us. Series editor Robert Atwan even characterizes it as "a gutsy form." Annie Dillard draws a neat distinction when she asserts that "the essay can do everything a poem can do, and everything a short story can do—everything but fake it."

VOICES THAT SHAPE THE ESSAY

Earlier we alerted you to the many voices from which a single writer may select, much as each of us may speak differently in a letter to a parent or another authority figure than we might in a letter to an intimate friend. An essayist's reputation revolves around the ability to forge a recognizable personality on paper so that we feel as if we are in that person's presence each time we read what she or he has written. At the same time, if we have read widely through that writer's essays, we begin to understand the essayist's different slants and ways of thinking over the course of time and how the writing has been affected by shifting historical, social, and personal conditions.

For example, the Alice Walker who wrote "The Civil Rights Movement: What Good Was It?" at the age of twenty-three is not the same person who wrote "Beauty: When the Other Dancer Is the Self" at age thirty-eight. In "The Civil Rights Movement: What Good Was It?" Walker is responding to those who doubt that the marches and sit-ins that characterized the 1960s have made any differences in the lives of Americans. Her language is forceful and precisely chosen to mix polemical assertion with illustrative example and detail. Near the end, she writes:

> What good was the Civil Rights Movement? If it had just given this country Dr. King, a leader of conscience, for once in our lifetime, it would have been enough. If it had taken black eyes off white television stories, it would have been enough. If it had fed one starving child, it would have been enough.

While describing a precious moment when her daughter Rebecca helped her see beyond the disfiguring scar tissue on her eye, Alice Walker's language becomes personal, even full of wonder: "There *was* a world in my eye. And I saw that it was possible to love it; that, in fact, for all it had taught me of shame and anger and inner vision, I *did* love it." One voice is more tuned to the public; the other retains the essence of the private voice that we are allowed to overhear.

Essayists write to inform readers about something of significance, to argue a position, to express their own personal response, to discover what they really believe, to explain why something is as it is or how it works, why something is important enough for them and for us to spend our time discussing. Whatever circumstances give rise to an essay, whether they are personal reflections or issues of public concern, authors have certain purposes in mind as they write. Sometimes authors even alert us to their intentions through an essay's title much as Virginia Woolf does in "How Should One Read a Book?" We call these intentions the voices that shape the essay.

Voices of Meditation

When Michel Montaigne wrote what has been recognized as the first essay (at least, the first one called by that name), he created a vehicle for sharing personal reflections written in an informal manner. His declared subject is himself: "Meditation is a powerful and full study for anyone who knows how to examine and exercise himself vigorously: I would rather fashion my mind than furnish it." This personal quality of the essay remains a powerful trait of the genre, although the essay today varies widely over a broad spectrum from serious formality—such as the American Declaration of Independence—to the informality found in popular journals and even daily newspapers. But Montaigne's essays exhibit an immediacy and lightness that have entertained centuries of readers, even in translation.

In addition, Montaigne's essays are expressions of personal opinions and views: in "Of Smells" he writes that "the best condition they [bodies] may have is to be free of smell." Their format suggests that his essays are reflections or meditations on various subjects that struck the author as worth interest, first of all to himself, and then to his public.

Taking a lead from Montaigne, imitators retain this meditative quality of the essay. Above all, the meditative voice is a personal one. Essayists find it appropriate as they turn inward and present to the world what they find out about themselves, about their feelings, sentiments, and attitudes. The meditative essay may deal with a person's own tastes in music, sports, or fiction, or with religious beliefs, or with attitudes toward sexuality. It may focus on the author's fear of riding roller coasters or making a love commitment or on his or her anger over environmental pollution or pride in receiving a coveted award. What makes these essays interesting to readers is that their meditative quality challenges us to look at our own values and perhaps to respond positively or negatively to those of the author.

Like Montaigne's self-examination, the contemporary essayist Annie Dillard's essay "Sight into Insight" allows us to witness her meditation on the subtleties of seeing and what different angles of seeing mean for daily living: "There are lots of things to see, unwrapped gifts and free surprises.... What you see is what you get." She takes us along as she surveys her local landscape, meditating on what it yields to the watchful eye: "It's all a matter of keeping my eyes open. Nature is like one of those line drawings that are puzzles for children."

One of the delights in reading a meditative essay like Dillard's is the way it allows us to follow the turns of an original and penetrating mind on an almost intimate footing. This essay's exploratory nature shapes its structure so that the writer almost free-associates by lighting on first one angle of the subject, then another. For example, Dillard begins with a childhood memory of hiding pennies and providing clues for someone to see this "free gift from the universe" and then explores the implications of nature as "a now-you-see-it, now-you-don't-affair." Sometimes she sticks close to the earth's surface, examining creek water "in a white china bowl," then skyward where she "can see two million light-years to the Andromeda galaxy." She ends the essay by pondering her own search for "'the tree with the lights in it.'" The vision came one day when she was not thinking of anything at all and saw a cedar tree "transfigured" by light—"a gift and a total surprise."

The spontaneity of Dillard's observations takes on added richness as we begin to see the carefully developed pattern of metaphors on which the essay builds itself. In her penetration into "what you see is what you get," Dillard takes us on a visual journey from "pennies cast broadside from a generous hand" and "the bright coppers at the roots of trees" to "the backyard cedar buzzing with flame."

Dillard's meditations are not developed into any arguments or recommendations for us to disagree with or to follow. Rather, it's as if we are asked to take a series of explorations to examine what it means to see the lights illuminating the world we live in. Our landscapes are necessarily different, but we look up from her pages better equipped to use our eyes and our minds on what's out there.

Voices of Response

We live in a world in which situational forces shape the human condition. These may be environmental or physical; social, political, historical, or economic. Sometimes the force may be simply a friend who takes issue with something we've said or an ad on TV that draws our attention for thirty seconds. Like the rest of us, essayists respond to these forces. For Virginia Woolf, "the art of writing has for backbone some fierce attachment to an idea." Occasionally essayists are affected so intensely by these cultural forces that they wish to explore their own response and to present it for readers to evaluate.

Although essayists are not necessarily trying to persuade us to agree with their reactions or to convince us they responded correctly to the situation at hand, the general intent of the responding voice reminds us that to react to what's going on around us is an important part of day-to-day living. This kind of essay reinforces a link between human beings as sensitive and caring.

Several years ago the biographer and essayist William Manchester was invited to participate in a Flag Day ceremony at Okinawa, commemorating one of the bloodiest battles in the Pacific during World War II. Manchester fought and was wounded in that battle. He intended to go to Okinawa. "But," he writes in his essay "Okinawa: The Bloodiest Battle of All," "when I learned that Japanese were also participating, I quietly withdrew. There are too many graves between us, too much gore, too many memories of too many atrocities." His response to the invitation prompts a very personal and frank essay in which Manchester exposes an intensely deep anguish and an unforgiving rage. He writes in part:

> On Okinawa today, the ceremony will be dignified, solemn, seemly. It will also be anachronistic. If the Japanese dead of 1945 were resurrected to witness it, they would be appalled by the acceptance of defeat, the humiliation of their emperor—the very idea of burying Japanese near the barbarians from across the sea and then mourning them together. Americans, meanwhile, risen from their graves, would ponder the evolution of their own society, and might wonder, What ever happened to patriotism?

No feigned patriotic fiction sentimentalizes this essay. Manchester recalls the phony patriotism portrayed in motion pictures dealing with World War II and ponders his experience that soldiers wage what they think are decisive battles only to discover that the folks at home can't pronounce their names. He criticizes those veterans who served in the military but never saw frontline action, yet in Memorial Day parades aggrandize themselves as war heroes. Combat itself is not worthy of praise; it is instead "cruel and squalid," Manchester writes, incorporating the words of Winston Churchill in his own essay. For this essayist, the war experiences continue to fuel a "primitive rage" that lingers within him and occasionally surfaces in response to meetings or chance invitations:

> In 1978, revisiting Guadalcanal, I encountered a Japanese businessman who had volunteered to become a kamikaze pilot in 1945 and was turned down at the last minute. Mutual friends suggested that we meet. I had expected no difficulty; neither, I think, did he. But when we confronted each other, we froze.
>
> I trembled, suppressing the sudden, startling surge of primitive rage within. And I could see, from his expression, that this was difficult for him, too. Nations may make peace. It is harder for fighting men. On simultaneous impulse we both turned and walked away.

This is a responsive although bitter voice growing out of a dialogue with his memory and reflection. The essayist is not willing to accept the irony that a political peace tries to force upon former combatants. His experiences will not allow it. Neither is the voice of the essayist trying to persuade us to accept its position nor to apologize for it. The anecdotes and brief descriptions of war scattered throughout the essay serve to measure the author's anguish.

This essay shows a responding voice in which the author discovers more about himself during the process of writing, a link with the meditative voice. The invitation occasioned a response. But it also brought back memories of the war and feelings aroused by public shows of patriotism and private personal experiences, all of which Manchester must sort out in his essay and in his life. He chose not to do this in a private diary or in a conversation with a close friend. He did not choose to write his response as a short story with some invented narrative voice. Instead, he preferred to use the public forum of the essay that he published for all to read. Through the medium of the essay, we vicariously share his response, even though we may or may not agree with it.

Voices of Dissent

In the June 26, 1989, issue of the *New Yorker* an essay appeared that addressed the American response to the Chinese student protest that eventually led to a military action killing numerous demonstrators. Many Americans watched on their televisions the brutal night attack on the students in Beijing's Tiananmen Square. To many Americans, what happened in China proved again the superiority of the American political system and allowed them to gloat over China's political failings. The essay took a different stance, however, arguing that Americans should not be so self-righteous. In part its author argued:

> Our system of government and the centuries of continuity that our nation has enjoyed are powerful forces of resistance against mass political violence. But our system is something we inherited; we aren't by definition better than other people because of it. Each of us in the United States today watching the events in China has reason for sadness and reason for gratitude, but no one has reason to feel superior. It's appropriate for us to refrain from helping oppressive leaders. It's appropriate for us to express grief. But it's not our job to punish oth-

ers, verbally or in any other way, and when a punitive tone creeps into our responses we no longer ring true.

Our founding fathers were idealistic, yet so were the founders of Communism. Our good fortune lies in that fact that ours were less ambitious, and more realistic about the corrupting nature of power, and wiser about the limitations of government in changing the human condition. We have been lucky. It is our job to realize that, and to stay clear of the blinding light of moral superiority.

The essayist argues that Americans might better temper their reaction to the China massacre by appealing to patriotism tempered by a historical perspective. This essay's method of argumentation is typical of the hundreds of editorials which appear daily in newspapers and magazines. The most successful persuasive essays meld convincing arguments with the artistry of solid prose. The enjoyment we derive from them ranges from the simple pleasure of reading well-wrought words to the intellectual satisfaction of having the essayists actually convince us of the merits of their argument.

A classic dissenting voice is that of Jonathan Swift, best remembered for raising political satire to such a high level that we continue to read his bitterly ironic essay "A Modest Proposal." This enduring argumentative essay appalled the credulous and provoked considerable consternation throughout England and Ireland. Even today, modern readers can be deceived by the serious tone that pervades the essay. They fail to catch Swift's ironic voice that, in turn, creates his argumentative voice.

In a departure from usual essayistic practice, Swift creates a fictive "I" who seems basically decent and compassionate. This narrator recognizes that something has to be done to alleviate the horrible suffering plaguing the Irish populace, especially the children. Wringing hands won't help, so, out of compassion, "I" responds with a plan. Seeing the huge number of starving Irish children and having been told "by a very knowing American of my acquaintance in London, that a young healthy Child, well nursed, is, at a Year old, a most delicious, nourishing and wholesome Food, whether Stewed, Roasted, Baked, or Boiled; and, I make no doubt that it will equally serve in a Fricassee, or Ragout," the speaker proposes creating an industry to raise and market children as food.

The success of this essay and its real message derive from the interplay between "I" and the second voice, that of essayist Swift. An ironic tension—saying one thing but meaning another—provides the lifeblood of this essay. The overt message of "A Modest Proposal" is outrageous and yet coolly, calmly, and logically written. While we cannot sympathize with the speaker's position, we do find ourselves siding with the bitter voice of Jonathan Swift and his covert plea for political action.

Voices of Explanation

Essays frequently serve as vehicles to provide specific information and to explore ideas. Informative essays are written by people who think they have unique knowledge—perhaps they are even leading authorities in a field or they have investigated and researched a topic in depth—and take it upon themselves to inform others who happen to read their essays.

Essays written as class assignments are very often explanatory or expositional in nature. For example, as you study literature you may be asked to compose essays in which you explain how a certain character's actions bring together the meaning in a play or why certain images control the way a poem should be read. As you write about what you read, you will be practicing literary criticism, a form of the essay in which readers—call them critics—explain their interpretations and understandings of a work.

A unique quality of this kind of essay is the authoritative voice of writers who speak because they are certain of what they write. Listen to Virginia Woolf as she asks us to consider her answers to the questions she raises in her essay "How Should One Read a Book?" She suggests to us: "Do not dictate to your author; try to become him. Be his fellow-worker and accomplice.... reading is a longer and more complicated process than seeing." As Woolf relies on her background as a book reviewer for newspapers and magazines, the expositional writer often draws directly upon experiences. They may come firsthand through personal observation and knowledge, through interviews of credible witnesses or other authorities, or through research and reflection on evidence. What makes the explanatory essay such a powerful literary form is the way it marries knowledge and personality.

What the explanatory voice does for readers is to bring them into ways of considering many subjects from unique perspectives. To explain things without condescension is what this voice aims for, just as Randall Jarrell does in "The Other Frost":

> Frost's seriousness and honesty; the bare sorrow with which, sometimes, things are accepted as they are, neither exaggerated nor explained away; the many, many poems in which there are real people with their real speech and real thoughts and real emotions—all this, in conjunction with so much subtlety and exactness, such classical understatement and restraint, makes the reader feel that he is not in a book but in a world, and a world that has in common with his own some of the things that are most important in both.

In his dialogue with us, Jarrell assumes we are sensitive readers well able to read Frost's poetry. He also expresses his own opinion by explaining what he considers significant to the experience of reading Frost. In the process of writing a critical essay, he opens up something of himself, and he draws each of us into the critical process as well. If we are actively engaged participants in what the essayist intends, we learn something about Robert Frost, Randall Jarrell, and ourselves.

Voices of Storytelling

At first it may seem a paradox to talk about essays as stories. Somehow, storytelling seems to be more properly a part of the world of fiction. But remember, many short stories are based on factual incidents and real characters, indistinguishable in the telling from autobiographies and other experiential essays. Whether a story is true or not, a memoir or a short story, an effective narrative voice is both clear and credible: If you do not know the author or the incident, you may not be able to distinguish fact from fiction.

A classic narrative essay is George Orwell's "Shooting an Elephant." While the author was a local police officer in a Burmese village, an elephant went berserk, killing residents and rampaging through the bazaar. Officer Orwell was called upon to slay the beast:

> But I did not want to shoot the elephant. I watched him beating his bunch of grass against his knees with that preoccupied grandmotherly air that elephants have. It seemed to me that it would be murder to shoot him. At that age I was not squeamish about killing animals, but I had never shot an elephant and never wanted to. (Somehow it always seems worse to kill a *large* animal.)

The storyteller's voice dominates this entire essay, and indeed, part of what Orwell is doing is simply telling a good story. But the reader perceives something else. In this essay, Orwell uses the incident in which a maverick elephant is slain to explore colonialism with its inherent racism and political subjugation. We finish the narrative entertained, but we also retain a deeper understanding of the racial arrogance that is a part of colonialism. Indeed, we come to view the shooting of the elephant as a symbolic act whose implications continue to shape world politics today.

In the passage from the Orwell essay is the parenthetic aside "Somehow it always seems worse to kill a *large* animal." David Leith, a student at our university, was struck by these words. It marked the beginning of a literary dialogue with Orwell. David thought about those words and about Orwell's feelings over shooting the elephant. He compared them with feelings he had had when he was forced to shoot a much smaller animal, and he disagreed with Orwell's aside: It is no easier to kill a small animal.

David began working on a narrative recounting a personal experience of killing a raccoon. In his early drafts, David wrote in the first person, but he eventually found that he could treat his material more effectively by casting the narrative in the third, "he" rather than "I." Nevertheless, "Where the Heart Should Be" is an autobiographical narrative essay, with David as "the boy."

One of the boy's chores is to gather eggs. One day he goes to the chicken house and notices that the hens seem somewhat unsettled and skittish. At first he pays no attention, but then

> opening the other laying box, the boy started as he saw a large raccoon eating eggs. It was a greasy mess of brown fur, its glassy eyes set into a black mask. A large raccoon about three feet long, it must have weighed over forty-five pounds. Without blinking, the raccoon, still clutching an eggshell in its front paws, looked up and hissed, snapping his jaw to reveal two rows of moist yellow teeth. The boy slammed down the laying box lid.

With a sense of certainty about what he must do, the boy goes for a gun. But as the essay unfolds, his efforts to kill the raccoon test his determination, and his initial failures test his own sense of self. Finally, he must confront his failure.

Leith's essay recounts what happened, but the telling, in its simplicity and directness, is a pleasure to read. Killing the raccoon becomes secondary to the story, which, like the Orwell piece that prompted Leith's essay, presents and develops character. We observe Orwell and the boy defining themselves by recalling in their essays their actions in demanding situations. And we respond to what they have written. Narrative provides the events and situations that essayists need in order to test and explore themselves in dialogue with the readers.

Other Voices

By this point, you've probably figured out for yourself that the essay "takes as many shapes as weather or daylight," to borrow the writer Maureen Howard's words, and there are many more voices giving shape to those essays than those we've described in this chapter. In our discussion we have explored some of the main characteristics that help us distinguish the essay from other literary genres. But we have surely not been able to pinpoint all the essay's characteristics, just those that appear major to us. Likewise, we have examined what seem to us to be major voices that shape the essay, but, once again, our discussion has not been exhaustive. Because the essay is such a vital form of contemporary literature, it is impossible to pigeonhole its process of disclosing the riches of human curiosity and self-creation.

We believe that essays begin out of very private observations or curiosities or experiences. Essayists do not remove themselves from the reality, but instead forge an authorial identity centering on the personal "I." Beyond that, the individual writer has many options in shaping the essay. Sometimes authors speak of "trying to find the right voice" that appropriately conveys and reflects their attitude toward their subject. The "I" shapes, speaks, and reaches out to engage its readers in dialogue, but it never loses its authority by compromising the accuracy of its material.

FINDING YOUR OWN VOICE

When asked to respond to fiction, poetry, drama, or film, you are seldom asked to create or mimic the very form you have just read or witnessed. Not so with the essay. To respond to an essay is to write an essay. In this sense, the essay is the most democratic and available of forms, as you are expected not only to understand the meaning of the essays you read, but to create your own meaning in the essays you write back. How you choose to respond to an essay may be personal, critical, or imaginative—or some blend of all three. That is, if asked for an open-ended response to an essay-reading assignment, you may write about any thoughts triggered by reading the essay in whatever voice you choose—serious or comic, meditative or satirical. No holds are barred in the essays you write just as none are barred in those you may read.

However, if you are writing in response to a school assignment, you may be asked to write a distinctly critical essay, in which you will be expected to analyze the logic, form, or style of the essay; or to write an argument back in which you agree or disagree with the essayist's position. In such cases, it may be wise to reign in your more subjective or outrageous voices and write your response essay in a more neutral academic voice.

No matter the voice in which you construct your response, you become an essayist yourself and enter the centuries-old conversation of essayists. And your readers will expect to find *your* voice, expressing *your* beliefs and values, being true to who *you* are and what *you* stand for. Finding your essay voice, then, depends on what your ideas are, what they mean to you, and how best to present them to others.

WORKS CITED

Atwan, Robert. Foreword. *Best American Essays 1986.* Ed. Elizabeth Hardwick. New York: Ticknor & Fields, 1986. ix-xii.

Didion, Joan. "Why I Write." *The New York Times Magazine* Dec. 5, 1976: 2.

Dillard, Annie. Introduction. *Best American Essays 1988.* Ed. Annie Dillard. New York: Ticknor & Fields, 1988. xv-xxii.

_____. "Sight into Insight." *Harper's Magazine* February 1974: 39-46.

Hall, Donald. "Winter."*Best American Essays 1987.* Ed. Gay Talese. New York: Ticknor & Fields, 1987. 116-30.

Hardwick, Elizabeth. Introduction, *"Best American Essays 1986.* Ed. Elizabeth Hardwick. New York: Ticknor & Fields, 1986. xiii-xxi.

Jarrell, Randall. "The Other Frost." *Poetry and the Age.* London: Faber & Faber, 1955. 36-42.

Le Guin, Ursula. "The Fisherwoman's Daughter." *Dancing at the Edge of the World: Thoughts on Words, Women, Places.* New York: Grove Press, 1989. 212-37.

Leith, David. "Where the Heart Should Be." *The Burlington Review* January 1983: 5-6.

Manchester, William. "Okinawa: The Bloodiest Battle." *Best American Essays 1988.* Ed. Annie Dillard. New York: Ticknor & Fields, 1988. 72-82.

Montaigne, Michel de. *The Complete Works of Montaigne.* Trans. Donald M. Frame. Stanford, CA: Stanford University Press, 1957. Passim. "Notes and Comment" from "The Talk of the Town." *The New Yorker.* June 26, 1989. 25-6.

Oates, Joyce Carol. "On Boxing." *Best American Essays 1986.* Ed. Elizabeth Harwick. New York: Ticknor & Fields, 1986. 204-18.

Orwell, George. "Shooting an Elephant." *Shooting the Elephant and Other Essays.* New York: Harcourt Brace Janovich, 1950. 3-12.

Porter, Katherine Anne. "St. Augustine and the Bullfight." *The Norton Book of Personal Essays.* Ed. Joseph Epstein. New York: W. W. Norton & Co., 1997. 91-102.

Swift, Jonathan. "A Modest Proposal." Cambridge, MA: Friends of the Harvard College Library, 1979.

Turley, Maureen. "Woman's Studies: My Right to an Education." *Angles of Vision.* Ed. Arthur W. Biddle and Toby Fulwiler. New York: McGraw-Hill, 1992. 1657-60.

Walker, Alice. "In Search of Our Mother's Garden." *Ms* May 1974: 64ff.

_____.The Civil Rights Movement: What Good Was It?" *American Scholar* 36 (1967): 550-54.

Woolf, Virginia. "How One Should Read a Book." *Collected Essays.* Vol. 2. London: Hogarth Press, 1966. 1-11.

"The Modern Essay." *Collected Essays.* Vol. 2. London: Hogarth Press, 1966. 41-50.

CHAPTER 6

Exploring Visual Texts

Tom Simone

While traditional English studies have concentrated on written texts, our contemporary world abounds in the visual representation of human activity. Partly in response to the broad presence of visual media in our culture, teachers and students have turned their attention to film and video texts with increasing frequency. This chapter is an introduction to some of the characteristics of visual texts that can be studied as logical and aesthetic extensions of written literature. For even though visual texts have evolved their own independent traditions, film and video can also be studied as parallels and developments of literary traditions. This essay introduces some of the major elements of visual media that, taken together, make visual texts such powerful means of story telling.

VISUAL TEXTS

What is a visual text? The word "text" derives from the Latin word for textile or web, and the concept of text implies the awareness that many single elements are interwoven to make up the complex object that we see as a poem, a short story, or a photograph. For while we often "read" photographs or films as presenting straightforward or instantaneous information, a little reflection or questioning can reveal a greater complexity than we had first suspected. And when a photographic image or a film or video comes under our investigation, we might say that it shifts from object to text.

Consider the famous photograph on page 81. This image clearly documents a public moment with an exuberant embrace of a sailor and nurse against a city backdrop. But while a kind of information is transmitted in this summary statement, a number of questions can be asked that go beyond the surface details of the image. Who are the two people in the photograph? What has allowed such a remarkably personal action to take place in such a public space? Have I seen this image before? Who took the photograph and why? Who are the people in the background?

This image, taken by Alfred Eisenstaedt, is called "V-J Day Kiss," or sometimes merely "The Kiss." While recording the tumultuous response of people to the end of World War II, Eisenstaedt, a photojournalist for *Life* magazine, shot this image in Times Square in New York in August 1945. So we learn that the image has an historical context, and we might find out that many people felt that this image symbolized the country's relief and joy at the end of a grueling war.

But we might also ask how this spontaneous moment was captured and what visual elements add to the dramatic element of the kiss itself. Eisenstaedt said that the couple seemed like a work of sculpture to him, and the forms of the man and woman do provide a strikingly graceful outline. The empty foreground of the picture showing the pavement of the street isolates the couple, yet their torsos are framed by laughing sailors on one side and women on the other in the middle background. And beyond that the couple and bystanders are framed at the top and back by city buildings and a billboard, so that this spontaneous event is situated in a visually interesting and focusing context.

In examining the photograph as a visual object, we can also reflect on the way that black-and-white patterns in this photograph contribute to the form and impact of the image. The dark foreground of the street, the sailor's black uniform, and the nurse's white one are part of the visual interest of the image.

By asking some of these questions and offering a few observations, we have begun to see a photographic image as a visual text. The kinds of questions that can be posed about this still image can be extended to the world of narrative film, a genre that has many connections to the areas of literary narrative and drama.

NARRATIVE FILM AS AN EXTENSION OF LITERATURE

Even though film, television, and video are strongly shaped by social expectation and commercial forces, they continue to share, in adapted form, many aspects of narrative art common to drama and fiction. While not all film is narrative in nature, the large majority of full-length popular films are: In them, human characters represent human action. In his *Poetics*, the first major work of literary criticism in the Western tradition, Aristotle says that a tragedy is an imitation of an action, by which he seems to mean that a play appears to us as a staged representation of a series of events that resembles the human world we inhabit. This is true of film as well, even though we are looking at projected images of human actors, rather than the actors themselves.

A film, even a fantasy like *The Matrix* or a farce like *Dumb and Dumber*, shows a represented world of places, actions, and characters that claims a kind of parallel reality to our own normal world. While we make sober distinctions between "reality" and "representation," we forget them when we gasp at some death-defying feat of Luke Skywalker or gloat over the folly of a character represented by Steve Martin or Woody Allen. In a visual story that appeals to us, we may even be so caught up that we wince or cry over the fate of the figures shown to us.

But the study of, or reflection about, narratives (whether literary or filmic) will include a consideration of the particular conventions of the medium—how effects are arranged, how certain characters and actions are portrayed, what special images or influences may be elicited from the medium's resources for storytelling. While the history of our literature and learning has developed through the civilization of the book, modern technology in the form of film, sound recording, and other electronic media have become the most widespread modes of communication in our time. And there continues to be a strong verbal element in the background of visual media. For example, the appetite of media for subject matter has drawn remarkably often on the heritage of literature, adapting plays or novels into films. And while we may not be fully aware of it, the spoken words and actions of *The X-Files* or *Ally McBeal* are usually scripted and distributed among cast members and production team, so that a "literary" or at least film script version of the show also exists.

When we watch a film like *American Beauty* or a television show like *The X-Files*, we generally absorb the story and action, along with advertisements and auxiliary material, in a defined period of time. A film like *Star Wars, The First Episode* runs for about two hours and fifteen minutes, and an *X-Files* episode occupies about 44 minutes during an hour that is laced with ads and enticements to stay tuned to other shows that will follow. We seldom sit back to reflect on the complexity of the preparation and refinement of a video entertainment. But, in ways that at least parallel literature, visual media are produced by elaborate working patterns and interactions and a large array of technical equipment and expertise as well as a wide array of cultural codes.

BEGINNING TO READ A VISUAL TEXT

Film is founded on the use of a camera to record a series of still photographs that are flashed quickly before the viewer. This rapid sequence blends together in the mind through the physiological phenomenon whereby the eye does not clear visual memory immediately but retains these individual images long enough for them to seem continuous. A child's flipbook, made of individual pages with separate still images, produces the illusion of movement when flipped at the right speed. In a similar way, film provides the illusion of movement by presenting a series of still images in rapid sequence. For standard sound movies, the camera records and the projector presents twenty-four images per second.

In its simplified fashion, the flipbook suggests some of the paradoxes in the apparent movement and seeming "reality" of visual media and the way it is created through mechanical means, manipulated by the shaping intention of the film maker and attendant assistants. The camera analyzes motion as a series of individual pictures and a soundtrack; the director conceives of a represented part of the action that is broken down into separate elements. And a larger story unfolds through the arrangements of acting, setting, and patterns of association in the process of editing.

Just as careful rereading of a printed text is an essential step in the process of analyzing and then writing about it, so in watching a film, repeated viewing of the same sequence can bring fuller opportunities for observations, understanding, and analysis. When we analyze, say, a sonnet by Shakespeare, we look at rhyme patterns, images, subject matter, small groups of words, and even individual words to excavate the complexity and suggestiveness of the poem. In the following discussion, I will use a few frames from George Lucas's *Star Wars* to suggest some of the elements of film that you might add to your personal inventory of film vocabulary and techniques for analysis.

The camera records in its visual field what has been arranged by director, actors, and technicians. Objects or actions outside the frame of the camera are usually irrelevant to the presented image. The actors and objects in the view of the lens can move in virtually any direction, but then, so can the lens itself. Thus, two kinds of motion are in play. While the camera is a machine recording the images in front of it, it can do so from above or below or from any angle, as well as head-on. The machine can also approximate the view of a person's moving vision, as if the camera were traveling at a walking pace or, as is often the case in an action film, the lens can record the quick shift of view as might be seen from a rapidly moving automobile. And of course, the camera may adopt whatever angle or pace of movement that the director and production team feel will portray the action effectively.

GEORGE LUCAS'S *STAR WARS*

If I tried to exemplify these principles with a film current at the time of this writing, the films of today become the films of yesterday all too rapidly and it might seem *passé* by the time you read it. A number of films, however, have become common currency for continuing popular culture and can provide examples of visual texts familiar to many of us. An example is George Lucas's first science fiction movie, *Star Wars* (1977), which has become a touchstone for the modern fantasy-adventure movie, achieving something like the status of a modern myth. The continuing popularity of *Star Wars* comes from Lucas's romantic interpretation of the science fiction genre of film and his sense both of the patterns of popular culture and of stories of growing up in America. His earlier film, *American Grafitti* (1973), was based on youth culture featuring hot rods and the California scene in 1962, and that appreciation of the lively world of high school adventure carries over into his space movies. As of this writing, the interest in the continuing saga of *Star Wars* material has led to a series of four films.

Lucas's ambition to show an epic series of adventures was signaled by the first image of *Star Wars*, not a scene, but a written narrative logo that accompanied the first release of the film in 1977: "In a galaxy far, far away. ..." Lucas added the fuller printed narrative, "Episode IV: A New Hope: It is a period of civil war. Rebel spaceships, striking from a hidden base, have won first victory ..." in 1980 to correlate *Star Wars* with the second film, *The Empire Strikes Back*.

By announcing itself as "Episode IV: A New Hope" *Star Wars* suggests an ongoing series of adventures and a kind of fantasy history. That sense of a previous series of events and the importance of the unfolding drama of the film suggests the scope of the enterprise from the beginning.

The first visual image in the first *Star Wars* is the depiction of space with stars and planets, and then a space ship being pursued by a larger vessel:

This opening frame begins the story with a powerful visual image. The surface of a planet spans the bottom of the frame, and a nearby moon is seen above the curved horizon, a view reminiscent of the reports from astronauts of the 1970s. Meanwhile, the appearance of the star cruiser coming in over the camera's view suggests menace, speed, and power through its descent from the top of the frame.

Mise en Scène

Perhaps the most important, if confusing term, for the discussion of film is the French phrase *mise en scène* (pronounced 'meez on sen'). The term literally means "put on stage," but for film it might be translated "staging for the camera." Whatever needs to be part of the visual text—and only that—must be arranged so that it makes sense through the camera and the audio recording mechanism. For instance, if you take a picture of your best friend, but there is an automobile commercial sign in the background, you will probably ask your friend to move so the sign does not distort the meaning of the photo.

In the opening shot of *Star Wars,* Lucas has arranged the special effects of planet and moon, then introduced in sequence the two spacecraft to suggest both the setting and the drama of pursuit and capture that forms the first sequence of the film. In addition to the image, the soundtrack with the now-famous music of the film and the roar of engines add to the "staging for the camera" of this opening shot. Great care and choice have gone into the opening images of *Star Wars.*

A lot is lost when you see a film such as *Star Wars* on a small overly square television screen. In considering a film that we might see mainly on a regular television screen, we might try to remember the effect of movie screen projection. While we are in a time of more large-screen televisions and projection televisions, most video viewing of a film reduces the size and impact of a film image significantly. In addition, cropping the image to "fit" a traditional television screen eliminates proportion and composition of the original "aspect ratio." The consideration of a film should acknowledge the original screen ratio of the image. The opening shot of *Star Wars* draws on film theater impact—especially through the use of images in a wide aspect ratio—for the establishment both of the atmosphere, the breadth of space, and of the narrative, the pursuit of one space ship by another through that space.

The Single Shot

The major element of visual media is the shot, a single continuous running of the camera filming the action that takes place before the lens. Derived from the physical nature of motion picture film, the shot represents one specific element in the film's narrative. While a large-production film may have some spontaneity depending on the development of the script or the accidents of acting and background context, many films are in fact described in full detail in the script describing what is to be shot in production. For instance, Alfred Hitchcock, the famous mystery film director, was noted for having conceived many of his films in complete detail, including camera framing and length of shots, before ever moving to the physical production of the movie.

Perhaps the key element in film narrative is the joining together, the editing of individual shots, into a continuous presentation of an action. *Star Wars* is particularly successful at balancing the strangeness and atmosphere of the space setting with strong components of traditional storytelling. My next example is taken from the moment when the Empire tests the terrifying Death Star on Princess Leia's home planet of Alderaan. After Leia tries to decoy General Tarkin and Darth Vader with the location of a former rebel base, the general proceeds to destroy the entire planet. In a parallel action, Luke Skywalker is traveling with Obi-Wan Kenobi toward that planet with the robot that has the secret plans of the weakness in the Death Star's defense system.

Using fairly simple special effects, models, and multiple exposure, Lucas introduces the sequence with a shot of the Death Star approaching the planet Alderaan, one that looks almost identical to pictures of Earth from space.

Second in this sequence, we see Princess Leia reacting with horror to the order to destroy the planet.

Lucas places Carrie Fisher as Leia slightly to the right of center in the shot looking to our left. In the next shot the death ray, to our right, focuses on the planet, shoots to our left and explodes the image of Alderaan. Because of the complementary placement of the images in the two frames, the effect is that we look along with Leia at the exploding planet.

In the progression of the narrative, Lucas then joins the devastating effect of the loss of Alderaan to the central Luke Skywalker story. The very next shot after the explosion of the planet, the third in this sequence, shows the Millennium Falcon with Luke and Ben or Obi-Wan Kenobi.

Obi-Wan, the wise man and teacher of young Luke from the older ethic of "Jedi warriors," is at the center of the frame, training Luke, who is on the left, to use the light saber. Following on the explosion of the planet, Obi-Wan, played by Alec Guiness, places his hand on his heart and says: "I've just felt a great disturbance in the Force." The famous "Force" is a generalized spiritual feeling that provides strength for the positive characters in the story. With clarity and strong storytelling, Lucas has shown the evil of the Empire and the need for Luke's role in strongly visual terms. These three shots, each independent images that differ from the others, are joined to create this dramatic moment of film narrative.

A sequence or episode in a film or video narrative will combine elements of the art form, both to tell a story and to elicit a committed response from the audience. In such a sequence the flow of character, action, and setting will be analyzed and segmented by the director into shots and edited links to be coordinated for the larger effects of the story.

Theme, Image, and Symbol

Like a play or a short novel, a film will have themes, recurring images, and symbols that intensify the story and its emotional or intellectual significance. One

Chapter 6 Exploring Visual Texts   **87**

important aspect of *Star Wars* is its combination of interest in storytelling along with its development of a moral world of good and evil. The film shows a fantasy world of space technology where individual adventure and daring are posed against huge, overwhelming forces of control. In this, *Star Wars* suggests the fight for personal and communal freedom in a modern world of technological and political intrusion.

Among Lucas's most famous creations are the serio-comic couple of "droids," or androids, C-3PO and R2-D2. These robots are introduced in the opening sequence with R2-D2, the short round-topped robot, having the distinction of containing the secret plans of the Empire's Death Star. His fate is thus connected to the film's climax, where this essential information and its transmission is what makes possible the final sequence of the Rebels' last minute battle with the Death Star:

Lucas uses these robots as images of a humanized technology. Where the Empire's storm troopers are anonymous under helmets and behind blasters—and so dehumanized—the two droids take on human fallibility and humor. The gold-toned C-3PO is a human-shaped machine programmed to speak more than 6,000 languages. His cautious nature and his desire to survive events beyond his control make him into a comic figure representing human dismay bowing before the forces of technology.

R2-D2 operates as a character who is both comic and loyal. His beeps and blurts, which must be translated by C-3PO, show that he has computer intelligence, but in a humorous way. R2-D2, though, becomes the loyal follower of Princess Leia, providing the link between the Rebels and Luke Skywalker's group. Lucas anthropomorphizes the robots—that is, he gives them human characteristics—so that they work not only as dramatic characters, but also as images of the conflict between technology and the human community.

Equally important in *Star Wars* is the drama of good and evil that centers around the ominous figure of Darth Vader. Within the fantasy world of the film, the categories of good and bad are almost always clear cut. A major sequence in the story concerns the sacrifice of Obi-Wan Kenobi to Darth Vader in order to allow for the escape of Luke and Leia from the Death Star:

This final duel between Ben and Darth Vader crystallizes the drama of self-sacrifice before the seemingly invincible Empire. In this shot, Lucas shows the combat of Ben and Darth Vader from Luke's perspective. The duel is framed by one of the launch bay doors, giving the effect of a staged scene.

While many of the images of *Star Wars* may be familiar to us, the film demonstrates an impressive range of the elements of a visual text. The combination of a pungently presented drama and the focused use of special effects and symbolism give the film a continuing resonance. Reflection on aspects of this famous film can lead both to a greater appreciation of this specific work but can also act as a bridge to exploration of other movies and visual texts.

ANALYZING A VISUAL TEXT

A film text, like Lucas's *Star Wars,* works from the smallest moment or frame to sequences of assembled elements and ultimately operates at the level of an entire narrative informed by choices of image and style. While the film or video maker uses aspects of drama found in character, acting, and script, the nature of visual media demands the use of carefully selected and assembled visual elements as well. Part of the process of inquiring into visual media involves heightening your attention to those elements particular to the medium and to the particular embodiment of the medium in a specific work.

You might continue to reflect on visual media as you watch a favorite film or taped television program for a second or third time by keeping a notepad by you and making a list of five distinct visual elements that intrigue you. Just as you can annotate a printed text, you can note down aspects of your chosen film. If you use either a video tape or DVD version, you can stop the video stream and even go back to segments that seem especially interesting to you.

Chapter 6   Exploring Visual Texts   **89**

If you stop the film at a visually arresting point, you can ask yourself about the composition of, say, a single frame. How does the selected frame work within the story or action of the film? What visual aspects do you see that connect this frame with other parts of the narrative in terms of the camera's point of view or the tone and symbolic suggestions of the frame? Does the film repeat or expand an aspect of your frame in other contexts?

Similarly, if you find a compelling short sequence, try to view it a number of times, asking yourself what elements of visual media are used to make this an effective part of the film or video. Think of the use of the camera, movement, and the linking of shots to tell the story and to emphasize theme, mood, or emotion.

By viewing one film critically and taking focused notes on it, you can prepare to write or report on the work with greater detail while adding to your own awareness of the visual elements that constitute both the medium and the particular film you have chosen. By adding reflection and focused observation to your first response to a film you will be able to develop and express a fuller understanding of the nature of visual media.

SUGGESTED FURTHER READINGS

Bazin, André. *What Is Cinema?* Ed. Transl. Hugh Gray. Berkeley: University of California Press, 1967.

> Bazin was the major critic for the French magazine *Cahiers du Cinéma* in the 1950s. His literate and far-ranging essays on the nature of film and its potential had a great effect on many major film makers of the French New Wave like Truffaut and Robert Bresson. His essays on the connection between theater and film in this volume are classics.

Corrigan, Timothy. *A Short Guide to Writing about Film,* 3rd ed. Boston: Addison-Wesley, 1997.

> This small book offers a common sense introduction to appreciating some aspects of film and making a transition to essay composition about film. Corrigan gives a sketch of film elements and a number of examples of student essays based on the analysis of film. While this book makes no claims to completeness or critical complexity, it offers one of the few usable introductions on film for a beginning student.

Monaco, James. *How to Read a Film: Movies, Media, Multimedia,* 3rd ed. New York: Oxford University Press, 2000.

> Monaco has evolved his substantial book on the history and aesthetics of film to include changes in the digital age. He surveys parallels of film to the other arts, the basic technology of film and media, the syntax of film, and a discussion of basic theories of film. In accordance with recent trends the book has both a Web page and a CD-ROM supplement to the print medium of the book. This is something of an encyclopedia of film and can be used for an efficient overview of most aspects of film.

PART TWO

Reading as Exploration

Literary theory plays a central role in contemporary English studies. At the same time, some of the assumptions and much of the language of literary theory can be intimidating when encountered for the first time. As one student, Chloe, wrote about her Introduction to Literary Theory class:

> I thought the course was going to be tedious and confusing. There are so many different theoretical approaches to be studied. I did not comprehend how I'd be able to write a paper using a theory I might not agree with.

By the end of the course, however, she was able to conclude: "My understanding of theory has influenced my understanding of other cultural forms by opening my mind and forcing me to think in ways that I might not have otherwise." Chloe's reaction is a fairly common one. Jess writes, "[Studying theory] has helped me so much. It makes reading for any subject interesting, while helping to break down complex ideas." And Jenny concludes, "My understanding of theory influences my understanding of literature and other cultural forms, in that it leads me to further acknowledge and understand issues such as gender, race, and class, and how they function within society and in literature."

But for many English majors, the study of literary theory remains a difficult prospect. Most people become interested in English studies in the first place because they enjoy reading and writing, but having to learn theories about how people read and write is another matter altogether and can sometimes feel like a barrier between a text and a reader's emotional responses to it.

Perhaps the best way to become oriented in this difficult terrain is with a brief historical review of the place of literary theory in North American English departments. A century ago, as English departments first began to proliferate in American colleges and universities, they imitated many of the practices of the already well-established departments of classical languages and literature—the study of Greek and, especially, Latin. From the late nineteenth century on, the English major was the new kid on the block, asserting that literature written in one's own language could be central to education, and not just a recreational activity. But if the subject matter was radical, many of the questions posed about English were borrowed directly from the study of classical languages: How can we establish dependable texts when several possibilities or variants exist? What prior texts may have influenced an author in ways that appear in a text? How does a given work reveal some aspect of the historical period in which it was written? How are literary periods defined and exemplified? How do the details of an author's biography illuminate an author's texts?

These historical or biographical approaches were challenged by, and ultimately supplanted by, a movement called "New Criticism," a term that is still used to describe the movement, even though the practice it describes has not been "new" for more than sixty years. The key instinct of New Criticism, its defining orientation, is its focus on "the text itself" as the primary object of study. (See Chapter 10, "Reader Response," which offers an additional critique of this attitude.)

While the earlier approaches provided interesting information about authors, texts, historical periods, and literary genres, they did not teach people the skills of "close reading," specific reading practices through which to draw meaning from the structure and language of the text itself. New Critics saw themselves as rebelling against contemporary orthodoxy in at least two ways: one against the reigning attitudes in academic circles, the other against the sloppy practices of a general reading public. On the academic side, they argued that background studies could not determine the meaning of a text. They rejected, for example, the notion that knowing an author's claims of what he or she tried to do in a work was relevant. By relying on these authorial assertions, a critic commits what they called *the intentional fallacy,* the notion that an author's intention should determine what a text said. If they rejected authorial intention, New Critics also rejected the notion that the facile, unreflective, "emotional" responses of "common readers" were important. To accept such readings was to commit *the affective fallacy.* New Critics were particularly challenging the perception that reading involved hunting for the underlying "moral" of a work, as though its significance could be reduced to an aphorism. As a consequence, New Criticism set about prescribing a set of reading practices to encourage a more precise reading of texts.

The underlying assumption of New Criticism is that good works of literature are tightly organized to achieve a unified effect. A term often used was that a well-written work of art had "organic unity," a metaphor borrowed from the world of nature: Just as every part of a natural creature—a plant or an animal—is essential to its life and function, when a text is successful no part of it can be removed or rearranged without altering the "organism." It's a sign of the long-term success of New Criticism that it continues to dominate the teaching of literature at the introductory level. (You will find, for example, that its assumptions and vocabulary are the basis for most of the chapters in Part One of this book.) But used in this way, where it is presented as how to "do" literature, New Criticism is not often acknowledged to be a theory of literature at all, so that individual students who first come to learn about theory often feel anew the challenge of subsequent theories aligned against New Criticism.

It is a theory, nonetheless, and like any theory it is simultaneously a lens and a filter: It lets you see some aspects of what you're studying with greater clarity, but it excludes other aspects that don't respond as well to its methodologies and values. In practical terms, New Criticism's assumption that good texts are tightly unified and that unity is an indicator of a text's value worked very well with highly complex and intricate works—especially with tightly constructed lyric poetry—but less so in addressing the effect of performance on drama, and less still with long multistranded narrative fiction whose structure seemed more episodic, less organic. In addition, it worked particularly well for certain historical periods, the metaphysical poetry of the early seventeenth century, for example, where some authors wrote poems of deliberate intellectual and technical complexity.

One of the most influential books of practical New Criticism, Cleanth Brooks's *The Well-Wrought Urn*, provides an example of this kind of focus by providing elegant and insightful, chapter-long readings of T. S. Eliot's notoriously difficult poem, *The Waste Land*, and of John Donne's metaphysical poem, "The Canonization," a poem from which the book's title, *The Well-Wrought Urn*, is taken. But readers who preferred other kinds of texts or who wanted to argue for their social, historical, or cultural significance inevitably felt the need to devise new theories of reading with which to do so.

During the period when New Criticism was dominant, a course in Literary Criticism or Theory would typically have been one in practical criticism; how to "do" new criticism; how to acquire and apply the skills of close reading that this approach prized, rather than an examination of competing theories. Alternatively, a course on History of Literary Criticism or Theory was likely to cover material from Plato and Aristotle up to some of the critical essays of T. S. Eliot written in the 1910s, 1920s, and 1930s. The course was likely to focus on texts speculating about the nature and function of literature written by figures such as Philip Sydney in the late sixteenth century, or John Dryden a century or so later, or Samuel Johnson a century or so after that, particularly with an eye toward how the attitudes expressed in them might illuminate the cultural assumptions underlying other texts written in those time periods. No need to bring the course up to the present, since that meant New Criticism. During the 1950s and 1960s, courses of this sort would typically have been a subspecialty of a single faculty member: someone in the department would have taught Shakespeare; someone else modern American poetry, someone else Romanticism, and someone else criticism or theory.

Challenges to New Criticism, the mainstay of most college English departments by the middle of the twentieth century, arose during the tumultuous 1960s, when all establishment doctrines were subject to scrutiny and doubt. By the 1970s, the serious theoretical challenges to New Critical orthodoxy could be found left and right, especially at the graduate level, the most prominent of which are still with us: structuralist, psychoanalytic, Marxist, feminist, and various related approaches. By century's end, these approaches to English studies had expanded so broadly that the only safe assertion now may be that there are multiple theories useful for exploring literature, that each is interesting, and that none is likely to become a new orthodoxy. What may well unite current English faculty is the assumption that there are many ways of reading texts and many texts written in English worthy of literary study, and that this pluralism is itself essential to intelligent literary study.

Most college English departments now offer courses on Literary Theory or on Literary and Cultural Theory, and nowadays, while some attention might be paid to theories from earlier historical periods, the courses will almost always focus on theoretical approaches developed since the mid-twentieth century. While the undergraduate curriculum in most institutions is still structured according to historical periods, genres, or major authors and texts, the way these courses are taught differs widely depending on the teacher's preferred theoretical approach. Usually the teachers in these classes make their theoretical approaches clear to you, but if they don't, you might do well to find a discreet way to ask. It might make you better understand what presuppositions your teachers bring to their own reading and to the structuring of your course, what kind of questions they might ask about literature, what kind of work they might be assuming that you understand you're being asked to do.

One last point: The humanities do not usually jettison outmoded ideas as new ones come along but incorporate aspects of what has been rejected into new conceptual models. Most modern theories, therefore, adapt to their own needs many of the questions posed a century ago by historical critics, using many of the rhetorical practices refined by the New Critics. That said, the newer theories raise questions about reading practices and the significance of texts that the earlier approaches ignored or vilified. The remainder of this introduction provides brief sketches of some of the major theoretical movements of the past thirty years. The five chapters that comprise Part Two explore selected theoretical movements in greater detail.

Psychological Criticism   Psychological critics challenge the intentional fallacy, arguing that it can be possible to explore authorial intent, but in a more subtle way than by using the old biographical and historical methods. Early psychological critics used the techniques of Freudian psychoanalysis, for example, to uncover ways in which an author might be repressing central concerns, desires, or anxieties, thus making many texts readable as expressions of subconscious desire. The works of other psychiatrists, psychologists, and the schools they represent have subsequently been applied to literary study, both to examine the ways in which an author's unspoken—sometimes unacknowledged—ideas and desires can be revealed in a text and to examine the ways in which psychology can help explain the structuring of readers' responses to them.

Sigmund Freud's works, such as *The Interpretation of Dreams* and *Introductory Lectures on Psychoanalysis* were key early works applied to literary analysis, and several of his specific case studies have also become widely read.

Norman N. Holland's work has helped structure psychological criticism for several decades, for example, in *The Dynamics of Literary Response*, and the work of Jacques Lacan has been widely influential in recent years for incorporating insights of other intellectual currents including structuralism into his refinements of Freudian thought. Feminist critics such as Nancy Chodorow, objecting to what seems to be Freud's presumption of male psychological development as normative, have proposed alternative models.

Structralism   Structuralists see literature itself, along with all other cultural forms, as having a structure analogous to language (and in fact one of the major sources of this approach is the field of structural linguistics). No individual symbol bears meaning inherent in itself. Rather, "meaning" requires a system of differentiation: The meaning of any one symbol is determined by cultural convention only and by contrast with other symbols from within the system with different culturally accepted meanings. Mixed with various other types of theory, several of which are listed below, this approach has led to the recent rise of "cultural studies," a notion that analogous techniques of analysis can be applied not just to texts but to other cultural forms as well, any of which might be seen as part of a language-like structure. Advertising campaigns, television talk shows, soap operas, rock videos, network news broadcasts, body piercing and tatooing, professional wrestling—all are structured cultural forms, and as such open to interrogation using the techniques of literary and cultural analysis.

Two of the seminal texts in structuralist thought come from fields other than literature: Ferdinand de Saussure's *Course in General Linguistics* and Claude Lévi-Strauss's *Structural Anthropology*. An early classic text for literary studies is Jonathan Culler's *Structuralist Poetics*.

Marxism   During the period of the Cold War, Marxist literary critics had an ongoing struggle to separate themselves from Cold War questions about the geopolitical distribution of power. Their concern has never been, however, to take sides in a bipolar struggle between superpowers, but to keep the focus of literary analysis on questions of class, especially on the distribution of power between a ruling class, which is frequently, perhaps even typically, oppressive, and the majority of people who are the victims of a political and economic system that distributes power and wealth inequitably. Marxist analysis generally examines the way literature can often replicate this power structure in such a way as to make it seem inevitable or "natural" or, at least, the best available alternative. Marxists are likely to focus on the content of works, but also on the means of their production and distribution, who has access to these privileges, and to what social end are they turned.

Works by such European scholars as Walter Benjamin, Theodor Adorno, and Georg Lucács remain influential and many are available in translation. Two important writers in English are Frederic Jameson (*The Political Unconscious: Narrative as a Socially Symbolic Act*, among other works) and Raymond Williams (*Marxism and Literature*).

Deconstruction   This philosophically-based theory is most identified with the work of Jacques Derrida and later with a group of professors at Yale University in the 1970s that included Geoffrey Hartman, Paul DeMan, and J. Hillis Miller. The central insight of deconstruction is that language is structured by a series of "binary opposites"—masculine-feminine, speech-writing, presence-absence—that seems to be necessary to facilitate thinking and language, but which ultimately simplify and misrepresent reality. In fact, this problem is so fundamental, so inherent in language, that unambiguous statements cannot be made about what a text might mean, since its own language is at so many junctures strained by these inherent linguistic contradictions. Like New Criticism, this is essentially a formalist approach to literature, one that examines the text itself rather than the way the text interacts with the outside world, but with the difference that a deconstructionist would challenge the very opposition between intrinsic and extrinsic in this context, since the outside world "exists" only insofar as we are able to construct it linguistically—with all of the ambiguity inherent in that process. Where a New Critic might see apparent contradictions in a text as an opportunity to demonstrate the way irony or paradox can resolve the contradictions into a subtle unity, a deconstructionist might demonstrate rather that the writer was trying to use language to impose a simplistic structure on an unresolved—perhaps unresolvable—conflict that may be personal, cultural, or inherent in literary form.

Derrida's work *Of Grammatology* remains influential.

New Historicism   New Historicists (as opposed to those who conducted more traditional literary history) tend to examine a wide range of texts, artifacts, and cultural phenomena and events, material ranging from the legal, political, or economic world to the way in which worlds are mapped to the structure of medical, military, or penal institutions—all while exploring the interrelationship between literary texts and other contemporary phenomena. On the one hand, they might examine ways in which the other cultural phenomena enter into and help shape the literature—how plays by Shakespeare and his contemporaries, for example, reproduce (and help produce) attitudes found in early written accounts from travelers to the new world about race and the foundations of what would become colonialism. But on the other hand, they are also at pains to suggest the symbolic structures underlying the social institutions themselves, using a close reading of the literary text to disclose meaning in the forms and practices of the wider culture.

Michel Foucault is the most important early figure in this movement, and his major works are available in English. Other major figures include Stephen Greenblatt, who has several influential works on the early modern period, especially as manifested in the works of Shakespeare; Sacvan Bercovitch, whose work has helped shape a rethinking of nineteenth-century American literature; and Edward Said, whose *Orientalism* and other works on the representation of non-Western cultures have helped define postcolonial theory.

Part 2   Reading as Exploration

Perhaps the most important warning to leave you with is the obvious: There is no one "best" theoretical approach for you to take when reading or writing about literature. The more theories you explore and feel comfortable with, the more you will be able to expand the kinds of questions you raise about texts, and this will increase the likelihood that you will find something of use in them, something more than your own reflection.

In the five chapters that follow, you will find more focused discussions of some specific approaches to literature. The first provides a general orientation toward the study of theory as an English major, and the others offer specific theoretical approaches that address the way the institutional structure of English departments and courses seems still to disempower large groups of people—women, people from various ethnic groups and from formerly colonized parts of the world, and individual (quirky) readers.

In Chapter 7, "On Not Being a Tourist, or Why It's Important to Study Literary Theory" Lisa Schnell addresses the anxieties some students feel about the difficulty (and relevance) of theory, arguing that it is engagement with the language of literary theory that helps define English as a discipline.

In Chapter 8, "Writing Feminist Readings: The Long and the Short," Mary Louise Kete differentiates feminist criticism from other forms of theory. She argues that feminist critics are unified not so much by a common methodology or canon, as by a commitment to raising as central to literary studies questions about the gender basis for the distribution of power.

In Chapter 9, "Expanding the Canon: A Multicultural Perspective," Helen Scott explores some of the challenges to the Eurocentric canon and model of reading, providing an argument for the value of an ongoing dialogue among texts from different cultures.

In Chapter 10, "Reader Response: The Value of Getting It 'Right' the First Time," Nancy Welch both argues for the value of Reader Response Criticism and provides examples and practical suggestions for implementing the approach in the classroom.

In Chapter 11, "Reading Film as Acts of Reading," Andrew Barnaby explains and illustrates his own theoretical position that acts of interpretation are acts of creation. For an example, he explores the film, *A River Runs Through It*, modeling for readers his own interpretative process.

WORKS CITED

Bercovitch, Sacvan. *The Rites of Ascent: Transformations in the Symbolic Construction of America.* New York: Routledge, 1993.

Brooks, Cleanth. *The Well-Wrought Urn: Studies in the Structure of Poetry.* New York: Harcourt, Brace, 1947.

Chodorow, Nancy. *The Reproduction of Mothering: Psychoanalysis and the Sociology of Gender.* Berkeley: University of California Press, 1978.

Culler, Jonathan. *Structuralist Poetics: Structuralism, Linguistics, and the Study of Language.* Ithaca: Cornell University Press, 1975.

Derrida, Jacques. *Of Grammatology,* Trans. Gayatri Spivak. Baltimore: Johns Hopkins University Press, 1976.

Freud, Sigmund. *Introductory Lectures on Psycho-Analysis.* Trans. Joan Rivière. London: Allen, 1922.

———. *The Interpretation of Dreams.* Trans. Joyce Crick; intro. and notes by Ritchie Robertson. Oxford: Oxford University Press, 1999.

Holland, Norman N. *The Dynamics of Literary Response.* New York: Oxford University Press, 1968.

Jameson, Frederic. *The Political Unconscious: Narrative as a Socially Symbolic Act.* Ithaca: Cornell University Press, 1981.

Lévi-Strauss, Claude *Structural Anthropology.* Trans. Claire Jacobson and Brooke Grundfest Schoepf. New York: Basic, 1963.

Said, Edward. *Orientalism.* New York: Pantheon, 1978.

Saussure, Ferdinand de. *Course in General Linguistics.* New York: McGraw-Hill, 1959.

Williams, Raymond. *Marxism and Literature.* Oxford: Oxford University Press, 1977.

CHAPTER 7

On Not Being a Tourist, or Why It's Important to Study Literary Theory

Lisa Schnell

THE ENGLISH MAJOR AS ANTHROPOLOGIST[1]

Almost every spring I teach a course called "Introduction to Literary Theory," a sophomore course required for our English majors. Each time I teach that course I face a room full of stony faces; a room full of students who think that I am about to ruin their experience of reading; a room full of students who are collectively thinking that they just need to "get it over with." One semester of theory and then they can get on with the real business of being an English major (whatever that is!). It is my job in that course to try to bring my students to an understanding first, of why the business of being an English major must involve some kind of encounter with literary theory and second, why that encounter need not be scary or, worse yet, inimical to their lives as readers and writers. But that assumes that we'll all be on the same page about what it means to be an English major, and that would be a false assumption.

A friend of mine, now a successful businessman, tells me that he chose English as his major because he could "speak the language." Things turned out well for him—after he went to Business School and learned *that* language. But as an English major, he was completely lost. Ironically, what my friend discovered was that he *didn't* speak the language. And I suppose, in the first instance, that's what literary theory is: a language, or languages, that allow us to work within a discipline. The problem with the English major—for many of our undergraduates—is that it is not perceived as a discipline. Like my friend, many of the students in my sophomore course are English majors by default. Almost all of them share a common enthusiasm for the written word, but beyond that, they have little idea about what the *discipline* of English is all about.

To be fair, the designation "discipline" is a little dubious; in fact, it may be that some of my students' misunderstandings about the "discipline" of

---

[1] I am indebted both to my extraordinary colleagues at the University of Vermont and to the students, so many of them also extraordinary, in all the English 86 classes I have taught over the past several years at UVM. Both groups have contributed, and continue to contribute in immeasurable ways, to my understanding and experience of the possibilities of intellectual community.

English is what leads them to speak with disparagement about, for instance, "dissecting" texts. Dissecting is something that a scientist does to reveal the truth about how an organism functions. And while literary criticism does often dig very deeply into a text in analyzing its forms of language, the "truth" of a text is just as deeply subjective as the digging we do. So what *does* it mean to think of English as a discipline?

One of the most helpful ways for me to think about what we do in English departments is to think of ourselves as anthropologists of language and literature. If we think about what an anthropologist does, this might begin to make sense. Typically, an anthropologist will travel to a culture—not usually her native culture—to study, describe, and then analyze cultural habits and social relations. She may be drawn initially to anthropology because of a love for travel, but that desire alone will hardly make her an anthropologist. In other words, an anthropologist is not a tourist. To succeed, she needs to learn another language, know how to position herself so as best to observe a culture not her own—which includes asking questions that will produce useful information—and then know how to translate her observations into a cogent and meaningful analysis.

My friend Sarah, for instance, is an anthropologist who studies birthing practices among Latin American women; she is also a mother herself. And indeed, she was partly drawn to her area of study because her own experience of birthing had been incredibly important to her. But no matter how fluent she is in Spanish, she's not going to be able to ask the right questions of her subjects simply from her own experience of giving birth in a big American hospital. She gains the trust of her subjects because she is, herself, a mom; but if she ever presumed to know Latin American women's experience through her *own* experience she would lose the trust of her subjects completely. She has to accomplish something very difficult to succeed as an anthropologist: She must continue to care about the issues she researches without resorting to the narcissistic temptation to re-create those issues only in her own image. She needs, in other words, to open herself up to all the possibilities involved in *learning*.

By extension, I might be drawn to the English major because I like to read and/or write, but by committing to the major I commit to being more than just a tourist in the texts I read or the writing I do. Like my friend Sarah, the cultural anthropologist, I have to start with a desire to know more about the culture I've chosen to study—in this case, the culture of language—and then I need to learn enough about it to be able to ask good, probing questions that will lead to good, probing analyses. But, while I need to continue to care about reading and writing as I always have, I also have to be willing to suspend my desire to make the text I'm reading always about me, to use only the knowledge that I already possess. Like an anthropologist, I have to continue to *care* about language but I also have to be willing to admit that the world of words is bigger than just my own lexicon.

The different models of literary theory are nothing less than the languages—or lexicons—we need to acquire to be able to ask good questions of the texts we read (questions that might elicit surprising answers), to be able to engage in

Chapter 7   Why It's Important to Study Literary Theory   **101**

conversation with the texts we read and, by extension, with their sometimes vast, and often truly diverse, communities of readers. Learning how to become an active part of this critical conversation is the whole discipline of the English major.

EXPANDING OUR FIELD OF VIEW

Many students who come to the English major because they love to read—I was one of them—find the experience of college to be just one big disappointment after another. Standing tall in the midst of my own experience is an eighteenth-century literature class I took when I was a sophomore. I remember, not without some embarrassment, how sophisticated I felt seeing that class on my schedule in September. There was something about studying the eighteenth century that made me an *authentic* English major. Then the course began, and that feeling of smugness was almost instantly replaced with frustration, even desperation. I did all the reading—I even read a lot of the books *twice*—but I didn't have the foggiest clue what was going on in that class. I developed a rash that I'm sure was caused by fear of being called on to say something in class; I anxiously considered switching majors; I hated every minute of it. I managed to get through the course somehow (probably purely on my ability to creatively regurgitate my lecture notes), and the eighteenth century remained pretty much a black hole in my literary world even after I had the tools that may have opened it up for me. Until, that is, I came to the University of Vermont as an English professor (my specialty is the seventeenth century, allowing me to avoid the eighteenth century entirely) and was assigned to teach a survey of British Literature that included the eighteenth century. An unmistakably familiar rash reappeared as I put Alexander Pope's *The Rape of the Lock* on the syllabus. Dread became pleasure, however, when we got to the poem and, in preparing for class, I discovered it to be not just about "heroic couplets" and "alexandrines" and "heroic convention" and the perfectly balanced metrical line—the things I had been taught about it as an undergraduate. The poem I read this time—though word-for-word the same poem I had read in 1981—was a wonderfully funny but biting critique of England's imperialist practices in the early eighteenth century, practices that included slavery. This was something that really mattered to me, and I got very excited about teaching the poem. To this day, though I no longer teach the survey course, I remember our few days on *The Rape of the Lock* as some of the most exciting, the most pleasurable of that course. What I felt was *intellectual excitement*, a marvelous feeling that comes from approaching a text (or a problem) armed with knowledge that, though it might not come directly out of our own limited personal experiences, does indeed *matter* in our lives and in our engagement with the larger world around us. It was literary theory that opened Alexander Pope's poem to me—without the vocabulary of Marxism and postcolonial theory (something Helen Scott writes about in Chapter 9) this marvelous poem would have stayed "locked" to me.

My experience with *The Rape of the Lock* implicitly addresses another issue that plagues the Introduction to Literary Theory classroom in its early weeks. And that is the misperception many students struggle with that "doing theory" will mean twisting and chopping a text to fit the needs of the theory. That, for instance, if I ask them to engage in a Marxist analysis of *Hamlet,* they will have to ignore what *actually* happens in the play and turn *Hamlet* into an early draft of *The Communist Manifesto.* I can identify with the resistance that comes from this misunderstanding because it was very much the way I felt when I was first introduced to literary theory as a graduate student.

Like many of my students, I loved reading, and writing about what I had read, and what I didn't want to do was to use theory to turn a text into something it wasn't. My own moment of "conversion" came when I was writing a paper on what had always been for me a very strange, but wonderful, early twentieth-century novel called *To The Lighthouse,* a novel that had, when I'd read it as an undergraduate, completely defied any literary description in my repertoire. Frustrating me was the fact that I really loved the novel but had no way to explain what it was that I was so drawn to in my experience of reading it. Working with this novel after I'd studied some theory, I realized that a good literary critic doesn't "do" theory to a text; instead, she uses theory to talk about what a text is *already doing to itself.* Using my new theoretical tools, I had a handle on what was strange and wonderful about *To The Lighthouse,* and I had an interesting way of talking about it. Which was not to suggest that Virginia Woolf, the writer of *To The Lighthouse,* had read all those late twentieth-century theories of "deconstruction" that I found useful in describing the odd narrative behavior of her novel, or that, if we go back to the *Hamlet* example for a minute, Shakespeare was a Marxist. Instead, our use of theory to talk about Woolf's or Shakespeare's work suggests that, in the case of *Hamlet* for instance, the twentieth-century vocabulary of Marxism—and the accompanying knowledge that that vocabulary stands for—can be used to talk about some of the sixteenth-century socioeconomic inequities that Shakespeare appears to have been very aware of. Marx, after all, did not *invent* the class system; he did, however, give us a new vocabulary for thinking and writing about it. A similar thing holds true for my use of the vocabulary of deconstruction—a philosophy of radical skepticism about the ability of language to fully represent "Truth" or even just lived reality—to talk about *To The Lighthouse.*

Philosophers like the famous French deconstructionist Jacques Derrida may have given us some very interesting ways of discussing linguistic skepticism that speak especially to late-twentieth-century ways of thinking, but skepticism about the power of language to represent is hardly a late-twentieth-century phenomenon. Using those theoretical languages, then, does not mean that we are insisting that Shakespeare was a Marxist or that Woolf was a Derridean; it does mean, though, that we have vocabularies that open up questions and lead to analytical possibilities that we may have previously found inaccessible.

The most surprising thing, however, is that new theoretical vocabularies allow us to talk not only about things we knew were there but didn't have the words to describe; those vocabularies can, in fact, open up for us aspects of a text that we simply did not know were there before. It's a little like the phenomenon I'm sure many of you have experienced in which you are introduced to someone for the first time, and suddenly you start seeing that same person everywhere you go. It's not a weird coincidence; in fact, chances are you've actually seen him in all those places before. But until you were *introduced* to him you could not have *recognized* him; he simply wasn't on your radar screen. I had read *Hamlet* a number of times before I studied Marxist literary theory, but certain prominent parts of that play, and arguably very important parts of the play—the gravedigger scene, for instance—never crossed my radar screen until my eyes had been opened up to the possibilities of Marxist analysis. For me, the play had chiefly been about a perversely triangulated relationship between mother, son, and father, and it didn't cease to be about those things. But it was now *also* about the way that family is even further complicated by its class position, and that made the play far richer than it had been before. Indeed, my experience of *Hamlet* changes every time I read it because new sets of ideas are constantly crossing my radar screen. And that means that every time I teach the play—which is at least once a year—it becomes richer and more pleasurable to me.

THE PLEASURE OF THE TEXT

This idea of "pleasure," or as I've also called it "intellectual excitement," is hardly one I take for granted in my classes. For I am well aware that one of the major reasons that students resent having to take my Introduction to Literary Theory course comes from their fear that "doing theory" will rob them of the pleasure they get from "just enjoying" a book (or a film, or a TV show). You may be one of these students—someone who loves the experience of getting lost in a big fat novel, or a beautifully evocative poem, or a very funny play—and you don't want that experience taken away from you by a teacher who insists that you have to "intellectualize" the text.

My own experience teaches me that we don't need to sacrifice pleasure on the altar of literary theory. In trying to communicate this to my classes I often tell them of an experience I had some years ago in which I took a friend to a favorite movie of mine. The film, *The Double Life of Veronique* by the Czechoslovakian filmmaker Krzysztof Kiéslowski, was one I had seen many times and that I found, for reasons that I didn't ever really try to articulate, strangely but deeply moving. Anxious to share my experience of the film, I drove with my friend 30 miles to see it at a little arthouse cinema a few towns over. Bad mistake. Not only did my friend *not* like the film, she was only too happy to share her scene-by-scene criticism of it all the way home. She didn't just dislike the movie, she *hated* it; she hated it for the whole 30 miles.

I felt pretty angry for a while, robbed of the pleasure I had previously taken in the film, and betrayed by my friend who, if she was really to qualify as my friend, *should* have loved that film. And I was furious with her that not only had she hated it, but that she'd actually made some persuasive arguments against liking it. I was furious with myself for agreeing with her, but I wanted my movie back. The only way to take it back was to try to name what I had not yet tried to name: I needed to counter her criticism with some criticism of my own. I thought about the film for a long time and, in subsequent conversations with my friend, eventually found ways both to articulate what I thought was beautiful and moving about it and to explain how her own critique of it had not taken into consideration those things. In these (surprisingly pleasurable) conversations, we found ways to agree with each other and still have some room for our original responses to the film. While neither one of us would completely change our positions, we found a way to *revise* them a little, opening up the door to other responses that had the effect of actually enriching our respective experiences of the film. In the end, it was a win-win for me: Along with identifying, and thus confirming, some of my original pleasure in the film, I was also reminded, during our conversations, of the genuine pleasure of belonging to a community in which every member does not think in exactly the same way but in which real conversation is a way of engaging in those differences.

Eventually, my one original pleasure—a wordless appreciation of a film—had turned into several pleasures: the pleasure of naming what I had experienced, the pleasure of a good conversation days after we had seen the film, and the pleasure I have had in subsequent viewings, viewings that have been made much richer by those conversations. I enjoy *The Double Life of Veronique* at a much deeper level than I did before; and while there is still something of the film's original, and perhaps largely inarticulable, effect on me that I want to preserve, I find that effect has not, in fact, been damaged by my intellectual involvement in the issues raised by the film.

THE MORAL CONVERSATION

But I also learned from my experience with my friend that there are two kinds of critical conversations: good ones and bad ones. If, eventually, conversations with my friend were enriching, the original 30-mile rant was not: with both of us dogmatically insisting on our own very different opinions there was no room for conversation at all. Theory should open up possibilities for us, it should not shut them down. And, to be sure, there have been some literary theorists who have given theory a bad name. Excessive use of jargon; dogmatic and defensive stances for or against a position; insensitive readings of others' work; insufficient exploration of issues that are foreign to us or seem repellent to us—none of these strategies results in a good conversation, not one of them results in knowledge that is truly *useful*. In an article called "Fostering Moral Conversations in the College Classroom," Robert Nash, an ethicist in the College of Education at the University of Vermont, quotes from the "memo" he writes to his students at the beginning of every semester. "You will know that you are engaging in good moral conversation," he writes, "when the following is happening more and more frequently in class discussions." I'll quote just the first six of his nine indicators:

1. You make an honest effort to read texts and to understand others *on their terms* as well as on your own.
2. You acknowledge that although you do indeed "construct" meaning when reading a text and listening to others, you also have biases and blind spots that can be exposed, and reconstructed, by others more objective and wiser than you.
3. You maintain an open-mindedness about the possibility of learning something from both the author *and* your peers in the conversation.
4. You show a willingness to improve your current philosophical language, because it may be incomplete.
5. You make a conscious effort to refrain from advancing your own current philosophical language as the best one.
6. You evidence an inclination to listen intently in order to grasp the meaning of other people's philosophical languages for expressing their truths. (88)

Nash's article—one that I have my own students read at the beginning of any class I am teaching—gets at the heart not only of the markers of good conversation, but at some of the most important aims of literary theory. If we reflect on Nash's assumption about learning—that we engage in intellectual (and other) conversations *not* so that we can advance our own limited viewpoints but so that we can learn from others' in order to broaden our own sense of the world—we end up right back at the anthropology example I began with. To my anthropologist friend, learning means acknowledging a set of experiences not her own; listening very carefully and with a fully open mind to the women she studies; resisting the temptation to *assume* things about her subjects based on her own set of cultural expectations and experiences; embracing the opportunities to revise those very expectations in the course of study.

Arguably, an anthropologist's job isn't primarily to enter into disputes with or even really to evaluate the culture she studies. Although there are all kinds of ways the current theory and practice of anthropology might complicate this model, we might still characterize the main work of anthropology as being a kind of description. And while description is also an enormous part of what we do in literature departments—and indeed, as I've argued, literary theory helps us first in *describing* what a text is doing—we are, in fact, literary *critics*. It is widely recognized that part of our job is to argue; part of our job is to evaluate. We are deeply involved in *active conversation* with the texts we read and with others who have also read them; like the anthropologist, we are not just tourists. And so if literary theory first allows us to describe, it finally allows us to speak for ourselves about things that matter to us, even as we open ourselves up to the possibility that those things can change as we listen to voices other than our own. The point of "doing" literary theory is thus to participate in a conversation, a conversation to which we bring our own theoretical positions (whether we know it or not, whether we can even identify them or not) and in which we weigh and consider the positions of others. The point of engaging in this conversation is *to learn*, which means only very occasionally learning that we were right in the first place; which *much* more frequently means learning how to revise a precious opinion and, consequently, enjoying an enriched understanding of the world we inhabit. When some of my students insist—usually at the beginning of the semester—that literary theory is superfluous, just a fancy way to "intellectualize" a text that takes all the fun out of it, I can't help but ask them two questions. What on earth would make them think that, at the ripe old age of 19 or 20, they've learned as much as they need to know; and, even more to the point (since they're all declared English majors), why would they want to *study* something they already claim to have mastered?

T. S. Eliot, one of the great poets of the twentieth century, was of the opinion that "Hell is where nothing connects." If that is true then, within the English major, literary theory—according to one dictionary definition, "the analysis of a set of facts *in their relation to one another*"—is the key to heaven's door. Used intelligently and responsibly, literary theory gives us the tools to make connections between texts, between ourselves and the texts we read, between our own readings and the readings of other interpreters, between the knowledge gained from our own experience and the knowledge that is bigger than our own experiences. "Doing literary theory" is hard work; good theoretical arguments involve a lot of background work—the learning of new critical languages included—and the careful and sensitive reading of a text. But the responsible use of these languages gives us access to the continuing discovery of our own constantly evolving place in the human community.

Two Questions for Student Writing

Many people have had the experience of revisiting a text (a book or a movie, for instance) that they thought themselves very familiar with and finding it quite different the second time around. Can you think of a similar experience in your own reading life (perhaps a text that you studied in high school that you revisited in a college classroom)? Can you speculate on what accounted for the differences in your reading experience?

How do you understand the work of the literary critic? What are your own reasons for studying literature (beyond the obvious possibility that you simply like to read)?

BRIEF ANNOTATED BIBLIOGRAPHY

Eagleton, Terry. *Literary Theory: An Introduction*, 2nd ed. Minneapolis: University of Minnesota Press, 1996.

The first of its kind and, despite Eagleton's obvious left-leaning political agenda, still arguably the best. The second edition (first edition was published in 1983) contains engaging and learned introductions to hermeneutics, structuralism, poststructuralism, psychoanalysis, and political criticism. The opening essay, "The Rise of English," is perhaps the most important piece in the book and should be required reading (and discussion) for English majors.

Barry, Peter. *Beginning Theory: An Introduction to Literary and Cultural Theory* Manchester and New York: University of Manchester Press, 1995.

Written, it would seem, as a response to Eagleton and notably less politically inflected. Barry includes excellent and very readable (and short) chapters on structuralism, poststructuralism, deconstruction, psychoanalytic criticism, feminism, marxism, lesbian/gay criticism, new historicism, cultural materialism, and postcolonialism, and stylistics.

Booker, M. Keith. *A Practical Introduction to Literary Theory and Criticism.* White Plains, NY: Longman, 1996.

As the title suggests, this book includes an emphasis on the *application* of literary theory. Booker supplements his introductions to the various schools of literary theory and criticism (Part I) with introductory essays that outline various approaches to five different works (Part II) and then formal essays by established literary critics on those same five works (Part III).

Bressler, Charles E. *Literary Criticism: An Introduction to Theory and Practice,* 2nd ed. Upper Saddle River, NJ: Prentice Hall, 1999.

Like Booker's, a textbook that both introduces different schools of literary theory and provides examples of practice. In this case, the practice takes the form of both a student-written and a professional short essay at the end of each discussion of a particular school of theory. Of particular interest in this text may be the "Websites of Exploration" bibliography that follows Bressler's suggestions for further reading in each chapter.

Makaryk, Irena R., general editor and compiler. *Encyclopedia of Contemporary Literary Theory: Approaches, Scholars, Terms.* Toronto: University of Toronto Press, 1993.

An absolutely essential resource for the serious student (and teacher) of literary theory. Thorough and admirably well-organized, it is a very user-friendly text.

CHAPTER 8

Writing Feminist Readings: The Long and the Short

Mary Louise Kete

"You're a feminist. We need you. Would you write a short essay for introductory students explaining feminist literary criticism and how to write it?" asked two, senior (male) colleagues as I passed down the hall one day. Since I didn't yet have tenure in my department, I responded with the only acceptable answer and, thereby, committed myself to a seemingly impossible task.

"It shouldn't take you long—you introduce sophomores to Feminist Literary Studies every year. Just write out your notes," assured my well meaning colleagues-cum-editors.

"But," I anxiously replied, "it takes me a whole semester to make this introduction and besides, I don't think I have anything really new to add to this subject."

"Oh, you'll do fine. Just give us the short answer."

THE SHORT ANSWER

The short answer is that one writes feminist literary criticism whenever one puts the issue of gender at the center of one's critical attention when reading and writing about texts. This *might* mean writing an essay on the differences between the way men authors and women authors in a certain historical period portray women. It *might* mean examining the way that femininity and masculinity are constructed in a particular literary genre. It *might* mean exploring the relationship between the representation of homosexuality and the representation of femininity in the various genres of a particular time period. It *might* mean analyzing the way that the narrators of texts assume a masculine voice even when the actual authors are women. It *might* mean studying the way men authors imagine how women characters might think and act. It *might* mean looking at how a particular author represents the differences between masculinity and femininity. All of these projects would be attempts to understand the very real consequences of how cultures imagine the differences between what they perceive to be masculine and feminine in identity and behavior. In other words, gender is at the center of all these critical projects. But there the similarity ends. For while it would be easier to give even the short answer to this question if there were just one, definitive, way to *write* as a feminist, there isn't. In fact, one of the greatest strengths of feminism as a political movement and feminist literary criticism as a kind of writing is that it is inclusive rather than exclusive. There isn't one definitive way to *be* a feminist, and there isn't one definitive way to write feminist literary criticism.

"Big help," I imagine you are saying to yourself just about now; and I'm sure you might appreciate it if I could just provide you with a recipe to follow. Perhaps it would be called, "Auntie Mary Lou's Feminist Literary Critique," and it would be preceded with a brief, engaging testimonial by the editor (a la *The Joy of Cooking*): "I stumbled across this dish at a Women's Studies Potluck several years ago and have been lucky enough to obtain the recipe. I'm sure your writing group or classroom will enjoy it just as much as we have!" All you would have to do, then, would be to follow the simple steps listed below and voila, one feminist essay! For whatever it's worth, here are the directions:

1. Take one text of whatever genre you prefer.
2. Read (or watch) three times or more.
3. Analyze slowly until you have rendered clear the forms and roles of gender in the text.
4. Toss lightly with personal perspective.
5. Contextualize in a relevant historical framework until malleable.
6. Articulate a clear thesis or argument that you can support with evidence from the text.
7. Organize your discussion in a persuasive manner.
8. Season with earnestness and humor.
9. Proofread, print, proofread again, and serve.

These directions sound simple enough, and would (possibly) give you a good start. You could, for example, take the anecdote with which I began this essay as a test case. As you read and reread it, you might make notes in the margins of your various reactions and responses. To what degree is such a dialogue familiar to you? What kind of essay does it make you expect? How are these expectations fulfilled or frustrated by the ensuing text? Have you ever felt like or known any of these kinds of characters? What are the sexes of the different characters? How is gender operating in this anecdote? What do you learn about gender from this anecdote? What differences do you perceive when you identify with the senior, male colleagues versus the junior, female colleague?

Having focused your response to the text on such questions of gender, now decide what you want to argue. Do you want to make an argument of how this personal anecdote does or does not serve the body of the essay? Do you want to make an argument about how this kind of beginning is or is not a convention of feminist literary criticism? Do you want use this anecdote to illustrate a claim about contemporary gender relationships in professional situations? Whatever you decide, begin to marshal your evidence as you experiment with different ways of convincing your reader. Check your assumptions and fill in any missing pieces of the context by reading historical, philosophical, or sociological references. Begin drafting versions of your argument for a reader. Choose whichever one promises to be the most persuasive and readable. Refer, again, to whatever resources you need to check, support, or amplify your interpretations. Draft your essay, revise, proofread, and revise. Done!

Sounds easy, doesn't it? Ultimately, however, such a recipe would be of limited help. Even if you were able to follow these formulaic directions (which sound simple, yet beg many questions), would you yourself really have learned anything about gender? Would you, yourself, want to read such an essay? Would it have taught you anything? Would it teach your professor anything? The answer to these questions is "maybe, maybe not," but you want the answer to all these questions to be "yes" not "maybe." Why read if not for the pleasure of learning? Why write if not for the pleasure of learning? Why write if not for the pleasure of teaching? I think you'll have a better chance of learning, enjoying, and teaching if I give you a brief introduction to the long answer. The long answer, I hope, will help you to formulate questions that are interesting to *you*, that will help *you* join other feminists who are challenging old assumptions, that will require new methods of research and of writing.

THE LONG ANSWER

The long answer is more complicated than the short answer because it involves having a sense of the history of feminism as a political and academic movement. The feminist writer doesn't pretend to be able to escape history even though she hopes to change the present and affect the future. It also involves developing a sense of the way that feminist approaches to the study of literature have actually changed what it means to study literature and, even, what literature itself is.

As a political movement in the West, feminism grows out of the same rich, composite soil of the eighteenth-century Enlightenment that produced such familiar political ideological frameworks as Liberalism, Nationalism, Socialism, and Capitalism out of a revolution in thought about the relationship between the individual and the state. Until this point, it had been generally assumed that the few strong were divinely appointed to rule over the many weak. This revolution posited that each individual has certain, inalienable rights and that the legitimacy of governments rests on the consent of the governed. Women, at first, were only theoretically (if at all) included, and it took women's right's activists in Europe and America well over one hundred years to extend the "rights of man" to women. The battle for the rights of women has been fought on two different grounds. One, an assertion of essential difference, prompts the argument that women deserve equal rights because of their fundamental differences from men. In other words, women need to be able to represent themselves (politically, artistically, and philosophically) because men are unable to do so for them. Otherwise, society is deprived of the very special and different wisdom that only women can provide. The other, an assertion of individual equality, prompts the argument that women deserve equal rights because of their fundamental sameness with men. In other words, women deserve to represent themselves because there is no reason they shouldn't. Society is, otherwise, deprived of the benefits of half its members who are illegitimately and arbitrarily ruled by the other half.

While the word "feminism" is a contribution of the twentieth century, feminist political activists have worked on the legal goals of guaranteeing women the legal rights of self-representation (the right to vote), self-support, and self-protection since the eighteenth century. In concrete terms this has meant the pursuit of the right to vote, the right to equal wages for equal work, and the right to make informed choices about health care and related personal decisions. By the last quarter of the twentieth century, women in most of the developed nations had gained the right to direct political representation, and feminists increasingly began to concentrate on the expansion of the right of women to self-support and self-protection. At the same time, women from the nonindustrialized nations began to embrace feminism as one way to improve their own and their nation's conditions. In the process of making feminism their own, women from economic, political, and religious cultures that differ significantly from those of the Western nations helped to make feminism one of the most broad-based, flexible and inclusive political movements of the twentieth century. To take this into account, the singular noun "feminism" has come to be replaced with the plural, "feminisms," in acknowledgment of one of the most important differences between this political movement and the many others that share the suffix "ism." This political movement recognizes that one answer will not be correct for all—justice for women may not look the same in Holland as in North Korea; it may not feel the same, and it may not be achieved the same way.

But thinkers we might also call "feminist" (because of their attention to the relationship between gender and power) have also been working in other areas besides the overtly political. These thinkers have been challenging the conventional and masculine-biased understandings of certain philosophical questions such as what does it mean to know, what does it mean to be, what is the nature of spirituality, and what is the possibility of communicating. Feminist literary critics are among this group. The plural word "feminisms" also signals that the work continues and is ongoing; injustice (both within the developed world and outside it) is still excused by the way people understand (read) and express (write) what it means to be a gendered person. Unlike many more organized traditions of literary scholarship, feminist literary critics aren't linked because of a shared concern with certain texts or with certain critical methods but are linked by a shared concern with the real consequences of how humans have imagined and expressed the differences between themselves and others.

The history of this field of study (unlike that of most academic fields) is strangely dramatic: The economic, institutional, and personal stakes were high and the battle was not fought merely with words. For almost two hundred years the secular universities and colleges of England and America (like the governments of those countries) resisted the efforts of women to be taken seriously as students and as humans. But in the last twenty-five years of the twentieth-century, feminists succeeded (not without struggle and huge personal costs for some) in getting many departments of literature to recognize that writings by and about women are serious subjects that are worthy of study. To a great degree, this is because feminists have succeeded in convincing at least some people that confining our attention to texts written by men and about men and for men has impaired our understanding of the human condition. But what has this definition of a political movement to do with the work of studying literature in a college classroom? The answer for most feminists would be everything; for no matter whether one thinks of oneself as an American or a Buddhist or a Communist or a fraternity brother or an artist or a girl; as a heterosexual, or as pretty or dumb or old or a boy, reading and writing are political acts because both are exercises of power in the world. I begin by discussing politics because one of the most important things that distinguishes "feminist" literary criticism from most other approaches to literature is an explicit commitment to political justice for women and a recognition that even our most personal acts (such as reading and writing) have political ramifications. Feminist scholars—students and teachers—not only try to be conscious of this but also explicitly try to examine the nature and consequences of this power.

But what would this mean? What does this mean? How does one bring concerns about gender together with concerns about literary history, genre, or plot? Conventionally, literary critics have asked certain kinds of questions about texts. These questions span a continuum marked on one end by those who try to focus exclusively on questions of text and marked on the other by those who try to focus exclusively on questions of context. Feminist literary criticism, on the other hand, tends to stress that text and context, form and content, book and reader are necessarily related and interdependent terms.

Because for so many years scholars paid attention primarily to the history of men as authors and readers, it is easiest to see how the answers to the questions on the context end of the continuum might be limited by the exclusion of women. As recently as the 1980s, when I was an undergraduate, most courses in nineteenth-century American literature would not have included more than one writer who was a woman. It was easy to think, then, that there had been no American women novelists (for example) worth reading from that period or even that there were no "real" novelists who were women. But even then, feminist literary scholars (women and men) were beginning to challenge this conventional wisdom by rereading the books of their childhood, such as *Little Women* by Louisa May Alcott and *Uncle Tom's Cabin* by Harriet Beecher Stowe, and by rummaging in the stacks of libraries and archives. These scholars asked questions such as: What else did these two, still remembered, women novelists write? What did they read? Who read their books? Who were the other women novelists, and where and when were they working? What was the relationship between men and women novelists of the nineteenth century? Why has the role of women novelists been excluded from the history of American literature? All of these specific questions are ways to get at the more general questions that had been so difficult to ask before: What *did* these women's novels mean? What *do* they mean now?

This kind of scholarship is fundamentally interdisciplinary because it depends on methods and insights melded together from history, sociology, and anthropology as well as on primary research in archives. This interdisciplinarity makes it difficult, but not impossible, to practice in the undergraduate classroom because it assumes the mastery of the very difficult skill of close, careful reading of individual texts *and* the very different skill of exploring the interrelationships among the various kinds of information we have about cultures.

Recently, for example, it has been getting easier for undergraduates to explore the kind of questions I posed above about once famous authors such as Stowe. There are now excellent sources for use in the classroom such as critical editions of *Uncle Tom's Cabin* that are heavily annotated with explanations of obscure historical references, excerpts of Stowe's private correspondence, and selections from the best recent essays on the novel. Almost all of her works, major and minor, are in print. There are also major critical biographies of Stowe that try to establish an historical context for understanding the connections between the biographical facts of her life and the content of her writings. The critical biography and the critical edition, per se, are standard academic sources. What is new, is the way that these conventional sources are turned to unconventional and feminist uses. These works summarize the painstaking primary research into questions such as what Stowe read and when, or what (as indicated in her private letters) she thought she was doing when she wrote *Uncle Tom's Cabin*. They provide insight into Stowe's changing opinions about the status of women, allowing undergraduates, as well as advanced scholars, to begin exploring her fictional explorations of issues such as the parallels between the condition of all black slaves and the condition of married white women. In addition, there are now several sociological studies of the status and role of women in Stowe's nineteenth-century America that provide a different kind of insight into what it meant that her 1850 novel, *Uncle Tom's Cabin*, outsold all other books that had ever been published in America except for the Bible. Who, for example, would have had enough extra money to buy a copy, and who borrowed a copy from a library or a friend? Would people read the book silently, to themselves, or listen to it being read in a parlor or kitchen? Sociological studies like these explain how difficult it was for a woman to have any kind of public voice at all (even regarding her own children's welfare or her own private property) and, therefore, help us to understand just how incredible Stowe's success was. At the same time, histories and sociologies such as these also help explain how understandable it is that Stowe was able to overcome the limits her society imposed on women. Finally, these studies acknowledge the importance of Stowe's own race, class, and gender, and they highlight the degree to which these categories may have been defined differently in the past.

Having begun by sharing the conventional assumption of the fundamental differences between texts and contexts, feminist literary historians came to reconfigure the relationship between what have seemed like two clearly different objects of study: literary forms vs. history. The nature of the American novel, for example, is beginning to look quite different now that the work of women writers and readers has begun to be studied. Scholars had thought they had a good history of the American novel, but what they had was a good history of the novels written by white, mostly northern, American men. In these *his*/stories the racial, class, and gender status of the authors was ignored, not to deliberately mislead, but because, for many scholars the race (white), class (elite), and gender (masculine) of an author was assumed. Race, class, and gender were noted only when and if there was some rare deviance from these norms. What was important, in any case, was the way in which an author transcended the contingencies of his particular life. Only in this way could a literary work attain universal significance.

To feminists, on the other hand, what a book *means* can only begin to be answered once writers remember that the meaning of books is created by the people who read, write, buy, sell, dust, or burn them. For many American women readers and writers until recently, this *his*/story had serious consequences. Given the apparent evidence that there have been no significant women writers in America, a woman who wanted to write felt that she must either break totally new ground or that she must pretend, in some way, not to be a woman. What is happening now, because of the attention of feminist scholars, is that the historical efforts of women writers are beginning to be recognized in lists of books taught in classrooms. Even more important, however, is the exploration of what had previously been the unexamined, yet powerful, assumptions about the nature and function of gender for both men and for women. If for a feminist what a book means and even what it is cannot be isolated from what it means to be a person marked by gender, then texts and contexts are reciprocally related, or even, interconnected.

But after all, isn't a novel a novel no matter what the gender of the author? Well isn't it? Or, is it? Again, take the question of how to define the American novel. The set of novels that used to be taught as the short list of nineteenth-century American novels used to look more or less like this: James Fenimore Cooper's *Last of the Mohicans,* Nathaniel Hawthorne's *The House of Seven Gables,* Herman Melville's *Moby Dick,* William Dean Howell's *A Modern Instance,* Mark Twain's *Huck Finn,* and Henry James's *The Ambassadors.* Such a list formed the basis of numerous generalities that helped students and teachers organize their thoughts about literature. The common wisdom was that these novels explored what it meant to be an American through a set of variations on a single plot. (Of course, the qualifier "American" shows that the political context had already been introduced even if not acknowledged.) The protagonists of each novel struggle to retain a sense of individualism and independence against the forces of convention. The ideal American hero (Twain's Huck Finn or Cooper's Natty Bumpo, for example) is a radical individual—a person without history, family, or responsibility—whose most important role is to be the innocent critic of corruption and whose most important challenge is to resist and to escape society. This hero's role is to "light out for the territories" where there might still be the promise of a utopian, perfect, America.

But when, for example, we include any of the following novels in this list—Maria Cummins's *The Lamplighter,* Susan Warner's *Wide, Wide, World,* Louisa May Alcott's *Little Women,* or Frances Harper's *Iola Leroy*—it becomes more difficult to say that the nineteenth-century American novel is characterized by variations on a single plot. The America of nineteenth-century American women's novel is very different—internal and domestic—from the America of the men's novels I mentioned earlier. Here, the task of the American hero (Alcott's Jo or Harper's Iola, for example) is to move from a position of social alienation or selfishness to a position of social integration and altruism by training the self to internalize values of self-sacrifice, responsibility, and virtue. The hero's task is to construct a sense of self that maintains individual integrity while nurturing the group integrity of the family or community. One thing that becomes immediately clear is that the kind of stories (or plots) told by nineteenth-century American men and by nineteenth-century American women tended to differ significantly from each other. The answers to even the most basic, seemingly formal questions (What is the American novel? What are its main components? How does it work?) become subject to exciting revisions once we take gender into account.

The political practice of feminism, then, revises conventional literary criticism by insisting upon the interrelated and mutually dependent nature of what had seemed like opposite poles. A feminist's concern with gender exposes what had seemed like an intractable opposition to be only a (sometimes) helpful, imaginary construction. To ask the formalist question of What? (from the art end of the continuum of conventional literary criticism) means also to ask the political questions of Who?, When?, Where? and To what effect? Similarly, for a feminist to ask political questions from the contextual end of the conventional continuum means also to ask the formalist questions of What? and How? Here, the two poles of the conventional continuum of literary criticism are brought together through the feminist concern with gender. The feminist literary critic (as opposed to the feminist congressperson or mathematician) explores these concerns in the realm of symbolic expressions (verbal, literary, or electronic texts), producing a reading or interpretation of how gender functions in the represented world.

The bad news I leave you with is that there is no one, set rule nor recipe for writing feminist literary criticism. This is not to say that there aren't currents of conventions. You can see these currents and learn from them by perusing collections of feminist essays or volumes of contemporary literary journals. But then you need to experiment for yourself, find models for yourself, explore and challenge the received assumptions about gender for yourself. The good news I leave you with is that there is no one, set rule nor recipe because the field of feminist literary criticism is still young and growing, and you are invited to be a part of it.

SUGGESTED FURTHER READINGS

Price Herndl, Diane and Robyn R. Warhol, eds. *Feminisms: An Anthology of Literary Theory and Criticism,* 2nd ed. New Brunswick, NJ: Rutgers University Press, 1997.

> A terrific, fully inclusive collection (meaning big—your library should have this on the shelves) of essays from which you can get a good sense of the various historical trends of feminist literary studies and of the range of critical questions and methods of the most important feminist writers of the last twenty-five years or so.

Gilbert, Sandra M. and Susan Gubar, eds. *The Norton Anthology of Literature by Women,* 2nd ed. New York and London: W.W. Norton & Company, 1996.

> This convenient, one-volume anthology provides samples of the English literary traditions organized by conventional historical and political categories.

Mankiller, Wilma, et al., eds. *The Reader's Companion to U.S. Women's History.* Boston and New York: Houghton Mifflin, 1998.

> A highly accessible book that helps fill in the gaps most of us have about the role of women in the American experience. Organized alphabetically by topic, it moves from the abolitionist movement through legal status to YWCA—offering well-written and succinct explanations.

CHAPTER 9

Expanding the Canon: A Multicultural Perspective

Helen Scott

EUROCENTRISM AND THE CANON

Some decades ago, American anthropologist Laura Bohannan found herself in a prestigious British university town debating the merits of Shakespeare. Did Shakespeare's plays represent the best of human culture, timeless and universal in their value and significance? While not everyone agreed, Bohannan felt sure that the answer was "yes" on all counts: These works, or at least their general plots and motivations, would speak to all people regardless of their place and time.

Before long, Bohannan had the chance to test her theories while in Western Africa. The village elders, themselves skilled and practiced storytellers, requested that she tell them a story from her own land in exchange for the many tales they had shared with her. Casting around for an appropriate story, Bohannan settled on *Hamlet.* No sooner had she started than she ran in to problems: Her audience had no equivalent terms for "ghost" or "scholar"; the villagers insisted on knowing genealogical details of the main characters; they believed it was only right and proper for a widow to marry the brother of her deceased husband. As she struggled to find ways to explain each puzzling concept she realized that she was moving further away from the core of the plot, until she was forced to admit to herself that perhaps the play was not so universally applicable after all; she reflects that "it no longer seemed quite the same story to me" (Bohannan, 32). We can speculate that she may have also suspected that she herself had misinterpreted many of the villagers' tales—imposing her own values and assumptions onto narratives that may have held very different resonance for their society.

Before her revelations, Bohannan had been under the influence of what is referred to as "eurocentrism": the idea that Europe's is the best and indeed the only culture in the world, and that the "canon"—or endorsed selection—of artistic works represents not the particular tastes of a certain section of a specific society but the objective pinnacle of the world's creative endeavors. This idea went hand in hand with European and American imperialism—as the powerful industrialized nations conquered and claimed large sections of the rest of the world for their own uses, they justified this domination with all sorts of racist ideas about the superiority of the "civilized" West and the inferiority of the "savage" colonized peoples.

The period of European formal colonialism, when European powers and especially Britain established political rule over huge areas of Africa, Asia, and the Caribbean, also saw the invention of the "canon" of English literature. From the end of the nineteenth century the idea that certain literary works together formed the "Great Books" of Western culture took hold in the English departments—which were themselves new—of universities across America as well as England. This canon was reflected in college curricula, literary anthologies, and critical studies that focused on those writers—from Beowulf to Virginia Woolf—who supposedly made up the literary achievements of the Western world. In recent decades, this idea of an objective canon of universally great works of literature has been challenged from many angles. I want to talk about some of those challenges from a multicultural perspective.

All of us have experienced at some time the way that plays or novels or poems we are told are "great" leave us unmoved or unimpressed. In any given classroom one group of students may enthusiastically devour Woolf's *To the Lighthouse*, while others experience the book as torture. These differences point to one problem with the idea of a canon of great works: The evaluation inevitably involves subjective tastes, not objective absolutes. The criteria used to determine greatness may also vary, so whether we see emotional power, ethical clarity, or technical sophistication as of primary importance is going to alter the verdict.

By the middle of the twentieth century another problem was being highlighted by a number of writers from non-Western countries and by minorities within the United States. They realized that the groups who decide what gets in to the canon, however indirectly, systematically exclude certain bodies of work. Eurocentrism insisted that the only culture, or at least the only one of value, was that of the West. As many colonized people challenged European domination of their countries, so did they reject eurocentrism. African writers, for example, pointed to the rich cultural achievements of African civilizations that thrived at a time when most of what would become Europe still consisted of little more than warring bands of primitive people with neither art nor literature. African-American William Leo Hansberry dedicated the middle decades of the twentieth century to researching the centrality of African culture to ancient civilization. He pointed out that the very idea of a distinct Western culture is itself a myth, as the cultural achievements of ancient and classical Greece, claimed as the foundations of the Western canon, themselves owed a great deal to the cultures of ancient African societies. As this recognition indicates, by its very nature art borrows heavily on a range of cultural traditions. So, for example, English modernists within the canon of great Western art were inspired by and incorporated into their own work the artistic products of many non-European cultures.

These polemics challenged the idea that *only* Europe has a culture, and that Western culture is a pristine and self-contained body. But, defenders of the canon argue, surely there are nonetheless literary works that are undeniably superior and universal in their appeal? Bohannan's experience would suggest that on the contrary, while some texts may speak to a broad range of people over a substantial period of time, any canon reflects the particular values of the people doing the selecting. This becomes very clear when you consider how the American canon has changed over time. Take Mark Twain's *Adventures of Huckleberry Finn*, for example. Along with *Adventures of Tom Sawyer*, this book was established as a "classic" founding text of American literature in the 1940s and 1950s. But when it was first published in 1885 the arbiters of literary taste hated it. The Library Committee of Concord called *Huckleberry Finn* "trash, only suitable for the slums," and the subject matter and style were broadly condemned as "coarse" and "common" (quoted in Kaplan, 269). The book itself did not change over time, but the criteria for evaluation did.

The example of *Huckleberry Finn* indicates that what is valued by the literary establishment in one period may be condemned in another. So the canon is based not on some unchanging aesthetic value, but on the particular tastes of the people—publishers, professors, critics—making the selection. In an exclusive canon, inevitably books that may be of value are rejected because they do not measure up to the particular criteria of evaluation used by these figures, because they do not fit the mold, or because they are hidden from view. As institutionalized racism was taken on by a new generation of African Americans and other minority groups, it became increasingly clear that there were systematic omissions from the canon. Certain groups of people—African Americans, Native Americans, immigrants, the poor, the working class—were not represented in the literary elite—upper class, predominantly white and male—who determined the canon. Just as the anticolonial movements challenged eurocentrism, so the civil rights movements of 1960s America launched further challenges to the existing canon of great books.

Many of you will have read African-American slave narratives such as *The Interesting Narrative of the Life of Olaudah Equiano, Narrative of the Life of Frederick Douglass,* or Harriet Jacobs's *Incidents in the Life of a Slave Girl.* These works made it on to your school curriculum as a result of such challenges to the Western canon. The history of this genre nicely illustrates the kinds of exclusions that can keep valuable literature out of sight. It is estimated that between 1700 and 1940 some six thousand ex-slaves produced narratives relating their enslavement and struggle for freedom. While many of these were orally narrated to others, a significant number of former slaves wrote and published their own stories. Yet during slavery the myth remained that slaves had inherent mental deficiencies that kept them illiterate. And while slave narratives were surprisingly popular in the mid to late nineteenth century (they were bestsellers among the growing literate audience in cities across the country), and together form a literary tradition of remarkable narrative and rhetorical power, they were not recognized as part of the American canon until relatively late in the twentieth century. In extension, the rich and diverse tradition of African-American literature had been ignored or marginalized until black scholars and activists fought for its inclusion in anthologies and course catalogs.

THE "CULTURE WARS"

No sooner had people begun to broaden the canon to include those authors and traditions that had previously been left out, than a battle broke out over the significance and consequences of what we now call "multicultural" expansion. In 1987 Allan Bloom, a conservative philosopher from the University of Chicago, published *The Closing of the American Mind*, which warned that in American universities the "disinterested" pursuit of truth was under attack. Questions of racism and sexism, the argument goes, should have no place in "objective" scholarship, and such "political" questions taint the impartiality of academia. In 1989 former Education Secretary William Bennett similarly attacked Stanford University for revising its freshman core reading list to include works by non-European, non-American authors. In reality Stanford's new Culture, Ideas, and Values program ended up with only one required book outside the accepted Western canon, but Bennett's protest unleashed a wave of panic about curricular revisions and attacks on the canon of Western civilization and culture. The underlying thesis of these critiques is that the inclusion of non-Western literature is at the expense of Western culture; the imagined or real response from multiculturalists is that because Western culture is racist (and sexist and elitist) it *should* be replaced.

But both of these positions take very narrow views of culture that would lead to restrictive teaching and scholarship. While Bloom, Bennett, and others place the study of non-Western and Western culture in opposition, in fact our reading of literature is enriched when seen in cross-cultural contexts. For example, the narrative of Olaudah Equiano, published in 1789, can be a wonderful partner text to the work of English Romantic poet William Blake, who wrote some of his best known poems in the same period. Reading Equiano is an important experience in itself: The narrative presents the powerful voice of a remarkable African writer. The slave context also allows us to understand Blake's call for equality in the context of broader debates about freedom, humanity, and liberation. Listen to this extract from Blake's "Visions of the Daughters of Albion." The speaker is a tyrant, Bromion, who has abducted a young woman, Oothoon:

> Thy soft American plains are mine, and mine thy north and south:
> Stampt with my signet are the swarthy children of the sun:
> They are obedient, they resist not, they obey the scourge:
> Their daughters worship terrors and obey the violent ...

Now consider this passage from Equiano:

> It was very common ... for the slaves to be branded with the initial letters of their master's name; and a load of heavy iron hooks hung about their necks. Indeed, on the most trifling occasions, they were loaded with chains; and often instruments of torture were added.... white people ... have committed acts of violence on the poor, wretched, and helpless females (27)

Blake's poem takes on a more concrete significance in the light of Equiano's description of slavery in the Americas: Bromion mirrors the real slave master;

Chapter 9 Expanding the Canon: A Multicultural Perspective

the "stampt signet" is equivalent to the brand of slavery; Oothoon parallels the actual enslaved women. The two writers also at times seem to speak to each other. This is Equiano:

> When you make men slaves, you deprive them of half their virtue; ... You stupify them with stripes, and think it necessary to keep them in a state of ignorance. And yet you assert that they are incapable of learning; that their minds are such a barren soil or moor that culture would be lost on them ... are ye not struck with shame and mortification, to see the partakers of your nature reduced so low? (29)

> ... If, when they (slave owners) look round the world, they feel exultation, let it be tempered with benevolence to others and gratitude to God, "who hath made of one blood all nations of men for to dwell on all the face of the earth" (14)

This is Blake, speaking now as the enslaved Oothoon:

> They told me that the night and day were all that I could see;
> They told me that I had five senses to inclose me up,
> And they inclos'd my infinite brain into a narrow circle,
> And sunk my heart into the Aybss, a red round globe hot burning,
> Till all from life I was obliterated and erased ...
>
> Arise and drink your bliss, for every thing that lives is holy!

Both use memorable images and metaphors to express the deadening consequences of physical and metaphorical slavery; both appeal to the sacred and common humanity of all living beings. These echoes give a sense of how immensely productive it can be to read texts from within the Western canon with those that have been outside it. Such pairings, which have become increasingly common with challenges to a restrictive canon, lead to an expansion of reading material rather than the replacement of one body of works with another.

Rejecting eurocentrism, then, does not mean getting rid of Western culture. Hansberry's work, as I mentioned before, reveals the multicultural roots of all cultures and indicates that even the category "Western culture" is misleading because it implies a homogeneity and consistency that doesn't exist. You may have heard disparaging talk of the works of "Dead White Men" (or DWMs). This term stems from necessary critiques of an overwhelmingly white and male canon, but is sometimes used in a way that implies that *anything* written by the white male authors of the past is oppressive or bigoted or has nothing to say to anyone outside this group. While it is clearly limiting to read *only* writers in this category, it is equally apparent that the color and gender of the author does not determine the content of the work and that white male writers can and do "speak to" different readers.

There are, in fact, many examples of non-Western uses of Western classics. One of the most striking is that in the late nineteenth century, Chinese rebels involved in the Taipei uprising against European and American imperialism distributed and read John Bunyan's *Pilgrim's Progress*. They saw in this story of perseverance in the face of suffering and seemingly insurmountable obstacles an inspiration for their own struggle for liberation.

As the example of Blake indicates, Western culture includes widely disparate literature not only in terms of form but also of content. Many of the writers who are seen as central to the Western canon have been overt critics of the dominant ideas of their societies. William Blake, of course, launched a passionate poetic opposition to what he saw as the stultifying and repressive mores of English society. We can add to him many of the writers who have been securely canonical throughout this century, periodic shifts in favor notwithstanding: Percy Bysshe Shelley supported the French Revolution and espoused women's liberation; Charles Dickens railed against the horrors of industrial capitalism in England; Wilfred Owen generalized from an exposé of the brutality of war to a critique of the entire class system, before he was silenced by the very guns he denounced.

Even those who weren't social critics often teach us something about their world, and the place of art in it, which is of value to opponents of Western domination. In recent years, for example, some critics have looked at Jane Austen's novels in terms of what they tell us about England's involvement in the slave trade and colonial expansion in the late eighteenth and early nineteenth centuries. In Austen's novel *Persuasion* the heroine, Anne, daughter of a landed gentleman, is dissuaded from marrying the man she loved, Frederick Wentworth, because he has no significant fortune. After a separation of some years, Wentworth reenters Anne's life, this time as a wealthy, propertied, and respected naval captain. We learn that he was "sent to the West Indies" where he "made his fortune." From this, and similar references in other books of the period, we can deduce that the "triangular trade" between Africa (slaves), Europe (manufactured goods), and the Americas (raw materials), was the source of considerable fortunes for English men without inherited fortunes, who then were absorbed into the ruling class of the period. Austen did not set out to educate subsequent generations about these things, but we nonetheless can learn much about them from her writing, and in turn gain further insight into the novels themselves.

POSTCOLONIAL LITERATURE

If multiculturalism has expanded the canon by drawing attention to works previously marginalized or ignored, and allowing us to see the existing canon in new ways, other social changes have altered the very category of English literature. If you look at the list of winners of the Nobel Prize for literature—one of the world's most prestigious literary prizes—from the award's beginning in 1901 up to the present time, you will notice a dramatic change. For the first six decades with only two exceptions—Rabindranath Tagore of India (1913) and Gabriela Mistral of Chile (1945)—the chosen authors were all from Europe or the United States. From 1965 to 1995, in contrast, eleven awards were given to authors from outside Europe and the United States, including Pablo Neruda of Chile (1971), Gabriel Garcia Marquez of Colombia (1982), Wole Soyinka of Nigeria (1986), Naguib Mahfouz of Egypt (1988), Octavio Paz of Mexico (1990), and Derek Walcott of Trinidad (1992). In that period not only has eurocentrism been challenged, but also new generations of writers have emerged from those parts of the world that were once colonized by Western powers, some of them writing from their countries of origin, some migrating to America or Canada or Britain.

Many of these writers have won awards because their work is exciting, powerful, and innovative in content and form. This is the area of literature that I chose to study when I was still an undergraduate student, because it moved me and challenged me in new ways. I remember first reading *One Hundred Years of Solitude* (in English translation from the original Spanish) by Gabriel Garcia Marquez and being mesmerized by a totally unfamiliar use of storytelling and language (which I later learned to call "magical realism.") Then I read Salman Rushdie's *Midnight's Children,* written in English by an Indian author, and found all sorts of similarities in how the novels were written and what they were about, despite the obvious and immense differences of origin, explicit subject matter, and form.

Both novels moved me aesthetically and emotionally: they used narrative techniques and figurative language that seemed to speak to me in new and powerful ways. These reading experiences taught me concretely how much we all stand to benefit from reading works from different cultures: As I read both Marquez and Rushdie I encountered references to places, customs, traditions, foods, names, religions about which I had known little. But I was also able to relate to so many of the questions they raised, about equality, justice, human perseverance in the face of hardship, the relationship between history and the forces of change in the modern world. Despite unfamiliar references and contexts, these contemporary writers were closer to me in experience and values than many of the authors I was taught to see as part of "my culture"—particularly the British modernists whose work I experienced as torture rather than pleasure. I started to see that my nationality did not guarantee a special relationship with British culture, which made me question the idea that the English own English literature, Africans African literature, and so on.

Before coming back to this question of cultural "ownership" I want to talk a bit about the debates around language and culture that these new postcolonial literatures gave rise to. Postcolonial literature can be categorized by language groups, including European languages. So it is common to refer to "Francophone" Caribbean literatures—those written in French—and "Anglophone"—those written in English—and so on. As Anglophone postcolonial literature is "my" field of study, I'll explore some of the debates around the English language and culture that have emerged in this area.

In 1988 Caribbean-American writer Jamaica Kincaid published a book called *A Small Place* (it is sometimes described as "prose-poetry" because of its particular mix of nonfictional content and figurative language). In it she uses imagistic and mesmerizing prose to describe the horrors of English conquest, slavery, and colonial oppression and to protest the new forms of "slavery," perpetuated by a corrupt government and exploitative tourist industry, in her native Antigua. At one point in the text Kincaid reflects on the fact that English is her first tongue and then asks "... isn't it odd that the only language I have in which to speak of this crime is the language of the criminal who committed the crime?" (31).

Kincaid here touches on a much broader debate that has preoccupied many Anglophone postcolonial writers: Do languages carry inherent values? Is English, the language of the colonizer, able to express the experiences of the colonized? Should writers use other languages when possible? These questions became central to an exchange between African writers in the 1970s. One of them, Ngugi Wa Thiong'o of Kenya, decided that although he had been writing in English, his second language, he would from now on write only in his native Gikuyu, precisely because English was imposed on him by colonialism and the only way he could resist the domination of colonization was through a return to his original and, as he saw it, "natural" language. He gave up writing fiction in English after 1977, but continued to write nonfictional prose in English until the mid-1980s, when his work *Decolonizing the Mind* marked his "farewell to English."

Ngugi was reacting against a specific set of practices, called cultural imperialism, that suppressed African culture and insisted on the superiority of all things English. In 1952 the British authorities declared a state of emergency throughout Kenya, in response to a growing movement for independence from colonial rule. All schools were placed under the direct control of colonial Education Boards, and the English language was brutally enforced. The Gikuyu tongue, for example, was outlawed at Ngugi's childhood school and speaking it was punishable with caning and humiliation. Many other postcolonial writers have spoken of similar conditions, particularly being force-fed British culture in the classroom even though it made no sense to the child's life. Trinidadian writer Merle Hodge humorously describes one such scene, through the eyes of the narrator, a schoolgirl called Tee:

> My reading career ... began with A for Apple, the exotic fruit that made its brief and stingy appearance at Christmastime, and pursued through my Caribbean Reader Primer One the fortunes of two English children known as Jim and Jill, or it might have been Tim and Mary ...
> We stood and counted in unison to a hundred or recited nursery rhymes about Little Boy Blue (what, in all creation, was a 'haystack'?) and about Little Miss Muffet who for some unaccountable reason sat eating her curls away ... (25–26)

Later on Tee creates an English double, Helen, for herself, in her desire to match up to the images of life held up in books and at school:

> Helen ... was the proper me ...
> For doubleness, or this particular kind of doubleness, was a thing to be taken for granted. Why the whole of life was like a piece of cloth, with a rightside and a wrongside, Just as there was a way you spoke and a way you wrote so there was the daily existence which you led, which of course amounted only

> to marking time and makeshift, for there was the Proper daily round ... which encompassed things like warming yourself before a fire and having tea at four o'clock ... (62)

In this case the Trinidadian children are being force-fed stories that bear no relation whatsoever to their experiences, to such an absurd extent that they are made to feel abnormal—and inferior—because in Trinidad it isn't necessary to drink afternoon tea or warm yourself at a fireplace. Such tales are recurrent enough in postcolonial literature to indicate that cultural imperialism was a central pole of colonial domination: Prohibition of native languages and cultures and the elevation of English language and culture serve to justify colonial rule and to divide and rule the colonized.

However, the experience of being alienated from your school curriculum is much broader than this. Certainly I remember feeling like I was reading a foreign language much of the time during my early school days in England. The "Janet and John" readers that we were given in primary school might as well have been about Martians for all they resembled my life. They described gracious, well-ordered suburban homes, inhabited by stay-at-home, elegant mothers, and austere-suited fathers. Both my parents had paid jobs, and the house I grew up in was crowded and chaotic. As I grew older this feeling of a gulf between my experience and the books I read was sometimes very pronounced, particularly, as I mentioned before, when it came to the English modernists. I had to force myself to finish Virginia Woolf's *To the Lighthouse*, and for years hadn't a clue what it was about. Many of the students in my postcolonial literature class admit to having felt the same way when they first read Nathanial Hawthorne or Herman Melville. They felt like they were the only ones not knowing what was going on, and found themselves asking, as my father used to say, "Is there a handbook for this conversation?"

This alienation is not necessarily the result of regional or national differences. Sometimes the gap is a historical one: English students today have no automatic connection to the language of Shakespeare or Dickens; no more do American students instinctively respond to Melville or Hawthorne. But sometimes the gulf comes from class divisions within a country; early school texts in particular disproportionately project the norms of an upper class life. This account by English writer and humorist Alan Bennett, of his working class Yorkshire childhood, for me captures this class-based distance:

> [I]t was soon borne in upon me that the world of books was only distantly related to the world in which I lived. The families I read about were not like our family ... These families had dogs and gardens and lived in country towns equipped with thatched cottages and millstreams, where the children had adventures, saved lives, caught villains, and found treasure before coming home, tired but happy, to eat sumptuous teas off chequered tablecloths in low-beamed parlours presided over by comfortable pipe-smoking fathers and gentle aproned mothers, who were invariably referred to as Mummy and Daddy.

In an effort to bring this fabulous world closer to my own, more threadbare, existence, I tried as a first step substituting 'Mummy' and 'Daddy' for my usual 'Mam' and 'Dad', but was pretty sharply discouraged ... (5–6)

Bennett's account always strikes me first because I identify with it strongly, but also because it is so like postcolonial accounts such as Merle Hodge's of the colonial classroom in Trinidad. Bennett's life was not reflected in the books he read at school; the tales he read were not of a different national culture, but spoke of a different world in terms of social class. The majority of people will at some time experience something like the feelings described by postcolonial writers—a sense that their everyday existence is not reflected in their school texts.

TOWARD A GLOBAL CULTURE

What these examples show more than anything is that cultures and languages are not homogenous and even within a national culture there is tremendous diversity. It is also the case that "English literature" is an amazingly flexible category. Ngugi's experience of cultural imperialism led him to reject English in favor of his native tongue. One reason for this is that he really was wrenched away from his mother tongue, and a return to it was an essential part of his struggle for autonomy. He also felt that he could better reach working class and poor Kenyans if he wrote, and produced plays, in Gikuyu. But other African writers have preferred to use English to express their particular realities. Nigerian writer Chinua Achebe insists on the pliancy of language and rejects the idea that only English people truly "own" English. Referring to African-American writer James Baldwin, who talks of making English "bear the burden" of his experience, Achebe writes: "I have been given this language and I intend to use it ... I feel that the English language will be able to carry the weight of my African experience. But it will have to be a new English ..." (103).

Achebe rejects the idea that only English writers can claim and use the English language. Multiculturalism can take this idea a step further, by refusing the idea of neatly divided national cultures. It has always been true that cultures borrow heavily from different traditions and that a comparative approach can reveal the rich interdependence of literature, but today culture is more global than ever before. Immigration patterns have brought people previously separated by oceans and continents together. Multiculturalism can be seen every day in the food, clothes, and popular culture—films, television, music—available in cities all over the world. While it is right to acknowledge the new forms of cultural imperialism that come with the concentration of ownership—of publishing houses, film studios, etc.—in the hands of a few corporations, many writers have embraced the idea of globalism and strive to produce an equally global literature themselves. Arundhati Roy, author of *The God of Small Things*, was accused of being "antinational" when she protested the nuclear arms buildup in India. Her response captures the international impulse of many contemporary writers: "I hereby declare myself an independent, mobile republic. I am a citizen of the earth. I own no territory. I have no flag" (109).

While Bohannan's tale is useful because it punctures the idea that Shakespeare's plays are universal, we should not conclude that they have no value *or* that no African can relate to them. Shakespeare's drama has remarkable breadth and range and does seem to hold meaning for many societies today. All of his plays have been translated and performed in different languages, and many have been adapted by postcolonial writers who emphasize some features and dispense with others. Shakespeare lived, after all, at the cusp of modern capitalism, the system that now dominates practically the entire world, and he was able to crystallize artistically some of the central contradictions and questions that continue to face us today.

Some writers are able to capture and express human experiences, desires, and conflicts in ways that speak to diverse peoples across many boundaries and eras. Some are able to manipulate language and create images in particularly beautiful or memorable ways that can move people from disparate periods and cultures. While something is inevitably lost in the process, good translations can capture much of an original work for foreign readers. Sometimes even literature that seemed meaningless at one point in our life can take on rich meaning at another time. While T. S. Eliot is still not one of my favorite writers, I can now recognize and appreciate the skill and power of his poetry.

Most importantly, T. S. Eliot's poems or Shakespeare's plays belong to the English no more than to the Japanese; Kurosawa's brilliant film adaptation of Shakespeare is but one illustration of this. At the same time, literature written by Rabindranath Tagore, Salman Rushdie, and Jamaica Kincaid can and does speak to Americans as well as Nigerians. Perhaps the true goal of multiculturalism is this recognition that the best of the world's culture past and present comes from and belongs to not exclusive groups, but all the "citizens of the earth."

WORKS CITED

Achebe, Chinua. "The African Writer and the English Language." *Morning Yet on Creation Day: Essays.* New York: Anchor, 1975.

Bennett, Alan. *Coming Home.* London: QPD, 1994.

Bohannan, Laura. "Shakespeare in the Bush." *Natural History* 75 (Aug/Sept 1966): 28–33.

Equiano, Olaudah. *The Interesting Narrative of the Life of Olaudah Equiano, or Gustavus Vassa, the African.* Rpt. in *Black Writers of America: A Comprehensive Anthology.* Ed. Richard Barksdale. New York: Macmillan Company, 1972. 7–38.

Hodge, Merle. *Crick Crack, Monkey.* Oxford: Heinemann, 1970.

Kaplan, Justin. *Mr. Clemens and Mark Twain: A Biography.* New York: Simon and Schuster, 1966.

Kincaid, Jamaica. *A Small Place.* New York: Plume, 1988.

RECOMMENDED READING

Boyce Davies, Carole. *Black Women, Writing and Identity: Migrations of the Subject.* London: Routledge, 1994.

> Boyce Davies explores the implications of considering literature cross-culturally, and considers how the physical relocation of people through migration has generated bodies of literature that defy categorization by nation or region.

Roy, Arundhati. *The Cost of Living.* New York: Modern Library, 1999.

> This slim book brings together two forceful essays by the internationally acclaimed author of the novel *The God of Small Things.* Protesting the inequalities that continue to define the world, Roy rejects the logic of nationalism and espouses an internationalist humanism.

Said, Edward. *Culture and Imperialism.* New York: Knopf, 1993.

> This broad-ranging text explores the formative impact of "distant land and peoples" on the Western canon of literature. Said also questions the idea of pristine, autonomous cultures and gestures toward a plural, hybrid approach to artistic production.

Takaki, Ronald. *A Different Mirror: A History of Multicultural America.* Boston: Little Brown, 1993.

> This invaluable history reveals the immense ethnic and cultural diversity of the United States of America and tells the story of successive waves of immigration with an emphasis on the commonalities rather than the divisions, between different racial and ethnic groups.

CHAPTER 10

Reader Response: The Value of Not Getting It "Right" the First Time

Nancy Welch

We look forward, we look back, we decide, we change our decisions, we form expectations, we are shocked by their nonfulfillment, we question, we muse, we accept, we reject; this is the dynamic process of recreation.
        Wolfgang Iser, "The Reading Process"

"Guigemar" follows the traditional chivalric romance ending. He saves the lady, kills his enemies, and he lives happily ever after. But what about the lady? Marie leaves many questions unanswered: What happened to the lady's husband? What happens if Guigemar leaves the lady? What will she do? How does society view her? Guigemar's pain has ended; what about the lady's pain?
        Tanya, response to "Guigemar"

NO APOLOGY NECESSARY

When Tanya, a student in my sophomore course Texts and Contexts, turned in her midterm portfolio, she did so with an apology. Her midterm portfolio contained an extended writing project—her reading of a chivalric romance called "Guigemar" by the twelfth-century writer Marie de France. Her portfolio also contained multiple drafts and close reading exercises that traced her changing views of this tale, lengthy notes to and from a peer writing partner, plus weekly letters about the course's readings and discussions. All of these writings offered a strong sense of a reader reacting, puzzling, arguing, questioning, and grappling. As Tanya examined how course texts like "Guigemar" spoke to and tugged at her contemporary context, particularly as a Women's Studies major, her writing also offered a strong sense of why such active reading matters, of what can be at stake in bringing to life and significance a tale written some 800 years before.

Active reading and writing with keen attention to the implications for our own lives and others'—this is precisely what Texts and Contexts, as an introduction to English studies, was designed to promote and precisely what Tanya's midterm portfolio dramatized. "What really surprised me," she wrote in a note accompanying her portfolio, "is that Marie wrote this in the late twelfth century. All the women's studies classes I've taken begin with the rise of feminist thought in the 1800s. People need to be aware that women like Marie, in the twelfth century, already had strong views ..." Here and elsewhere, Tanya demonstrates the work of a reader to form a relationship with a particular text *and* place that text in relationship to her other studies, communities, and concerns. In the process of reading a twelfth-century tale, she discovers something new and vital to introduce into her conversations beyond this single classroom. Forging a relationship between Marie's "Guigemar" and the discipline of Women's Studies, Tanya begins to speak, I think, not as a student completing an assignment ("Here's what I think 'Guigemar' is about") but as a scholar speaking passionately and persuasively to her field ("Here's why I think Women's Studies should expand its scope to consider the work of writers like Marie").

Even so, Tanya felt the need to apologize for her work. Specifically, she apologized for her very first response to "Guigemar," written in the semester's second week. In her midterm note, Tanya wrote:

```
I think you might want to ignore my reading letter of
"Guigemar." I really did not see or understand [Marie's]
stance at that particular time. The letter is basically
very unthoughtful and also kind of embarrassing.
```

With this note, Tanya points to the many revisions that have taken place between the penning of her initial response letter (where she dismissed Marie's tale as a "typical chivalric romance" that "reinforces male dominance") and the completion of her midterm project (an essay in which she argues that "Guigemar," far from typifying the genre, exposes chivalry and its literary/social confinement of women). Tanya no longer agrees with her first reading of the tale. Indeed, her whole midterm project can be read as an argument *with* that first response. But does this mean that her first response was "unthoughtful," "embarrassing," *wrong*? Is this first reading letter a misstep that a "good reader," somehow, would have managed to avoid? The reader-response theorists I'll highlight in this chapter all suggest no, not at all. For these theorists, not "getting it right the first time" isn't the mark of failure but the start of real reading.

READER RESPONSE: AN OVERVIEW

"Reader response theory" is a term I use loosely to refer not to a unified school of literary criticism but to a diverse group of literary critics, theorists, linguists, and educators who believe (despite the many differences among them) that what is read cannot be separated from who is reading. Jonathan Culler, for instance, working from the assumptions of structuralism, argues that practiced readers, despite personal differences, all share the same reading conventions—tacit literary competencies—that set the boundaries of possible, permissible readings. In contrast, psychoanalytic reading theorist Norman Holland argues that what determines the boundaries of possible readings of a text aren't shared conventions but one's individual "identity theme" that a reader imprints, unconsciously and without variation, on every text encountered. For feminist literary theorist Judith Fetterley, paramount is that readers—particularly those concerned with the (mis)representation of women in literature—become very conscious indeed, learning to question the social conventions of reading and learning to resist the representations of gender and politics a text might otherwise seek to imprint.

How these theorists construct readers, their activities, and their consciousness of their activity of reading has as much to do with their other critical communities (structuralism, psychoanalysis, feminism) as with any set of assumptions we might attribute to reader response theory. Yet all of these theorists, their differences aside, stress the presence and the role of the reader. "Every time a reader experiences a work of art," writes Louise Rosenblatt, "it is in a sense created anew" (113). "One must take into account not only the actual text but also, and in equal measure, the actions involved in responding to that text," writes Wolfgang Iser (50). Readers, Iser and Rosenblatt believe, don't simply "receive" an author's "intended" meaning; they are actively and equally involved in *creating* a text's meanings. For reader-oriented theorists, there is no "work of art" without the artistry of a reader. There is no meaning in the text apart from the context in which it is read.

That the significance and impact of a story, an essay, a poem has at least something to do with who is reading (and when and where) isn't really news. Many of us have had the experience, for instance, of reading a novel in a middle or high-school class, then rereading it some years later in college and discovering that this novel has greatly "changed"—even though we know, of course, that we are the ones who have changed. Recent writing and reading technologies have sought to creatively exploit such reader participation. Hypertext fiction, for example, calls on readers to pursue multiple, embedded links that change not only a story's order but, profoundly, just what the story is.

We may also have experienced moments in which, far from passively receiving some fixed "intended" meaning, we *resist*, argue with, and even begin to *rewrite* the implications of a story. Tanya is acting as such a "resisting reader" (a phrase I borrow from Judith Fetterley) in her first response to "Guigemar." In her first reading letter, she resists the cultural work of the chivalric romance to reinforce a captive, passive role for women. Marie's tale, Tanya concludes, is typical of the genre and of the gender representations that a Women's Studies major would want to actively rewrite, not passively accept. Later, as Tanya begins to identify odd moments in the tale in which the nameless female character also struggles with her confinement, she begins to imagine Marie as a resisting reader as well. Tanya begins to imagine Marie as someone who has likewise "read" the problems of the chivalric romance, who may be penning "Guigemar" in resistance and response. Resisting, rethinking, revising, rewriting: At this point in Tanya's reading and writing with "Guigemar," it is difficult to separate author from reader, reader from text, these dancers from the dance.

Yet even if it seems apparent that we can't separate a dancer from the dance, adherents to the twentieth-century's most popular and enduring school of literary criticism, the New Criticism, believed that to regard a reader's responses as part of a text's meaning was to fall prey to the "affective fallacy." In their famous essay arguing against reader participation in meaning, William Wimsatt and Monroe Beardsley describe the affective fallacy as a "confusion between the poem and its *results* (what it *is* and what it *does*)" (21, Wimsatt and Beardsley's emphasis). Like other New Critics, Wimsatt and Beardsley emphasized attention to a text's formal features. They would be interested in what creates formal "unity" within "Guigemar" (the plot pattern of arrivals and departures, for instance) and what creates "ambiguity" (love ambiguously represented as both cure *and* lasting curse). Above all, New Critics feared that a shift in critical attention away from such formal features and toward its effects on readers would eclipse the poem altogether. "The outcome," Wimsatt and Beardsley warned, "... is that the poem itself, as an object of specifically critical judgment, tends to disappear" (21).

The New Critics had reason to worry. Late nineteenth-century critical practices tended to view literary texts as either disguised author biographies or as reducible to trite moral lessons: "love conquers all" as the sum meaning of "Guigemar," for example. The school of New Criticism developed, in part, in response to such critical practices that did indeed eclipse the text. But in their eagerness to emphasize a poem's stylistic complexities, they shut out any discussion of a poem's equally complex cultural work. In seeking to prevent a reader from simply imposing her or his own wishes on a text, they shut out any consideration of how a text might challenge a reader's social position and views. In trying to keep the poem squarely in view, the New Critics tried to make the reader disappear instead. (For a fuller history of the cultural conditions that gave rise to New Criticism and its fears of reader involvement, see Jane Tompkins's essay "The Reader in History.")

Louise Rosenblatt, considered a primary founder of reader-oriented criticism, sympathized with the concerns of New Critics; she did not believe that a reader's response should be taken as an "absolute" that's celebrated rather than investigated. At the same time, in a direct counter to the "aridity and sterility" of New Critical text-focused readings, she sought to restore the reader to the reading scene (xi-xii). Instead of accepting the either/or choice between attending to a text's impact on a reader or attending to a "close reading" of the text itself, Rosenblatt argues that both must be done. "We can broaden the concept of close reading," Rosenblatt writes, "to encompass the reader's close attention to his [or her] responses to the text" (xii). Such close attention, in Rosenblatt's view, prevents a reader's response from becoming a simple matter of wish-fulfillment as Wimsatt and Beardsley feared. Such close attention also greatly complicates the popular idea of a reader-response classroom—students and teacher in a circle, each saying, "This is what the story means to me" and nothing more. A close reading of our responses takes us beyond *voicing* our reading experience to *examining* our reading experience, an examination requiring that both text and reader remain in view.

How is it possible to consider both what a text is and how a reader experiences it? Russian language theorist Mikhail Bakhtin, who also should be included among early advocates of the reader's role, argued that as we examine the experience of reading, we should consider that any given text offers us not one story but two:

> Before us are two events—the event that is narrated in the work and the event of narration itself (we ourselves participate in the latter, as listeners or readers) ... at the same time these two events are indissolubly united in a single but complex event that we might call the work ... (225)

Here Bakhtin, like Rosenblatt, demonstrates that we don't have to make an either/or choice. There *are* events within the text—the story that is told, the different actions that take place. There is also, inseparable from the events "in" the story, the event of a reader experiencing this story, a reader experiencing, reacting to, and making sense of these events. In Bakhtin's view, a text does not become a literary work until there are readers and until these readers begin to respond—their responses necessarily shaped by who they are and where they are.

In other words, we can look at a text like Marie's "Guigemar" and claim that there are facts and as yet unrefuted theories *about* the writing of this text that do not change with time and readers: facts about how texts were produced, circulated, and authorized in the second half of the twelfth century, about the status of women and literacy, about Marie's prominence and success as a courtly writer, about the social use of chivalric romances to justify the leisure of the nobility. We can also claim that there are events *in* the text that do not change with time and readers. The tale starts, for example, with a prologue, Marie's argument for why she is authorized to tell such a story despite many detractors; the tale ends with Guigemar riding off with his lady, "all his pain ... now at an end" (line 882). In between a series of actions take place in a particular order:

1. Guigemar, a young unmarried knight, kills a magical fawn during a hunt. Before dying, the fawn places a curse on Guigemar: He will suffer the wounds of love until he finds a lady who can heal him through her care and suffering.
2. Guigemar immediately meets and falls in love with a married noble woman (referred to only as "the lady" throughout the tale) who is held captive by her jealous husband. He lives with her undetected by her husband for a year.
3. When discovered by the lady's husband, Guigemar leaves and returns home to the rejoicing of his family and friends.
4. Meanwhile, the lady endures two years of suffering in a locked tower, then frees herself and is soon captured by another lord who invites all the knights in the region to try to remove the chastity belt Guigemar has girded her within.
5. By chance, Guigemar shows up, fights for the lady, and, victorious, takes her (though she is still married) away.

Although the presentation of these events can vary, depending on whether we read the text in its original Old French or in modern English prose or poetry translation, readers can more or less agree that yes, this is "what happens" in the tale, these events are "in" the text.

But what happens in a tale, as Bakhtin reminds us, is only half the story. Still to be attended to is the experience of encountering and considering these events. Take the lines near the conclusion of "Guigemar," as an example. Here the text tells us that Guigemar rode off "rejoicing" with his lady, "all his pain at an end." This is the story's final event, and it seems straightforward enough. Not so straightforward, however, is what this event means, how we might feel about it. In Texts and Contexts, students' widely varying responses to this ending show how much readers and their contexts participate in creating meaning:

> It shows that the two characters were meant to spend their lives together, and because of this, they were brought to each other again. (Cat)

> I am left with a sense of relief that the two lovers have found each other again, but the lady is still married to another man ... Marie showed the world that the power of a good story can override moral values. (Nicole)

> I see their relationship as a shady affair. (Lee)

> Guigemar's pain has ended; what about the lady's pain? (Tanya)

What may first appear as a typical happy ending becomes, through the differing responses of readers like Cat, Nicole, Lee, and Tanya, the subject of classroom debate. They agree on what happens at the story's end but don't agree on what this ending means. For reader-oriented theorists like Bakhtin and Rosenblatt, what's needed in this debate isn't a determination of just which of the above responses is "right." Rather, what's needed is an investigation into the text and into the contexts that are creating each response—close attention, as Rosenblatt puts it, to how we and how others are imagining this tale.

What does this idea of close attention mean in actual practice? How can the examination of our responses lead to expansion, complication, and revision, not just insistence and defense that our first reading is the "right" one? Tanya's attention to "Guigemar" and the debate she experienced within herself as well as with her classmates offers one example.

READER RESPONSE IN ACTION

Tanya's first written response to "Guigemar" is a reading letter that she writes in response to both the text and to my "reading preview" letter to class. In the preview letter, I ask the class to consider what they associate with words like "chivalry" and "chivalric romance." I also ask students to consider how "Guigemar" does and doesn't seem to fit with these associations. Tanya writes at the start of her reading letter:

> I feel that stories of chivalry strengthen our patriarchal society. These stories often portray women are help-

less creatures that are saved by the love of an extremely
masculine man. Even though this was written by a woman,
it still portrays that image.

Tanya's first responses to this story, both in her letter and in class discussion, are of disappointment and muffled frustration. She was expecting, she says in class, *more* from a woman writer like Marie.

Here it should be apparent that Tanya doesn't come to this text as a blank slate, with no expectations and preconceptions. Instead, she and her classmates come to reading with some knowledge of chivalry and its conventions—knowledge that comes as much from popular culture (enduring ideas about gentlemanly conduct, for instance, and Hollywood films like *The Last of the Mohicans*) as from past experience with knightly tales. Tanya also brings to "Guigemar" her familiarity with feminist critiques of chivalric rescues and marriage plots. She comes, too, with the tacit expectation formed through her experiences as a Women's Studies major that this romance by a woman should offer something else.

While many of us have been taught over the years that we should avoid bringing to a text any preconceptions about what it will say and do, reader-oriented theorists like Wolfgang Iser and Frank Smith emphasize that reading *depends* on a reader's ability to make predictions—and then read to find out how these predictions are confirmed or upset. Reading doesn't just happen in a forward word-by-word direction, writes linguist Frank Smith in his books *Reading* and *Understanding How We Read*. Instead, drawing on past experiences and associations, we constantly make guesses about what will happen next. We skim ahead to see if our guesses hold true. We circle back to reread when we realize that wait, no, something unexpected has taken place instead. It's this process—of reading forward and back; of forming expectations, then feeling the shock (and frequently pleasure) when they aren't fulfilled or the satisfaction (and sometimes boredom) when they are; of reacting, looking again, changing our minds—that begins to transform a text from a static artifact to dynamic event. Such a process is not smooth, fast, and flowing (as many of us have also been taught that good reading should be). Instead, this dynamic, revisionary, back-and-forth reading depends on *"interruptions* of the flow," on moments of what Iser calls "the defamiliarization of what the reader thought he [or she] recognized" (62–63, Iser's emphasis).

This back-and-forth defamiliarizing process is what Tanya begins to experience as she works with a partner, Lee, in class on how "Guigemar" matches and departs from chivalric romance conventions. They make a list of the general conventions with which they're familiar that "Guigemar" does indeed fulfill: damsel in distress, handsome knight, brave rescue, the two riding away at the end. As they search the text for moments that depart from these conventions, though, they find some surprises. "The 'damsel in distress' becomes not so distressed after Guigemar leaves," Tanya notes in an update to her initial reading letter. "She lets herself out of the tower. She takes control back of her life and sets out on a quest." The list of surprises she and Lee find grows. There's the depiction of a frank and matter-of-fact sexual relationship between the lady and Guigemar that begins within minutes of their first meeting; the early representations of the lady as active and decisive, the knight as passive and vulnerable; the lack of resolution at the end because while the two ride off together, the lady remains married to another.

"Maybe," Tanya writes in another update to her initial letter, "this was a first step to bring awareness to women. To subtly let the reader know that women can take control over their lives and unhappiness." Her partner, Lee, wonders, though, if control is what the lady really has. "How does the ability to heal and save a man empower the woman?" she asks. The question turns them to other odd and surprising events in this tale: the very unromantic appearance and consequences of the chastity belt, the lady's increasingly captive position, the complete absence of her voice and perspective by the end. At the very bottom of her reading letter, Tanya lists her questions that the tale has left unanswered: "But what about the lady? ... Guigemar's pain has ended; what about the lady's pain?" Fifty minutes earlier, "Guigemar" was for Tanya a familiar, predictable, and disappointing tale. Now through rereading, through discussion, and through considering both expectations and surprises, the tale has become strange, perplexing. Tanya had thought she recognized here a typical masculinist romance—end of story. Now she is not so sure.

This is the letter, with its increasingly unsettled reading of "Guigemar," that Tanya apologizes for at midterm. My own view of this letter (and, I hope, Tanya's now too) is that far from unthoughtful, this letter is thought-filled. It offers not one but at least three readings of the tale. It seeks to unsettle, not just confirm her initial reading. It ends with that list of *What's going on here?* questions that turn Tanya to imagining the focus of her midterm project. Here is a letter that needs no apology because it marks the start, not the end, of reading.

SO WHERE DOES IT ALL END?

The concern of the New Critics was that readers would simply make a text say anything they wanted it to. Tanya, Lee, and other readers dramatize, I believe, that the opposite can hold true. These students bring to the tale particular concerns, yet instead of simply defending their varying readings, each learns from the complications others raise. Tanya, persuaded by Lee's view that appearances of the lady's autonomy are deceptive, argues in her midterm project that "Guigemar" demonstrates both the potential for a woman to take action and how patriarchy works to recontain her. Cat, persuaded by Lee and Tanya that here is no ideal fairytale, is also increasingly drawn to the theme of containment, but in a midterm project that imitates Marie's tale in form and style, she is primarily concerned with how a writer such as Marie negotiates a tricky rhetorical situation, telling a story that her noble audience most likely does not want to hear. A third student, Nicole, feels that too much emphasis is being placed on social restriction without considering how this is also a tale about chance, coincidence, and magic despite a restrictive reality. From her interest in folklore and folk tales, she focuses her project on the use of magic in the tale to make possible actions and relationships that would be otherwise prohibited. Lee, just emerged from a troubled love relationship herself, takes a critical view of anything that has the appearance of magic; she views "Guigemar" as a cautionary tale against "selfish love," emphasizing particularly the lady's complicity in her confinement.

So which view of "Guigemar" is the right one? Most reader-oriented theorists would say this isn't quite the right question. "The potential text," Iser says, "is infinitely richer than any of its individual realizations" (55). Each of these realizations of "Guigemar" has merit. None can represent, however, all that this tale has the potential to say—including Tanya's reading that highlights Marie's potential liberal feminism but doesn't consider the conservative work of chivalric romances (with their presentations of beautiful ladies and gallant knights too busy with love and adventure to actually work) to justify feudal class divisions. So even if there is no one "right reading," we *can* evaluate our "individual realizations" by considering both the richness we're tapping into and, simultaneously, the complications of text and context that our reading ignores. What passages in "Guigemar" did Tanya, Lee, Nicole, and Cat highlight in their reading? Which did they overlook? How are our contemporary contexts shaping what we can and cannot see? How do our contexts converse and conflict with Marie's? These are the questions that, at my prompting, Tanya, Lee, Cat, and Nicole ask of their drafts and of each other's as they work toward their midterm projects through in-class revision activities, feedback sessions with draft partners, and conferences with me. These are the questions that led each, with their individual and varying realizations of "Guigemar," to increasingly responsive, responsible readings of this text.

There's a further step we can also take in considering the value of our interpretations: *So what does it mean to read the text this way? What are the implications of such an interpretation then and now?* Tanya pursues these questions when she places her reading in the context of Women's Studies, her project not just about what "Guigemar" *is* but what this tale might *do* in our renderings of feminist history. Contrary to the counsel of New Critics like Wimsatt and Beardsley, her work tells me we must consider a text *with* its results. The question, *What is my experience of this text?* leads to, *So what does this experience allow us, with this text, beyond this text, to recognize and do?*

ACKNOWLEDGMENT

I'm grateful to Tanya Rodrigue, Nicole Jochec, Cat Nigro, and Lee Mathers, who all asked to be cited by name, for giving me permission to include their work in this chapter.

WORKS CITED

Bakhtin, Mikhail. "Forms of Time and of the Chronotope in the Novel." *The Dialogic Imagination.* Ed. Michael Holquist. Trans. Caryl Emerson and Michael Holquist. Austin: University of Texas Press, 1981.

Culler, Jonathan. "Literary Competence." In *Reader-Response Criticism: From Formalism to Post-Structuralism.* Ed. Jane Tompkins. Baltimore: Johns Hopkins University Press, 1980.

Fetterley, Judith. *The Resisting Reader: A Feminist Approach to American Fiction.* Bloomington: Indiana University Press, 1978.

Holland, Norman N. "Unity Identity Text Self." In *Reader-Response Criticism: From Formalism to Post-Structuralism.* Ed. Jane Tompkins. Baltimore: Johns Hopkins University Press, 1980.

Iser, Wolfgang. "The Reading Process: A Phenomenological Approach." In *Reader-Response Criticism: From Formalism to Post-Structuralism.* Ed. Jane Tompkins. Baltimore: Johns Hopkins University Press, 1980.

Marie de France. "Guigemar." *The Lais of Marie de France.* Trans. Robert Hanning and Joan Ferrante. Chapel Hill: Labyrinth Press, 1978.

Rosenblatt, Louise. *Literature as Exploration* (1938), 4th ed. New York: Modern Language Association, 1983.

Smith, Frank. *Understanding Reading.* New York: Holt, Rinehart, and Winston, 1971.

———. *Reading.* Cambridge: Cambridge University Press, 1978.

Tompkins, Jane. "The Reader in History." In *Reader-Response Criticism: From Formalism to Post-Structuralism.* Ed. Jane Tompkins. Baltimore: Johns Hopkins University Press, 1980.

Wimsatt, William Jr., and Monroe Beardsley. *The Verbal Icon: Studies in the Meaning of Poetry.* Lexington: University Press of Kentucky, 1954.

CHAPTER 11

Reading Films as Acts of Reading

Andrew Barnaby

This chapter has two purposes. First, it aims to offer students a particular interpretive methodology by which to think critically about films. There are, of course, many other ways of working with filmic texts. But it is important to get students to recognize that some kind of critical orientation is necessary even for a popular art form that might, initially, seem immediately accessible. The methodology offered here will not work for every film, although it will work for many films being studied in the context of traditional literature courses. It would be especially useful for any film whose core material is adapted from a literary work (play, novel, short story, autobiography, etc.). Second, this chapter asks students to give some thought to what it means to read *as a writer* or, conversely, to write *as a reader.* We will consider this possibility by focusing our attention on an often-neglected fact: that one of the most powerful impetuses to creative writing is thoughtful, reflective reading. Exploring what this means in the context of film adaptation will also enable students to see more clearly that revisionary reading is the source of many types of creative work.

READING AS A WRITER, WRITING AS A READER

Let's take up this last issue first before we get back to the particular issue of interpreting a filmic text. Think for a moment about your experiences reading a story or a poem or a novel or a play. None of these activities is particularly complicated in itself. By contrast, thinking of something to say about one's reading can be very difficult. Certainly one of the central premises of this book is that studying literature is an outgrowth of reading it. But if studying *derives from* the experience of reading, it is also different in some significant ways. The key difference, of course, is that as students we are asked to reflect on our reading experiences. This is precisely the *work* of studying literature: distinguishing the reading experience from the process of finding our own words by which to respond to that reading, discovering if we have something to say, something we feel is worth saying, and some way of saying it. In short, when we read as *students* we always, whether explicitly or not, read as *writers*.

139

Of course, we can think about this process in a number of ways. On the one hand, we might observe that reading as a writer can mean that, when we read, we conceptualize images, storylines, characters, narrative point-of-view, dialogue, figurative language, and other literary qualities from the perspective of the person writing them: What did it require to locate these possibilities? How is this writer's personal "signature" (to borrow a phrase from Raymond Carver) stamped on things? By what means and in what contexts did this writer give voice to this experience? On the other hand, reading as a writer might mean that we sustain an awareness of how our own writing might derive from the reading experience: How might we describe our responses in words, in an essay or a report or a journal, as a theoretical discussion, historically based research, or a personal narrative?

One way to understand just how closely related these two ways of reading-as-a-writer can be is by focusing attention on the fact I noted in the opening paragraph: that one of the most powerful impetuses to creative writing is thoughtful, reflective reading. The evidence for this is everywhere, though it sometimes surprises us. In a recent interview, for example, Bruce Springsteen makes the rather startling admission that his life as a serious reader has been a transformative catalyst to his development as a songwriter:

> I go through periods when I read seriously, and I get a lot out of what I read, and that reading has affected my work since the late Seventies. The really important reading that I did began in my late twenties, with authors like Flannery O'Connor. There was something in her stories that I felt captured a certain part of the American character that I was interested in writing about. They were a big, big revelation. She got to the heart of some part of meanness that she never spelled out, and that dark thing—a component of spirituality—that I sensed in her stories set me off exploring characters of my own…. So right before the record *Nebraska* [1982], I was deep into O'Connor.

Springsteen's statement is certainly thought-provoking: O'Connor's work represents "some part of meanness … that dark thing" in the "American character" that yet mysteriously reveals "a component of spirituality." But because the validity of Springsteen's claim is not immediately self-evident it is also requires some critical unpacking. Thus, if you were writing an essay on O'Connor, you might use Springsteen's own interpretive act as a *starting* point—but not the endpoint—for your own explorations. You might, for example, examine the violence of O'Connor's "A Good Man Is Hard to Find" in such a way as to link the "meanness" of the story (it is, after all, a story about a serial killer, the "Misfit") to something in American culture that paradoxically manifests a "spiritual" condition. Of course, you might also try to understand the lyrics on Springsteen's *Nebraska* album as somehow revealing how he "set … off exploring characters of [his] own" because of what he discovered in his reading of O'Connor. You can, in short, think of what Springsteen wrote as a conversation with what he had been reading. In this way you can begin transforming your own *triple* reading experience—reading O'Connor and reading Springsteen and reading Springsteen reading O'Connor—into a critical act, an act where you join the critical conversation as a writer by being an attentive reader.

Although students tend to be a bit dismissive of this fact, the artistic impulse often begins precisely with a reading experience so powerful that the reader feels compelled not just to consider the implications of what has been read but also to discover his or her own words to speak back to that text. As a tool for our own learning, moreover, recognizing the adaptive impulse at work when artists themselves read as writers is important to the extent that it allows us to understand literary works as existing in dialogue with each other. From the perspective of our own reading and writing, such a recognition can serve as a powerful catalyst to our own inquiries, producing unique possibilities for discovery.

For example, we might come to understand something of how we ourselves read by reflecting on how others read as evidenced by what they subsequently create. Or, we might come to recognize that critical and creative work are not so at odds as we typically think precisely to the extent that we can see an artist's creative response to a source-text as at once deriving from and demanding interpretive, analytical, and comparative labor: How is this story already the story an artist wants to tell yet one still somehow in need of retelling? Clearly, there is a kind of paradox in this process in that we have a source-text that simultaneously satisfies an artistic need and frustrates it, or stimulates a need to say more. From the perspective of critical work, focusing our attention in this way helps us learn to trace out something of the creative impulse by following an artist's reading into acts of construction and reconstruction, interpretation and revision, extension and change, part of the perpetual conversation between works.

At the same time, we should understand how our own creative ventures might be prompted and sustained by serious reading. Indeed, in the context of college courses, the discovery of our own words might in fact take explicitly creative form: write a missing scene from a play; write out the diary entries for a character from a favorite novel; develop a storyline that will retell a famous story from the perspective of a minor character (as Tom Stoppard does in *Rosencrantz and Guildenstern Are Dead*—a play that revises Shakespeare's *Hamlet*). In short, whether our work is creative, critical, or a mixture of the two, exploring creative adaptation as an interpretive act helps us to grasp how all art forms seek the means of giving voice to what would otherwise go unsaid.

REVISIONARY READING AND THE IMPULSE TO FILM

We are certainly not unfamiliar with this notion when it comes to film adaptations of novels or plays or some other source material. Indeed, in a literature course we are quite likely to encounter a film precisely because it has a literary precursor: film versions of Shakespeare's plays or of Jane Austen's novels, for example; and such acclaimed films as *A Streetcar Named Desire, The Godfather, The Color Purple, The Name of the Rose,* and *The English Patient* are all based on modern literary sources (plays or novels).

There is, of course, another category of adaptation altogether: films that radically recontextualize the source material, as Stoppard's play transforms the Shakespearean original. Thus, for example, Amy Heckerling's *Clueless* relocates Jane Austen's *Emma* in the context of modern American teen culture, Francis Ford Coppola's *Apocalypse Now* reimagines Joseph Conrad's *Heart of Darkness* in terms of the Vietnam War, and Gus Van Sant's *My Own Private Idaho* translates Shakespeare's *Henry IV* into a dark fable of the American dream.

No doubt when most of us watch film adaptations of works we have previously read we are likely to begin our inquiries by asking if the film is being faithful: Is it true to the spirit of its source if not to the precise letter? In posing this question, we are probably most attuned to the specific content the adaptation borrows from its source, or, perhaps more accurately, to whatever changes the film makes to the source's content. We tend to notice changes especially when a film leaves out or condenses material we take to be essential to the original. But while the content of a story is always important, to focus too much on this is to misunderstand the artistry of adaptation. Indeed, as in the case of Springsteen's encounter with O'Connor, a film maker's act of reading prompts a response that is at once interpretive and creative. Film makers, that is, do not simply aim to replicate the written word in a visual medium; rather, they employ all the expressive capacities of film—sight and sound, word and image, plot, character, dialogue, camera angles, cinematography—to represent in an artistically compelling way those ideas, emotions, intuitions that have been elicited by the reading experience. Film adaptations, in short, are always talking back to their sources and not merely translating them into a different language. Thus, when we watch a film adaptation of a literary source, we are not looking at a simple visualizing of what already exists. As I suggested earlier, we are, instead, listening to a dialogue. And our own responses, whether these are creative or analytical, should be understood as our own efforts both to listen to this dialogue and to participate in it.

With all that in mind, it might be helpful here to give sustained attention to how a specific film's adaptive processes can be understood as an extension of the act of reading itself. That is, we need to consider an actual instance of how, in a way similar to Springsteen's songs, a film adaptation yet reveals imaginative borrowing as a catalyst to a truly creative process. Our test case will be Robert Redford's screen adaptation of Norman Maclean's autobiographical novella, *A River Runs Through It*.

A RIVER RUNS THROUGH IT

Briefly, Maclean's story recounts the rather shadowy events leading up to the murder of his brother, Paul, who, as the novella and film both tell us, on one fateful night in a small town in Montana was "beaten to death by the butt of a revolver and his body dumped in an alley." However momentous Paul's death is in the lives of the Maclean family, as narrator Norman keeps the actual circumstances discreetly on the margins of the story. Indeed, while the novella is especially concerned to foreshadow Paul's tragic fate—"and in the end, I could not help him," Norman tells us by page 6—both the novella and the film con-

Chapter 11 Reading Films as Acts of Reading   **143**

centrate on other matters, especially a parallel struggle that Norman's wife, Jesse, has with her own brother, Neal, and Norman's own struggle to connect to Jesse and to Paul.

In a general sense, then, Redford is clearly being faithful to the novella's content. But our observation of the obvious similarities—same characters, same basic storyline, etc.—should only serve to heighten our awareness of all the things Redford is doing differently. First, start by noticing things: What is he altering, expanding, omitting? What is he adding to the original? If he retains something, does he keep it in the same place, or does he shift its location? A student should try to be very specific about the details of these changes because a good list of details can very quickly be translated by a short list of rather generic questions into the foundation of a productive inquiry. The best question to ask is simply "Why?"—why is that here or why is that not here—but perhaps it is easier to ask what effect the changes have on our perception of the story; or, to use a theoretical concept, how does the film maker's version of the story "defamiliarize" it (that is, take what is familiar and force us to see it in a way that estranges us from what we think we already know)?

From asking these questions we can move on to formulating some tentative ideas by discovering connections and patterns within the work. These tentative ideas can then be linked together in a series, and the series as a whole can then be shaped into an argument that will at the same time force us to revise many of our original ideas. The best thing about taking advantage of the availability of film adaptations is that the very process of considering two versions of the same material is by its nature comparative. It thus offers great opportunities for linking close, careful consideration of what texts explicitly say and how they say things to an awareness that when we read as *critical* readers we are always trying to translate what we notice about texts into what we might understand about them. We pay attention to two or more texts individually, but we are also listening to the conversation between them. That conversation automatically gives us critical perspective.

So let's consider some of the specifics of the novella and the film as a way of exploring their dialogic encounter. Although the novella is really a finely crafted fictionalization of actual events, it is told as though it were simply a memoir. As is appropriate to that genre, the novella reads as a collection of memories loosely organized first, by a general proximity in time—the summer of 1937 in the novella, about twelve years earlier in the film—and second, by the frequent scenes of dry fly-fishing, a highly repetitive and individualistic activity perfectly suited to deep and long contemplation. Not surprisingly, then, in Maclean's version almost the entire story comes to us as he is mulling over issues, problems, and uncertainties in the privacy of his own thoughts. The very dominance of Maclean's voice throughout the narrative represents a major problem for a film adaptation, however, because, despite its brilliantly conceived characters and a few emotionally charged scenes of interaction between them, the novella offers very little by way of sustained, externalized action. How, in short, is a film to match aesthetically the intense personal presence of the narrator whose powerful revelation of his interior consciousness is at the heart of his telling?

One can easily see just how much effort Redford puts into capturing the essential voice of Norman Maclean as the centerpiece of his adaptation in his choice to employ voice-over narration at critical junctures in the film. These segments are significant, in part, because they help us understand something of the complexly collaborative nature of filmic art. The voice-overs combine new material from the screenwriter, Richard Friedenberg, with some of the most moving passages from the original novella, all read by Redford himself. We will consider some of the deeper implications of these segments a bit later, but for the moment we might simply note that, at their simplest level, Redford uses them to celebrate the world of words—a deeply felt and expressive language—that was so much a part both of Maclean's life and of his storytelling.

Redford's celebration of Maclean's language is not confined to voice-overs, though. Indeed, in one particularly powerful moment, Redford represents Norman and his father sharing the good news of Norman's new job as an English teacher at the University of Chicago by reciting Wordsworth's "Immortality Ode" to each other, a scene that is not in Maclean's original. Besides adding yet another layer of "borrowing"—and it is certainly worth considering why Redford chose this particular poem (That's a hint: A student should read the poem to understand something of Redford's own reading of Maclean!)—the scene offers us a telling, somewhat sad glimpse of how men in the Maclean family interact: The respectful, almost reserved distance they keep from each other, even at times of high emotion, is no small cause of their inability of help Paul. At least, that is how Redford seems to understand the situation. But is this reading confirmed by Maclean's own way of representing matters, or is Redford's view shaped by other concerns?

Consider the following account provided by Timothy Foote in his fine essay on the making of the film:

> Redford grew up in a Scotch-Irish family full of emotionally charged silence … When I talked to him he seemed to identify with Paul…. "Did you have a son or a brother in danger like that?" I asked. "I *was* that son," he said. "I *was* that brother." And he went on to say that in his family, silence was used as a weapon of disapproval…. But Redford also sees the old-fashioned habit of shutting up about your problems as a source of inner strength, part and parcel of a stoical frontier toughness, now vanishing into the past, that younger generations "can hardly relate to."

As we'll see in more detail shortly, Redford is at pains to insist that this story really belongs to Norman, and not just because he wrote it. But he admits that he identifies with Paul and not Norman, and we might reasonably ask just what effect such identification has on the film he produces. Is Redford's version of either Norman or Paul significantly different from Maclean's own version (more or less sympathetic, for example)? To the extent Redford does present us with different kinds of characters, how does this alter the central conflict of the story? Furthermore, what Redford tells Foote suggests that his reading of the novella

Chapter 11   Reading Films as Acts of Reading   **145**

was profoundly influenced by his own experience with, and ambivalent feelings toward, the "silent treatment": It was at once a "weapon of disapproval" and "a source of inner strength." But, at least on the surface, Redford's view seems surprisingly at odds with Maclean's own way of representing the family dynamic:

> Undoubtedly, our differences [that is, between Paul and himself as boys] would not have seemed so great if we had not been such a close family. Painted on one side of our Sunday school wall were the words, God is Love. We always assumed that these three words were spoken directly to the four of us in our family and had no reference to the world outside.

Certainly the scene that Redford adds involving the Wordsworth poem does not contradict Maclean's portrayal of a loving family. But it does suggest that we should be on the lookout in the film for moments when a darker, and deeper, tension cuts across the surface of the action. I must insist that the point of this special attentiveness would not be to show where Redford got things wrong; as I noted earlier, film adaptations do not merely try to replicate their sources. More to the point, if Redford makes adjustments to Maclean's story, it might be because he is picking up on things that Maclean himself is unable to address, even unable to fully imagine. That is, it may be that, at points at least, Redford's reading is more attuned to Maclean's text than Maclean himself is.

Before considering this possibility, let us then simply observe that, despite a general effort to be faithful to the novella, like any adaptor Redford cannot avoid altering his source-text in some fundamental ways. And indeed, there are major changes in the film: deletions, additions, shifts in emphasis. As attentive readers of Redford's own reading, we might note that many of Redford's choices open up room for critical discussion and exploration. For example, what are the effects—positive or negative—within the narrative core of setting the main storyline back more than ten years earlier? What is the effect of representing Norman and Jesse during their days of courtship rather than as a married couple? Does Paul's self-destructiveness seem qualitatively different to us if we see him as a man in his mid-twenties rather than, as Maclean shows him, as a man in his late-thirties? What do we gain and what do we lose in Redford's decision to represent Jesse's mother as rather comical whereas Maclean himself represents her as a powerful, intense figure? And, finally, how are we to make sense of deliberate alterations of the actual words used by Maclean?

Consider the following passage from the end of the novella, a passage that, in subtly but significantly altered form, Redford redeploys in a voice-over at the very opening of the film:

MACLEAN'S ORIGINAL:

> "You like to tell true stories, don't you?" [my father] asked, and I answered, "Yes, I like to tell stories that are true."
>
> Then he asked, "After you have finished your true stories sometime, why don't you make up a story and the people to go with it?
>
> "Only then will you understand what happened and why."

REDFORD'S REVISION (VOICE-OVER NARRATION AS WE SEE AN IMAGE OF RUSHING WATER):

> Long ago when I was a young man, my father said to me, "Norman, you like to write stories," and I said, "yes, I do." Then he said, "Someday when you're ready, you might tell our family story. Only then will you understand what happened and why."

It is interesting to note that the actual opening of the film is different from the screenplay; Friedenberg's original voice-over opening simply used the first three sentences from the novella. But at some stage those three sentences were pushed back a bit and the new opening was imported from the end of the novella. It would certainly be interesting to know who decided on that change and what prompted it. But even if we cannot find the answer to those questions, we can yet consider the effect of moving the passage from the end of the story to the beginning. Moreover, starting from some important distinctions that Maclean himself seems interested in making—what are the differences between "true stories," "stories that are true," and a made-up story that enables one to understand where the other kinds might fail—we can certainly ask how we should understand Redford's own sense of storytelling from the fact that he leaves these distinctions out entirely.

I make no effort to answer those questions here. They simply represent a list of possible starting points. Of course, they are precisely the kinds of questions we need to formulate as a way of prompting the shift from reading to reflecting, from simply enjoying literature and film to loving the critical engagement as well. Any adaptive work—a performance of a Shakespeare play to the most obscene parody (my own favorite is "The Skinhead Hamlet")—offers us material that, by its very nature, sustains critical thinking: It enables our own thinking as a process of comparing and contrasting. As a way of concluding this exploration of film adaptation and the critical thinking that attends it, I want to return to Redford's use of voice-over narration as a way of registering how revisionary reading can also clarify or even intensify a source by a process of adaptive representation. Along with the voice-overs, we will also give special attention to the use of flashbacks as a way of structuring the film narrative.

LISTENING AND SEEING VERSUS READING

Earlier I suggested that Redford uses voice-overs as a way of celebrating Maclean's own life of language. But while it is Redford who is actually reading these passages, conceptually they stand in for the presence of Norman Maclean as the narrator of the story. Most films do not employ narrators since that role is taken up by the camera itself, which tells us where we are to look at all times. But Redford wants us to know that this story is not simply passing in front of us. Rather, Norman's consciousness already possesses the full story, and what we are seeing is being very deliberately presented as a flashback. This fact becomes clear at the end of the film when we discover that the hands tying the fly to the fishing line in the film's opening scene are really the hands of Norman Maclean as an old man.

Sustaining, even *foregrounding,* Maclean's narrative presence is certainly part of Redford's way of honoring Maclean's memory as well as his memories, an issue that was very much part of Maclean's decision to let Redford have the rights to the story rather than another director. As Maclean himself once explained, "Unless you can see and feel about my brother as his father and brother did, I have no story to tell." And in trying to capture how Norman feels about his brother, Redford needs to use any film technique that can give the viewer the sense of an interior perspective even as we are watching exterior action. The flashback framework and the voice-overs thus enable Redford to clarify for us that the real story here belongs not to the more charismatic and energetic Paul but to the more reserved Norman, a fact much more difficult to establish in film than in prose. Indeed, the novella can simply rely on Norman's constant presence as narrator to unify many disparate memories; the film, by contrast, must go out of its way to insist that the story, including its central conflict, is actually taking place in Norman's mind. Moreover, as I just noted, the narrative presence is the consciousness of a much older Norman. Redford wants to present his version of the story as the retrospective ruminations of an older man who is looking back on past events from late in life. In short, Redford deliberately structures the film so as to make Norman's struggle to understand his own memories the central conflict of the story.

Shaping the story in this way enables Redford to give expression to the most powerful aspect of Maclean's own telling but something that, perhaps understandably, Maclean himself is uncomfortable with stating directly. Despite the fact that the story concerns Paul's death, *A River Runs Through It* is less about Paul than about Norman's troubled, guilt-ridden memories of his failure to save his beloved younger brother. With respect to Paul, we never really know "what happened and why," but both novella and film—in fact especially the film—lead to a compelling awareness of how Norman, by the end of his life, must find a way to forgive himself even while he accepts the mystery of his brother's life and death.

There are many elements within Redford's framing of the story that serve to intensify our awareness of this struggle in Norman's own psyche. But let me just point to a couple of these. For example, as background to the opening credits, Redford provides us with a ramble through what might have been someone's personal album of black-and-white photographs but that reads more like a mini-documentary of life on the Montana frontier at the turn of the century. Toward the end of film, Redford moves us quickly through a seamless weave of closeup images of Norman's face at different moments in his life: when first confronted with the reality of Paul's death, then, several years later, when listening with his wife and his children to his father's farewell sermon before his Presbyterian congregation, and finally, to a much older Norman who is out on the river fishing one last time (the scene that frames the entire film). In between the last two of these closeups Redford gives us black-and-white images of Norman and Paul as boys, growing up together beside the rhythms of Montana's Blackfoot River. The return of black-and-white images in conjunction with the closeups suggests that what has been "documented" in the film is not the full life of the Montana frontier but that life as mediated through the personal experiences of one man. What Redford's film narrative gives us, in short, is the narrative memory of a man documenting his own life and working to make it all come together in some meaningful way.

FINAL THOUGHTS

Of course it is this same work—the work to make experience meaningful—that Redford himself is struggling with as a film maker. Indeed, viewed in this context, we understand how Redford is presenting an analogy of sorts between his own work—struggling to read and revise source material—and Maclean's effort to make sense of what has happened in his life. We might think that this effort is primarily an aesthetic issue for Redford, whereas it is more an ethical issue for Maclean himself: As I previously noted, the central conflict for Maclean is his struggle to come to terms with his own feelings that he is somehow responsible for his brother's death. But one wonders if the very reason Redford wanted to make this film was because he too had an ethical struggle of his own to work through, a struggle to make sense of his own life. Did he make the film because he needed some catharsis of his own? After all, when he read the story he identified with it very powerfully and the feelings it evoked were not all pleasant ones.

This possibility also suggests that film makers choose material to make into their new creations for much the same reasons that we cherish those works we love most: They at once challenge and invite us to speak back to them. And the very artistic success of great works comes partly in their capacity to help us discover what we want to say and how to say it. Trying to understand a revising artist's work as at once an interpretive and a creative act enables us to see that our own best interpretive insights might come precisely through creative engagement, through the awakening of what Raymond Carver refers to as the reader's own "artistic sense." Finding our own words to express that sense—whether in critical or in creative ways—is what reading as a writer, or writing as a reader, is all about.

Questions to Ask When Comparing Films to Books

- What events, scenes, or characters does the film omit that the book includes?
- What events, scenes, or characters does the film add that are not in the book?
- What events, scenes, or characters does the film change or modify in some way?
- In your opinion, what is the effect of each omission, addition, or change?
- In your opinion, what is lost, what gained, by the changes you have noted?
- What secondary sources are available to shed additional light on the differences between the film and the book: Interviews with author, director,

or screenwriter published in film journals or Web pages, or broadcast on TV? Supplemental material on a DVD version of the film? Film or book reviews?

WORKS CITED

Carver, Raymond. "On Writing." In *Fires: Essays. Poems, Stories.* New York: Vintage Books, 1989.

Foote, Timothy. "A New Film about Fly-Fishing—and Much, Much More." *Smithsonian* 23 (1992): 120–32.

Friedenberg, Richard. *A River Runs Through It: Bringing a Classic to the Screen.* Livingston, Montana: Clark City Press, 1992.

Maclean, Norman. *A River Runs Through It and Other Stories.* Chicago: University of Chicago Press, 1976.

Redford, Robert. *A River Runs Through it.* Columbia Pictures, 1992.

Springsteen, Bruce. "Rock and Read: Will Percy Interviews Bruce Springsteen." *DoubleTake* 12 (1998): 36–43.

PART THREE

Writing as a Reader

The same kinds of *shoulds* surround writing as reading. That is, many students have come to believe that writing privately is one thing, but writing for an academic public quite something else. Melissa, a sophomore, describes it this way in her journal: "Writing, Writing, Writing! Umm, I love it, but I'm told that I'm not allowed to use the verb "to be." I've also been told to never use "never" and never use "always"! Write with description. Action verbs are best." Writing for an academic audience *is,* of course, different from writing for oneself, but maybe not quite in the way Melissa describes.

In the first section of this book, we explored the concept of reading as a writer. In the second section, we looked at different approaches to reading texts. In this third section, we examine ways to write your own texts, or what we call, writing as a reader.

We write as readers in at least three distinct ways: First, when we learn how and in what contexts and with what struggles literary works were created; second; when we remember that much of what we write is directed ultimately at other readers whose needs we must anticipate; third; when we write to please ourselves, using all the techniques at our disposal to help generate prose and poetry that satisfies our own sense of rightness. Let's look at each of these perspectives in turn.

LESSONS FROM THE MASTERS

One of the problems with literary study is the distance we often feel between those who write the great works of literature and the rest of us who write *about* them. That's why it can be helpful to remember that the great writers themselves were once students of other great writers, and that they too worked hard on their writing to get it just right. When you read the finished works of Jane Austen or Henry David Thoreau or T. S. Eliot, keep in mind that these writers filled notebook after notebook with observations and ideas that only later, and sometimes after many drafts, bore fruit as the finished works we so celebrate today. Keep in mind also that many published authors had mentors—friends, spouses, teachers, editors—who helped them clarify and refine their ideas, images, characters.

Learning to write well—and continuing to do so—is often a messy, frustrating business. Once you've mastered the conventions and forms of written composition, you need to remember that each time you set out to write something new—a critical essay, a personal narrative, a research proposal, or a poem—each time you need to start all over to develop and order your ideas, always asking: Have I said this as clearly, concisely, believably, or gracefully, as possible?

Most of us who have learned to write with some competence consider writing a fairly unpredictable, multistage process, in which we need to find and capture ideas in the first place, develop them in some reasonably clear sequence according to some reasonably clear logic, support them with good examples remembered or researched, and make sure the whole composition is written in a style appropriate to the audience and purpose. Along the way, many of us have learned to rely on the same tricks that helped Austen, Thoreau, and Eliot: to record our insights and observations informally in notebooks or journals; to begin writing before we have fully developed our ideas, trusting that the act of writing itself will help work them out; to plan to write more than one draft of anything important; to receive a little help from our friends; and to edit ceaselessly to get the final product just right. We've also learned that there are few guarantees in the act of writing: Sometimes ideas that seemed brilliant in the shower or on the jogging path look pale on paper; at other times, ideas that start out routinely develop into something quite original and pleasing.

So it may help you, as it helps us, occasionally to remember that writing well wasn't necessarily any easier for the masters than it is for us and that the techniques that helped them may help us as well.

WRITING FOR OTHER READERS

When we write for other readers, we need to write with care, with courtesy, and with doubt. We write carefully that they may follow the thread of our thought and not be thrown off by distractions. We write courteously out of respect for our readers and in order to be taken seriously. And we write with doubt, anticipating that our readers will be curious and ask questions. We'll look briefly at some of the techniques writers use when they think carefully about their readers.

Conventions Writers who use the standard conventions of written English treat their readers with respect and care. At the same time, they usually guarantee a fair hearing for whatever they have to say. To misuse the conventions, whether punctuation, spelling, grammar, or format, is to violate your readers' expectations and therefore to distract them. This is not to say that the violation of expectations has no place in writing, for we know it does. Just keep in mind that when it's done by a Walt Whitman, or an e. e. cummings, it's done deliberately and with purpose. So, when you violate convention, you too need to know what you are doing.

Information and Explanation In writing notes to ourselves, we often use shorthand and abbreviations because we fill in the rest from our heads. But as soon as we begin writing to others, we start asking: How much do my readers already know? What else will they need in order to understand me? Many college students writing to academic audiences don't know how much to assume of their readers. If you are not sure, we recommend that you err by providing too much information rather than too little: When you mention literary works, at least the first time, give full titles, authors, dates. When you use literary terminology or concepts (like *point of view, existentialism,* or *pastoral*), either define them or make sure your examples do that for you.

Evidence As you write, try to consider the kind of evidence *you* require in order to believe someone or be persuaded to accept their perspective. As a reader yourself, you may find that you are seldom convinced by vague generalities or unsupported assertions—at least we seldom are. This means that when you write personal narrative, remember to create belief by supplying concrete detail of character and situation from remembered experience. When you write critical essays, give specific evidence from texts or documented support from experts. And when you write imaginatively, support your imaginings with details and facts—or the illusion of details and facts.

Language and Style The language in which we write makes it easy for our readers to understand us, or it doesn't. It demonstrates our understanding of our subject, or our ignorance. When we write letters to friends, we use a fairly informal talky style. When we write term papers for a Shakespeare professor, we adopt a more formal, analytical style. (And when we write books for college students, we try to fall somewhere in between.) In thinking about who is going to read our writing (our audience), we adjust word choice, sentence structure, perhaps even punctuation and paragraphing to match our intentions with their expectations.

Transitions The more we become attuned to the needs of our audience, the more important become the little words that connect one sentence to another by showing the relationship between ideas—words like *so, thus, then, however, meanwhile, nevertheless, and, but, first, next, last, on the one hand, in other words, in addition, finally.* These words do not always show up the first time we write a draft, when we're worried more about getting the basic ideas down. But as we rework drafts to make our text as clear as possible, we add signals and cues like these to point readers—as unmistakably as we can—in the right direction.

Documentation Documentation is another reader courtesy, necessary whenever the writer uses the words, data, or ideas of another. Through in-text references or footnotes, we tell where to find all the assertions and expert opinions used to support our arguments. We explain who said what, where, and when. Readers who are curious can trace these references and find out still more. *The MLA Handbook for Writers of Research Papers* (fifth edition) explains the conventions for documenting academic papers in the field of English. (See Appendix.)

Titles and Headings   We're amazed at how often novice writers ignore some of their most powerful tools—titles and headings. A good title (both descriptive and provocative, if possible) not only announces your subject, but creates a favorable attitude toward your piece. Section headings (like those you see in this) guide your reader through an essay. We find that creating subheads *as we write* helps us understand where we are in our writing task, tells us where to go next, and even gives us a marked block of text to relocate elsewhere if revision demands it.

Document Design   It is now common for college papers to look every bit as professional and polished as articles published in established periodicals. Such papers may incorporate **different fonts** in varying point sizes, *italics* for book titles or emphasis, **boldface** for subheadings, and visual illustrations including charts, graphs, clip art, and photographs. In addition, some college papers are no longer paper, but electronic texts published as Web pages and incorporating not only varied fonts and illustrations, but also hyperlinks offering a variety of ways in which a document can be read and understood. Writers who master the design potential of powerful computer programs increase the comprehension and enjoyment of their readers.

WRITING FOR OURSELVES

Our first audience is always ourselves. Remember this, especially when you're blocked or confused or uncertain of exactly what you want to say. At such times, it can actually be a hindrance to worry about your audience. Instead, you must ask yourself: Where do *I* want to go? What is the point *I* want to make in the first place? Do *I* understand where my text leads so far? Where does it need to go next?

While we have been describing writing that is primarily academic, we think the same suggestions hold true for imaginative writing—maybe even more so. Before a fiction writer can worry too much about "reader cues," she or he needs to be pretty certain that his or her "writer cues" are in order; in other words, the writer needs to see *for himself or herself* that the character development is consistent, the setting true to imagination or memory, the plot one the writer believes in. Before a poet can think about potential reader responses to images, rhymes, or rhythms, he or she first has to see them in his or her own eye, hear them with his or her own ear to test their ring of truth. As writers, we are readers, first and last—readers of our own language, whether it be directed through letters to family and friends, through essays to teachers, or through journals, intended from the outset to stay quite close to ourselves.

OPTIONS FOR WRITING

The chapters in this part examine the conventions of college writing assignments in the field of English Studies. They look at both the rationale behind the most common assignments as well as strategies for successfully completing such assignments. These chapters are illustrated with samples of writing by students in a variety of classes at the University of Vermont over the past few years. No chapter is meant to be the last word on writing college papers, but each offers thoughtful approaches and lucid guidelines to aid college writers in constructing interesting and coherent papers.

In Chapter 12, "Writing Critical and Interpretive Papers," Sarah E. Turner looks at the most common and, perhaps demanding, writing assignment in typical college English classes, the critical essay. The chapter explains the importance of such assignments and offers suggestions for making convincing literary arguments, finding and documenting evidence, using quotations, and observing the conventions of voice and tense.

In Chapter 13, "Writing Personal Essays," Mary Jane Dickerson focuses on the more subjective writing sometimes asked for in both literature and writing classes. The chapter treats autobiographical writing as a serious and especially honest form of academic writing and includes an autobiographical questionnaire as a prompt to draw out meaningful personal experiences for further exploration.

In Chapter 14, "Imaginative Writing and Risk Taking" William A. Stephany argues that substantial writing, reading, and learning experiences derive from taking unusual or experimental approaches to otherwise conventional assignments. The chapter looks at writing in alternative forms, styles, and voices, and suggests that the skillful writing of parody, satire, and even fiction has much to offer in academic settings.

In Chapter 15, "Writing with Research," Richard Sweterlitsch makes the case that all academic writing is strengthened when students become serious researchers. The chapter includes suggestions for making both library and Internet research critically substantial and interesting; it makes an especially strong case for the value of field research to enliven academic writing.

In Chapter 16, "A Web of One's Own," Katherine Anne Hoffman explores the possibilities and limitations of electronic texts for the field of English studies. Readers are offered ways to critically evaluate Web pages as well as guidelines for constructing their own.

In Chapter 17, "Examining the Essay Examination," Tony Magistrale looks at the rationale behind writing essay examinations and investigates both strong and weak responses to essay exam questions. The chapter suggests ways to cope with writing under pressure and offers strategies for writing both timed and take home examinations.

CHAPTER 12

Critical Essays: Engaging with the Text and the World Around You

Sarah E. Turner

Your English professor has just assigned the first paper of the semester, and you are being asked to write a critical analysis of a text you have just barely finished reading. How will you start? What does it mean to be critical or to write critically? Before you panic, think for a second. You know what being critical means. Every time you walk into a store, you are taking on the role of the critic.

Imagine yourself ready to buy that new snowboard; think about the steps that brought you to that store. At the end of last season, you decided you were ready for a new board. Why? Well, maybe you decided that you will concentrate on the park this year. Or the pipe. Or maybe you want to try the Boarder X series at the local mountain. Whatever your riding style, you know you have a new board in your future. So, there you are, listening to the salesperson's pitch. Part of you is wondering if this person even rides. The credibility or authority of this person will definitely affect your decision. However, would you ever buy based solely on what someone else tells you? No! Instead, you enter into the discussion, making clear that you prefer free-riding to pipe, or that you have some concerns about the construction. You might mention the review you read in *Transworld* or in *Outside Magazine.* Very likely you have talked to your friends and gotten some additional input. Each of these steps have immersed you in the critical process.

If you don't snowboard, think about the process you go through when you determine whether or not a film is worth seeing or a CD worth buying. What do you ask yourself? Does the movie have a good storyline? Big name actors? Original or plausible plot? Is it too predictable? Do the good guys always win? Should they? Look at this excerpt from Rick Kisonak's review of the film *Gladiator:*

> *Gladiator* is simply a great movie. Great wronged hero. Great demented pervert emperor. Great camera work, art direction, and dialogue. And, as I mentioned, the greatest use ever of computerized special effects. If you're going to spend $100 million on a movie, *this* is what it should look like.

Kisonak's critique of the movie is based on both his personal reaction to the text—note his use of "I"—and his evaluation of the components of the film: camera work, dialogue, characters, special effects.

Or, in the case of music, you might ask: Is the sound new or too derivative? Too much drum and bass? Too electronic or not enough? Lyrics I like or that speak to me? Voices that appeal to me? Why it is that you are willing to line up at midnight for the latest Phish release but use that new Madonna disk as a drink coaster? And, aren't you being critical each time you make a purchase or a decision? You weigh the evidence, think of the pros and the cons, maybe ask for someone else's input, surf the net to see what others have said or done, and then analyze the evidence and commit one way or another. In other words, whether you need to buy something or write something, the process of critical analysis is similar.

To describe or interpret or evaluate a literary text, the first step is to know your own voice. By voice I don't simply mean a comfortable style. I mean how your language resonates with your beliefs. Remember, your interpretation or evaluation is based on your response to the text as a reader. That doesn't mean you can't draw from other published scholars or theorists, but make sure it is your voice and your interpretation that comes through in the end.[1]

But how do you do this? And what do you say about a text that hasn't been said before? This seems especially true if you are reading older, more canonical texts such as Emily Dickinson or Harriet Beecher Stowe, Shakespeare or William Faulkner—about whom so much has been written already. A good place to start is to decide not what you are going to say, but why. Ask yourself why you did or did not value this story. Given the amount of time and work a critical text demands, if you aren't invested in the direction of the paper, then the writing will become a tedious and painful process. Your answer to why you do or do not value the text will become the driving force behind the research and the evolution of your ideas. The "why" of your paper must reflect your investment in the topic and will explore what it is that you as reader bring to the text.

BEING CRITICAL: DESCRIBE THE TEXT

The simplest or most direct way to arrive at a critical understanding of a text is to describe it. To do this, you need to look at how a text works—literally how it says what it says. What, you ask yourself, does the text tell you about itself? Think about your reaction to a text that begins with the familiar "once upon a time"; you expect a fairy tale or children's story, complete with good and bad characters and some sort of a lesson. If you are looking at a poem, do the last words in each line rhyme? Is there repetition of certain sounds or words that seem to add emphasis to what the poet has written (see Chapter 3)? If a piece of fiction, look at plot, point of view, character, setting, symbolism, style, theme (see Chapter 2). What the authors of these chapters have done is to provide you with access points for your entry into an analysis or critique of a particular piece of literature.

[1] For an in-depth discussion of the way to approach and incorporate secondary sources (research) into your writing, look at Chapter 15.

Chapter 12   Critical Essays: Engaging with the Text and the World Around You   **159**

Look at Emily Dickinson's "My Life had stood—a Loaded Gun—" and ask yourself what you might say if someone asks you to describe the text:

My Life had stood—a Loaded Gun—
In Corners—till a Day
The Owner passed—identified—
And carried Me away—

And now We roam in Sovereign Woods—
and now We hunt the Doe—
and every time I speak for Him—
The Mountains straight reply—

And do I smile, such cordial light
Upon the Valley glow—
It is as a Vesuvian face
Had let its pleasure through—

And when at Night—Our good Day done—
I guard My Master's Head—
'Tis better than the Eider-Duck's
Deep Pillow to have shared—

To foe of His—I'm deadly foe—
None stir the second time—
On whom I lay a Yellow Eye—
Or an emphatic Thumb—

Though I than He—may longer live
He longer must—than I—
For I have but the power to kill,
Without—the power to die—

1863

In the first place, you might describe its basic structure: a poem with six 4-line stanzas and an irregular rhyming pattern. Looking more closely, you might notice that she seems to use capital letters in unexpected ways. Why capitalize the final words in the first two lines—"Gun" and "Day"—but not the next two—"identified" and "away?" The former are nouns and the latter a verb and a direction marker; that is a good distinction and you see it repeated again in the next stanza. Then it all breaks down in the third. Why? And why use dashes in the place of commas and periods throughout until the second to last line? By simply looking at how the text is written, you can discover a litany of questions and possible readings that will contribute to your understanding of it.

BEING CRITICAL: QUESTION THE TEXT

To interpret is to decide what a text says and means to you as the reader; others, many others, may have reacted to and written about the same text but you bring to it your own voice and experience.[2] For example, when asked to interpret this poem, the students in this particular class argued and wrote quite convincingly that this poem was about a lament on the death of traditional religion; a woman's first sexual experience; a celebration of capitalist culture; a feminist critique of patriarchal society; an insomniac's long night; a mother's love for her child; a widow grieving for her now-dead spouse. And yet, when you look at this poem, chances are you see none of these. You wonder: Did they read the same poem? Who is "right"?

The student who felt that the poem talked about the death of traditional religion brought her conservative religious upbringing to her reading. She saw the speaker in the poem as the defender of the faith and justified her reading with the lines "To foe of His—I'm deadly foe—" and the capitalization of His, He, Him, My Master as indicative of a powerful religious figure. However, another student argued that the gun was clearly a phallic image and therefore represented a woman's first sexual experience. The feminists in the class read the Owner/Master figure as representative of patriarchal society guilty of oppressing women, as depicted in the submissive "I" of the poem who "guard[s] my Master's Head—" and who is dependent upon the patriarchal figure to free her through death: "For I have but the power to kill, / Without—the power to die—."

In one small class, these are just some of the reactions students had to the text—reactions that they were able to justify through a close reading and analysis of the lines and images of the poem. These students did not simply run to the library or the computer, pull up several books or articles on Dickinson, find a series of quotations that seem connected to their topic, and then fill in the blank spaces around those quotations until they reached the necessary page length. Instead, they decided what it was they wanted to demonstrate, or argue for, and then they turned to the text to find the evidence they needed.

The question of interpretation is difficult—students frequently want to know the "right" answer (sometimes felt to be synonymous with what the professor says) as if literature could offer a definitive or "correct" reading. And yet, the appeal of reading literary texts is that there is no one definitive answer. Remember, each reader reads with his or her own unique perspective, a perspective shaped by each reader's unique blend of education, experience, and circumstances. In other words, interpretations of texts are bound to vary to one degree or another. If you are unsure of your initial reaction or interpretation, or confused by what you read, test possible hypotheses by writing in your journal or talking to classmates before you write the paper. Look to the text for evidence to substantiate your claim; focus on specific lines or images and ask: does this really illustrate or suggest my reading? Will others be able to understand my argument through the evidence offered by the text?

---

[2] At this point, you may be asked by your professor to incorporate a particular literary theory or critical approach with your interpretive paper. See Chapter 7 for more insight as to what this means and how you undertake it.

For example, one of my students in an American Literature class wanted to argue that Nathanael West's 1933 novel *Day of the Locust*, an apocalyptic condemnation of Hollywood, could be read and understood by listening to the Red Hot Chili Peppers' *Californication*. Despite the almost sixty-year gap between the two texts, not to mention differences in the historical context, politics, diverse artistic styles, and possible audiences, Spencer sensed and successfully argued that the overlaps between the two texts suggested that the band was familiar with West's text and that today's readers of West can identify with and comprehend West's criticisms by listening to the contemporary reiteration of the same condemnation of society. Spencer substantiated his argument by quoting from and then explicating passages and lyrics from both texts.

That is not to say that Spencer's reading of West is the "right" reading; instead, it is one of many possible readings stimulated by the text, clearly articulated and substantiated by evidence from the text itself.

BEING CRITICAL: "SO WHAT?"

To evaluate a text is to ask the "so what" question about it: So what makes this text important or interesting? So what's it worth? Your answer to the "so what" question explains why a text is worth reading or why it isn't. One of the most insightful papers I read this year explained the author's ambivalence about the latest Dream Works production *The Road to El Dorado*, an animated "children's" film about Spain's exploration/exploitation of Central America. Neil begins his paper with the acknowledgment that he himself is a "pro-Disney man"—implying an anti–Dream Works stand. In addition, he read several Internet sites arguing that the film perpetuated negative stereotypes of Latina/Latino people:

```
Armed with the angry e-mail and my preconceived notions
of this movie, I sat in the theatre ready to rip the film
apart. As soon as the credits started I tried to find neg-
ative images and misconceptions, anything that could be
construed as perpetuating the stereotypes I had learned in
school. But I was disappointed; the first part was in Spain,
where the heroes of the film taught kids that cheat[ing]
at dice games was okay and funny. I figured I would use this
as a side note in my paper, that the movie taught chil-
dren that dishonesty was okay. I figured that as soon as
they reached "El Dorado" the really offensive stuff would
begin. However, somewhere in the boat ride over, I lost
my negative view of the movie and started to enjoy it.
```

Neil's initial evaluation of the film, before he saw it, was based solely on what others had said about the film, and so he started to interpret armed with someone else's ideas. However, he discovered that his reading of the film differed greatly from the secondary sources he had read, so it was not until he let go of those other opinions that his own interpretation of the film became pleasurable, positive, and authoritative.

BEING CRITICAL: PULLING IT ALL TOGETHER

Although the previous pages present the acts of description, interpretation, and evaluation independently of each other, in reality, most acts of critical reading and writing contain elements of all three, as it is almost impossible to interpret a text without some evidence of evaluation or to describe something without your interpretation or evaluation making itself known.

To illustrate, look at Caitlyn's analysis of the role and use of vernacular language in *The Adventures of Huckleberry Finn* as an extension of her study of the role of Ebonics in contemporary culture:

```
In terms of writing, one of the great American novels, The
Adventures of Huckleberry Finn, by Mark Twain, would lose
much of its meaning and representation if Ebonics was
replaced with Standard English. Ebonics, in the following
example, was the language spoken by Jim, a slave in the
novel: "En when I wake up en fine you back agin', all safe
en soun de tears come, en I could a got down on my knees
en kiss' you' foot, I's so thankful." (68)
```

Caitlyn's reading of Twain focuses on the role that an author's creative dialogue plays in shaping our understanding and perceptions of cultures in ways that are both enabling and disempowering. In this case, it is obvious that her argument about the text, based on a description of its specific language, calls upon some element of evaluation as well.

In another critical piece that relies heavily on description to enable both evaluation and interpretation, Katie picks up and chooses to emulate the short, highly visual structure of the texts that she is critiquing: We can almost "hear" the protest against rape, chains, and oppressions that she is describing:

```
A paint brush has the strength of the proverbial pen. As
artists use this power to mirror the chains that bind them,
and "us." The Social Protest Art Festival used the strength
of one individual piece of protest to form a broader shout
of protest. A shout of protest against rape. The beauti-
ful model. Male dominance. White dominance. Cages. Chains.
Oppression. Each piece of protest, each piece of art, held
the protester's own consciousness, memories, experiences.
In exhibiting these individual truths, a broader, more
intimate concept is shaped.
```

Here, the form that she uses underscores the effectiveness of her analysis of the texts; moreover, look at her careful and deliberate word choices. Why do you think she shifts from the "them" of the artists to this "us"? By incorporating this term, she has pulled "us" as readers and audience into her text and into her experience; she is showing us, making us feel a part of the experience, instead of merely telling us about it.

Chapter 12   Critical Essays: Engaging with the Text and the World Around You   **163**

ESTABLISHING A CRITICAL DIALOGUE

In the same way that carefully buying a snowboard is an active, back and forth, critical process, so, too, are reading and writing. Being critical about anything means participating in a dialogue about the object of your critical stance, asking—then answering—both pro and con questions: What's good about it? What's not so good? How does the evidence prove one or the other position? And if you, the writer, don't ask critical questions, you can bet some of your readers will. Therefore, the critical writer anticipates critical questions from the reader at the outset. The critical writer acknowledge what others have said before and makes clear what he or she brings the interpretation that is new—age, sex, sexual preference, politics, religion, race, ethnic group, linguistic group, socioeconomic status, life experiences, and so on. And it is this personalized experience that enables the critical writer to say something or to disagree with what someone else may have said about the same text.

Most critical essays written for English classes will require you to work with the primary text—the book or poem or play or film you are reading. In some cases, you will also be asked to examine secondary materials—articles, book reviews, biographies of the author, interviews, online as well as printed journal material. What this doesn't mean, however, is that you let someone else's ideas speak for you or that you rely on someone else's words to make your point (see Chapter 15 on Research Writing). What this does mean is that you find your own voice and interpretation, whatever that may be, and then work to substantiate that view with evidence from the text itself and from other sources if necessary.

Your place of entry into a text may be a point about which you disagree, question, or are confused. Starting with your own personal conflict about a text is a good strategy because it suggests that something truly bothers you about the text. It also encourages the use of "I" in your essay. Don't worry that you have been told in the past not to use "I" in formal writing; I find that my students have an easier time becoming invested in a paper if they can hear and see their own voices in their argument instead of reading the more neutral and distant "one" or "s/he." That is not to say that all professors want to see "I" in your paper. Some may legitimize your first-person presence in early drafts of critical papers or in more personal writing such as journals, but not in final papers.

In the following example, Sindia enters into a dialogue with Latina writer and theorist Gloria Anzaldúa's text "How to tame a wild tongue" in order to question and to clarify what it is she feels Anzaldúa is saying:

```
I did not experience the life that Gloria Anzaldúa had.
She was confused on what dialect of Spanish to use: I knew
that at home, I spoke Spanish and when I was out, I spoke
English. I never questioned why others did not understand
```

> what I was saying before I learned English. I just knew that
> I had to learn the language due to the area that I was
> living in. I never had anyone tell me directly "If you
> want to be American, speak 'American.' I also did not have
> anyone telling me "*Que vale toda tu educacion si todavia
> hablas ingles con un* 'accent.'" Although I never had any-
> one say these things to me, I guess that was what was being
> done to me. I was learning English and at the same time
> learning how to speak without an accent.

She starts with a reaction to Anzaldúa's piece that suggests that she is disagreeing with what she just read, but ultimately, through her questioning and critique of Anzaldúa's text, Sindia discovers that she comes to the same realizations as Anzaldúa. However, it took her personal interaction with the text to get there. Had Sindia not combined the personal voice and experiences with her interpretation of the text, her paper might have gone off in an entirely different direction, one that might not have taught Sindia something about herself as she worked through Anzaldúa's ideas. In this case, she surely experienced the idea that we write to learn.

The use of "I" as demonstrated by Sindia's essay may not be a strategy for all students; the following is an example of a dialogue between a student and two texts that avoids the "I" voice, but conveys a personal commitment to the subject nonetheless. Travis, a film aficionado, explored the influence of T. S. Eliot's 1922 *The Waste Land* on the 1991 movie *The Fisher King*. He began his paper with the following:

> In their works "The Waste Land" (T. S. Eliot, 1922) and
> *The Fisher King* (1991, directed by Terry Gilliam), both
> artists approach the Grail Myth from a decidedly twentieth-
> century perspective. Though similar, Eliot tantalizes us
> with the hint of redemption, like the promise of a coming
> spring, whereas Gilliam, in his indefatigable optimism,
> actually unfurls spring like a triumphant banner.

The direction and "so what" of Travis's paper is clear; his use of "us" draws the reader into the essay implying an interactive dialogue between reader and writer, and he delineates the premise of his argument by offering examples of overlap and divergence through his opening lines. Like Sindia, Travis made clear his personal voice and investment although through an implicit rather than explicit strategy that might be more comfortable for many students.

Several years ago, I had a Russian student in one of my classes who was preparing for medical school and who told me he had no time or tolerance for the study of literature. He wasn't interested in meter or alliteration; he wanted to know the reason that someone would actually bother to sit down and write poetry. Because he was so used to reading facts and technical pieces, his resistance to poetry was the first obstacle he had to overcome to become a critical reader. Although unhappy when I asked him to write about his reactions to a poem, he realized he had much more to say than simply "this sucks." Trying to articulate why he didn't like the poem and all its images and irregular punctuation, he discovered that in fact he really was a good critical reader because he was able to talk about individual lines and metaphors and engage in a dialogue with other possible interpretations. For him, recognizing that reading and writing are inherently connected was an important step, and one that enabled him to see that no piece of writing exists in a vacuum. Even though the meaning of Emily Dickinson's "My Life had stood—a Loaded Gun—" continued to frustrate him, he explored his reactions to Dickinson and the text in his writing. Through his writing, he discovered that both reading and writing are active and engaging dialogues between the reader and the text, dialogues that pose a problem or seek to answer or respond to it. And so, armed with the understanding that being intellectual is a means to engage with the real world and not a way to live outside of it, he was no longer reluctant and unable to enter into a dialogue with a nineteenth-century poet or an early twentieth-century writer. For him, access to a text was still, in a sense, a search for the "why bother" answer, but in doing so, he found his voice and two A's on his way to medical school.

Another one of my students, Katie, as part of a larger piece exploring the role of written and visual texts of social protest, chose as her starting point the definition of "oppression" as offered by the *New Webster's* dictionary. Now, this is a fairly common strategy among student writers, to rely on the authority of the dictionary as a means to add authority and credibility to what it is they are discussing:

```
My friend Webster and his answers are not needed. I find
my own definition as I think of all the reasons why it
sucks to be a girl. The weaker sex, the fairer sex, blue
is for boys and red is for girls. I don't feel weak or
fair. I love blue. I feel weak only when I remember how
vulnerable I am to rape, as a female as well as a col-
lege student. One of three, Kate, one of three. Be care-
ful not to be the one of the three to get raped, and
remember don't give any boys the wrong idea. The iceberg,
just the tip of it all. The floodgates open to my defin-
ition of being a female, a minority. I know that my friend
Webster cannot answer it all.
```

This is an acceptable strategy if you are able to start with the definition but ultimately move to a definition that is clearly your own. However, what made Katie's paper both powerful and effective in my eyes was the fact that by the end of the paper, she came to the realization that *Webster's* wasn't enough, that she could move beyond the reliance on another's words to discover the power in her own. Look at her use of the first person "I" and how she juxtaposes it with the distant and distancing third person "he" that she associates with the *Webster's* dictionary.

Ultimately, what you are doing when you write critically is engaging with a text in such a way that you enter into a larger discussion with the world around you. As I have tried to demonstrate, you produce acts of interpretation every day, whether in writing or in speech. To be able to organize those ideas, to substantiate them through evidence, to convince your audience of the validity of your point of view, to decide upon and in some way answer the "so what" question— is what it means to think and write critically, and it is a skill and a practice that extends far beyond your experiences as an English major.

SUGGESTIONS FOR WRITING CRITICAL ESSAYS

No matter how exploratory, tentative, and loose your early drafts of a critical essay, your final draft needs to respect certain academic conventions:

1. Support all assertions with textual evidence. While I have said that interpretation is very subjective, in order to add validity to your reading of a text, you need to support what you say by referring to specific passages in the text itself. Support may also come from secondary sources that discuss that particular text or author. Use direct quotes as well as paraphrases and summaries, and acknowledge all such references with the proper documentation (who said what, where, and when).
2. Use signal phrases to introduce all quotations in your essay. A signal phrase tells (signals) the reader that someone besides you is about to speak, identifies who it is, and avoids plagiarism (using sources without acknowledging them). Frequently, you will need to draw on the primary text for substantiating evidence; in this case, you will also need to use signal phrases and provide a sense of context for your reader. For example,

   In Ruth Ozeki's *My Year of Meats,* the Japanese-American documentary maker Jane Takagi-Little makes clear her opinion regarding the American image she is to "sell" to Japanese housewives with the following statement: "During my Year of Meats, I made documentaries about an exotic and vanishing America for consumption on the flip side of the planet, and I learned a lot" (15).

   Introducing both primary and secondary source authors by name into the body of your text informs and clarifies your essay as well as it tells an academic reader that you know how to write academic essays.
3. Use the present tense to refer to actions that take place in the text itself. Whether you are discussing Mark Twain's nineteenth-century books or twenty-first-century films, write as if the text is alive in the present. To illustrate, look again at Caitlyn's reading of *Huckleberry Finn:* she says "Jim speaks in Ebonics in the text" not "Jim spoke in Ebonics in the text."

   Use the past tense to refer to historical events in the past. If she were to discuss the role of slavery in the nineteenth century, as an historical reality, she would use the past tense: "The American institution of slavery was an oppressive and unjust system based on assumptions of racial inequality."

4. When in doubt about format or documentation matters refer to the MLA Appendix at the end of this text; for additional information, consult the most recent edition of the *MLA Handbook for Writers of Research Papers*.

WORKS CITED

Dickinson, Emily. "My Life had stood—a Loaded Gun—" in *The Complete Poems of Emily Dickinson*. Ed. Thomas H. Johnson. Boston: Little, Brown and Company, 1960.

Edmundson, Mark. *Nightmare on Main Street*. Cambridge, MA: Harvard University Press, 1997.

Kisonak, Rick. "Talking Pictures: Review." *Seven Days* (vermont) 5, no. 37 (10 May 2000).

Ozeki, Ruth L. *My Year of Meats*. New York: Penguin Books, 1998.

CHAPTER 13

Writing Personal Essays about Literature

Mary Jane Dickerson

It was only after I descended from the trees, and tasted the joys and sorrows of becoming a scientist, that I began to meditate upon the magic city and to see in it a mirror image of the big world that I was entering. I was plunged into the big world abruptly, like Philip. The big world, wherever I looked, was full of human tragedy. I came upon the scene and found myself playing roles that were half serious and half preposterous. And that is the way it has continued ever since.

Beginning with the vivid memory of a childhood reading of Edith Nesbit's novel *The Magic City* and his identification with Philip, Freeman Dyson narrates his development as a nuclear scientist in terms of the many interrelationships between his life and what he reads. In *Disturbing the Universe,* Dyson writes his autobiography as a scientist against the act of reading Nesbit's book and many others as he was growing up in England. Writing personal responses to literature often assumes such autobiographical frames of reference with some similarities to what Jane Tompkins describes in "An Introduction to Reader-Response Criticism" when she says "Reading and writing join hands, change places, and finally become distinguishable only as two names for the same activity" (x). But writing a personal response to literature differs from reader-response criticism because the interrelationships between life and literature are themselves the focus rather than the interpretation of literary texts. In this chapter, we will look at ways students of literature can weave life experiences into reading experiences to create a new kind of text—the personal essay about literature.

    This kind of personal essay can resemble the human voice talking just as the mind works—in a natural outpouring without the more systematic ordering of argument and ideas usually associated with literary criticism, even less formal reader-response criticism. Indeed, each act of writing may generate a difference in perspective and voice according to the needs and the constraints of the particular piece of writing, because each of us possesses many selves. Behind every essay *about* literature or *in response to* literature, but especially in the personal essay, there exists such an "I" informing the whole.

Chapter 13   Writing Personal Essays about Literature   **169**

Learning how to place yourself at the center of writing about literature beyond the formal critical essay also gives you ways to speak to audiences beyond students and professors. Because this essay writing is exploratory in nature rather than expository, you are able to discover your personal connections to the literature you study in order to make these works and their words a part of your life. This process of discovery is what you make real through putting it into words—or, to put it another way, in the personal essay you combine what you think with what you are. Such a personal approach to writing literary essays has a long history that continues today as readers delight in sharing with each other the pleasures of poetry, fiction, nonfiction, and drama. From the sharp wit of Addison and Steele in the eighteenth century decrying such poetic practices as composing poems in the shapes of wings and altars to the genial and open tones of John Updike as he describes our times through what he reads and shares with us, personal reactions to reading enlarge the possibilities of literature to inform our lives.

CREATING A NEW TEXT

Since the personal response to a text merges the act of reading with the activity of making an essay, you also have the opportunity to create literature through the discovery of the "I" in your prose—who you are in relationship to what you are writing about. It happened to one student of mine as she reflected on being an English major against the texts and contexts she has met along the way. Here is the opening paragraph of Maureen's essay "Women's Studies: My Right to an Education":

> It seems my education has always been strictly divided into male and female subjects. I remember in high school telling my mother that I might be interested in being a veterinarian. She frowned at this and told me that I wouldn't really like being around sick animals. I began to wonder if my fondness for biology was abnormal because even though dissecting a crayfish was not a milestone in my life, my parents trivialized my enthusiasm about it in comparison to the praise they lavished on my maudlin poetry and oil paintings. While my parents and teachers forgave my incompetence in mathematics, they encouraged my interest in literature.

Maureen's life experience—her story—sets up an autobiographical frame of reference for the story of her educational experience.

In the following paragraph, Maureen's personal experience merges with what she has read to create a richer context for synthesizing meanings and implications for women studying a body of literature largely determined by and taught by men:

> My college introductory course in British and American literature contained a token selection of poems and essays by women. While we spent four classes on Wordsworth's *Prelude*, we only spent one class on Virginia Woolf. While we read Hemingway's *The Sun Also Rises*, we ignored *Jacob's Room*, *The Waves*, and *To The Lighthouse*. Instead, we read Woolf's essays, "A Room of One's Own" and "Professions of Women." In doing so, we acknowledged Woolf as a woman who wrote and not as the innovative writer of fiction that she is. Ironically, even though Woolf has a chapter next to Joyce in the *Norton Anthology of English Literature*, she can be, like Shakespeare's sister, a "lost novelist" because of the perfunctory treatment she receives in the classroom.

This essay reflects a process of intellectual integration as Maureen examines her educational experience since childhood through a lens that allows her to organize meaning in a powerful way.

Maureen has listened to the voices of the writers included in her English courses as she has listened to the voices of her family and teachers. And from the integration of these voices into her own experience, she has forged a personal perspective by writing an extended essay in which she examines how far our society has yet to go before all its citizens have the same rights and freedoms of education. The final paragraph of "Women's Studies: My Right to an Education" illustrates how far she's moved from the details of her own educational experience toward the kind of insight she needs to pose imaginative and important questions:

> Intellectual integration from grammar school through college is most important. It took until 1948 for women to gain the legal right to learn as stated in the United Nations Declaration of Human Rights. Not only should everyone have the right to education, but "Education shall be directed to the full development of the human personality and the strengthening of respect for human rights and fundamental freedoms." I wonder how long it will take until the world decides that Women's Studies, as a discipline, should be instrumental in the development of these rights and freedoms.

In this essay, Maureen has engaged an audience beyond the confines of classroom, academic major, and even college or university.

MY STORY

As a first year college student, when I was assigned to read Faulkner's story "A Rose for Emily," I immediately recognized that not only was I reading about a character in a small town in rural Mississippi but I was also reading about a woman who lived as close as two houses down the road in my own rural North Carolina. What I was in the act of reading merged with the shocking memory of Miss Vera McLean, who, like Miss Emily Grierson, was found dead days later, cloistered in a shuttered house and whose life also generated speculative gossip. It was as if from that moment on, writing about a work of literature was no longer an abstract exercise, but one that held possibilities of knowing unlike any other I had ever encountered. In "A Sketch of the Past," Virginia Woolf describes this sort of experience for herself as a writer: "It is the rapture I get when in writing I seem to be discovering what belongs to what.... It proves that one's life is not confined to one's body and what one says and does; one is living all the time in relation to certain background ... conceptions" (27). Since I first glimpsed these connections through reading, I have also written about those characters who peopled my childhood by filling my poems with them. Writing and living have continued to overlap through both reading and writing.

All serious readers undergo such shocks of recognition and find themselves forever altered by what they read. No matter whether we are writing about a fictional life, an actual life, or indeed our own lives, what autobiographer Wallace Fowlie says rings true: "Writing is indeed a process of self-alteration. Living belongs to the past. Writing is the present" (275). We make connections with the voices in fiction, in autobiography, in poetry, in our own various texts, and of those people surrounding us as part of our everyday lives. We keep reading, we keep listening, and we keep writing.

William Faulkner's representations and visions of reality have offered me ways to make sense of my own "postage stamp of the universe." Perhaps you can name the writer who has done the same for you. Although I have never recovered from that powerful initiation, the "I" who writes occasionally about Faulkner and other American authors has undergone transformations and has learned to listen to the many potential and possible voices that enable writing literary criticism as well as poems, essays, letters, and journals as the need and desire arise.

PERSONAL ESSAYS

Let's pause for a moment to list some adjectives that describe writing personal responses to literature through the personal essay:

- **Autobiographical:** Use "I" frequently even when autobiography is not central.
- **Conversational:** Create a friendly sense of equality between yourself and your reader (or audience).
- **Exploratory:** Be reflective, even imaginative, rather than explanatory or analytical (or persuasive).
- **Creative:** Whenever appropriate, consider how reflecting on the act of writing might allow you to participate in the creative process of the literary work—in the production of meaning itself.
- **Open:** Rather than coming to a conventional kind of conclusion that ties things together, try, instead, to follow where the central idea might lead you

toward other possibilities, thereby encouraging the play of ideas that resists the finality of usual conclusion or closure.

Of course, not all personal essays about literature exhibit each of these features, but I think you'll find many of them present in contemporary essays published in places like *The American Scholar, The New York Review of Books, Shenandoah, The Georgia Review,* and *The New Yorker.* Here's an example from *The New York Times Book Review,* "Staying Alive by Learning to Write," an essay in which Swiss writer Adolf Muschg reflects on the exclusion of the writer and "creative writing' from the Swiss university:

> Until fairly recently, for a European professor to admit that he or she was secretly doing some "creative writing" was tantamount to academic suicide. One could do serious work *on* writing or writers, but they had better be dead. Knowing something about current literature, if you claimed to be a scholar, implied the proud modesty of not even trying your own hand at it—or it would wither from the sacrilege.
>
> I happen to write and teach German literature ... (1).

From the beginning, Muschg engages our attention from his own perspective as both teacher and writer in the university and as both a scholarly and an imaginative writer.

Autobiography

To stimulate a rich identification between students and their literary subjects, I often distribute an autobiographical questionnaire to help students generate their reponses during the entire semester as part of their course journal. For my literature courses, autobiographical reflection encourages students to connect the narratives they see within their own lives to the narratives that they are reading in various literary genres. Responding to these questions can stimulate richly conceived essays in which you actively integrate your experience into your understanding of others' texts. Questions about the self can arm you with a powerful invention tool to create textual forms that may uniquely represent your writerly identity. At least, posing such questions is worth a try. Here is a list of questions that you can use as a guideline and add to as you read:

Autobiographical Questionnaire

1. Is there any dominant physical trait, gesture, or feature in a character that gives you special insight into yourself? Of others close to you? How does this recognition affect your response to the character? The work? Consider the reverse as well: For example, do you exhibit a dominant trait, gesture, or feature that helps you understand a character?
2. Is there a character who resembles you in important ways? Describe the similarities.

Chapter 13   Writing Personal Essays about Literature

3. What physical objects in your reading—such as the flowering pear tree in Zora Hurston's *Their Eyes Were Watching God* or the broken pocket watch in William Faulkner's *The Sound and the Fury*—do you associate with yourself, your parents, or others? What does their appearance make you think about?
4. What are you most passionate about in your reading—such as those human interrelationships with the natural world depicted in Ernest Hemingway's "Big Two Hearted River" and Annie Dillard's *Pilgrim at Tinker Creek?* How does this recognition affect your response?
5. What of your major fears do you also find in literary characters—such as the sudden death of a parent in Charles Dickens's *David Copperfield?* What inhibitions or desires?
6. What patterns or events in your own life do you see reflected in your reading—such as the adolescent's desire for the transforming power of beauty and romance in James Joyce's "Araby"? What similarities and/or differences?
7. What are the motivating forces of your own life that set up particular responses to the literary work—such as John Wideman's need to explore how brothers could come from the same family yet take such opposing paths in his memoir *Brothers and Keepers?*
8. What place or setting (interior, landscape, street) in your reading do you identify with most and why?
9. What have you found most disturbing or disquieting (or pleasurable and satisfying?) about what you are reading—such as the rendering of the Holocaust through cartoon in *Maus* by Art Spiegelman? Why?
10. What connections do you see between some aspect of political or social life in the present and political and social life in an earlier work—such as the entrenched racial inequities reflected in, for example, Richard Wright's *Native Son?*
11. How do you see the past affecting the present in your own life? In the lives of those in your reading?
12. What is your earliest memory of reading or being read to—such as Freeman Dyson's memory of Nesbit's *The Magic City?* Do you remember the book's title? What are your favorite books and those that remain most vividly a part of you? How might these earlier reading experiences have affected your responses to literature in the present?

What follows are some journal explorations students have made in response to the autobiographical questionnaire; in each case, the writer found possibilities for the personal essay. One student describes his obsession with his running in answer to the question about being altered in some way by what he is reading, here Annie Dillard's *Pilgrim at Tinker Creek*. Remembering Dillard's meditation on what she learned of consciousness in contrast to self-consciousness while seeing a cedar (the "tree with the lights in it") caught in the rays of the setting sun, Adrian muses on his own moment while running, akin to Dillard's own heightened sense of "time, which had flowed down into the tree bearing new revelations like floating leaves at every moment" (80, 81):

> The syllable ME was not the center of my thoughts this fine October afternoon. Orange, red, and brown captured my imagination. I stared at the sun through the trees. Looking up at the sun, patches of color registered in my head. I felt daring enough to close my eyes for an instant; imprinted on my eyelids were kaleidoscopic images of the leaves. The death grey bark of the white birch, which is my favorite tree, reminded me of winter. I had found my own "tree with the lights in it." It had come in the form of loosely connected observances and recollections. My "tree" was not as profound or cohesive as Dillard's, but that did not matter. It was my own. (Adrian)

This material from his own daily experience finally turned into an exploratory essay titled "Running After Dillard," in which Dillard's sojourn at Pilgrim Creek altered Adrian's own running attitudes and habits.

In another journal entry, a student describes the experience of hearing Hayden Carruth read his own poetry:

> I had never gone to hear a poet speak or read his poetry before in person. But I got what I expected. I expected to feel special because I was in the same room as an excellent poet. I expected to hear other works not in the book we read and to get more meaning from poems I had already read because he would be speaking the voice that originally spoke them before they were written down on paper.
>
> You know, after reading the above paragraph, I wonder about myself. My ability to communicate is almost nonexistent in that paragraph. (Brian)

Most of us would probably disagree with Brian and regard his intense experience of seeing, hearing, and remembering coupled with the writing and reading in his journal as a revelation of what it means to experience a poetry reading. Using oneself as a vehicle to explore the meanings of literary tests makes reading a co-creative act: acts of reading *and* writing the self. Brian later wrote an essay in which he drew on his own knowledge and performance of jazz to explore its influence on the composition of many of Carruth's poems in "Brothers, I Loved You All."

Conversation

Since writing about literature is like engaging in a personal dialogue with writers and their texts—as both Maureen and Muschg do throughout their essays—this sense of conversation, with its strong use of "I," creates a friendly relationship between writer and audience. One of the most powerful places for such dialogues to occur is in the journals described in Chapter 1. The many and varied conditions of journal writing provide a framework that encourages free-ranging writing activities that engage the self. It's as if the autobiographical journals create ideal conditions for conversations to take place between you and what you're reading—between who you are and what you think. These conversations, in turn, help bridge the gap between reading and writing that all of us experience to some degree whenever we are faced with a writing assignment.

When we write as frequently as we read, we enlarge our potential to make connections with facets of our own lives. Many writers acknowledge the pleasure they get when readers communicate just how much their works have affected their lives. Surely Alice Walker would appreciate what this reader expresses in a journal entry about how sharing *The Color Purple* with her mother enriched that reading experience for her:

> I haven't had much in common with my mother for a while, and that seemed to crumble away this weekend. She has read *The Color Purple* and we spent the whole day talking about women, her relationship with my father, her job, her education, and all that she feels about such things. For the first time in a while I found myself caring about her thoughts and listening to what she said. She talked about the book and how she would like to borrow mine to read more by Alice Walker. I told her I would send her some of her own which I promptly did when I got back to Burlington. I sent her *Once* and inscribed it with one of A. W.'s musings from "Mississippi Winter II":
>
> When you remember me, my child,
>   be sure to recall that Mama was
>   . . . . .
>   not happy
>   with fences.
>
> I think I started to really love my mother again this weekend. (Patti)

For Patti, the reading of Alice Walker encourages her to engage in conversation with communities of voices outside those she hears in the novel: she creates an informing context to enrich her own reading experience. Through conversation with her mother about a shared reading experience that, in turn, stimulates a journal reflection, Patti gets in touch with her own mother's life and reestablishes a vital connection.

Alice Walker's voice sets into play the voices of a mother and daughter that Patti meditates on in her journal. But what's even more significant here is that the student's major piece of writing for the semester turned into an examination of the nurturing and inspiring influence that earlier writer Zora Neale Hurston has had on the contemporary writer Alice Walker—another variation of mother-daughter relationships. For Patti, reflecting on the role of family as she reads Walker, whose fiction and poetry speak to all women as they explore their bonds with both their real and their adopted mothers, provides her with a perspective for writing an essay about Hurston's influence on Walker. The thematic concern in the journal entry provides the central thematic concern in an essay in which Patti traces the intertextual relationships that exist between Hurston's *Their Eyes Were Watching God* and Walker's *The Color Purple*. Through using your journal as the site for personal explorations about the literature you read, you practice the kinds of conversations that enable you to speak about yourself in the act of reading in equally powerful ways.

Exploration

Because you may not be trying to prove a point about a literary work, the form of the personal essay may take on a different shape than the exposition you are more accustomed to in which you develop a thesis and marshal support toward a persuasive and reasoned conclusion. Consider the following scenario: Your teacher makes an assignment similar to one given in a British literature course when the teacher asked students to write a personal response to their reading of a Wordsworth poem. This assignment demands a careful reading of the poem, but the interpretation must also be informed by the student's own life.

In "Expostulation and Reply," Wordsworth writes that "The eye—it cannot choose but see; / We cannot bid the ear be still; / Our bodies feel, where'er they be, / Against or with our will" (227). In response to Wordsworth's urging that we can learn much of value from nature as well as from books, you might open your essay with a description of a memorable instance of productive inner reflection or daydreaming. From this personal anecdote, you might compare the progress of Wordsworth's own process of learning from nature in a state of daydreaming as he narrates it in his poem. You might interweave other scenes from your own childhood and schooling to show how children learn from their environments as well as from formal education. In the ending of your essay, you might speculate on what we might learn from Wordsworth's poem of 1798 as contemporary educators consider lengthening the school day and going to a year-round schedule.

For a similar kind of assignment, another student recognizes in Maxine Hong Kingston's *Woman Warrior: Memoir of a Chinese Childhood Among Ghosts* about growing up with Chinese-born parents implications for his own cultural identity:

```
Since I am a third generation Chinese-American, I am fur-
ther removed than Kingston from a Chinese past. Both
of my parents speak Chinese, but I lost my ability to speak
Chinese as I grew up … and now I am unable to have any
```

> lengthy conversation with my grandmother. She does not speak English and I do not speak Chinese. We communicate through limited vocabulary and creative sign language…. I really feel a tremendous loss. Now I am learning the Chinese language and searching for my roots. For the first time in my life I am considering myself Chinese. (Jason)

As Jason considered his reading of his own life alongside reading Kingston's memoir of growing up female with "ghosts" of a Chinese past, his choice of "I" became a natural, even an inevitable act as he faced the dimension of loss in his own life. He could not write a convincing critical essay about the nature of Maxine Hong Kingston's search for gender, familial, and cultural identity without exploring and acknowledging his own Chinese-American history. It's as if these autobiographical connections prompt conversations between writers and readers so that readers also become writers of their own stories in the flexible form of the personal essay.

Writer Julian Barnes creates these conditions as he explores the sequence of events that led him to write a novel about Flaubert rather than a biography in his essay "The Follies of Writer Worship":

> I once owned a piece of Somerset Maugham's gate. Well, not exactly Somerset Maugham's gate—it wasn't pillaged from the Villa Mauresque—but near enough. My chunk of literary wood came from the vicarage at Whitstable where Maugham spent part of his unhappy childhood. (1)

From the "piece of Maugham's gate," Barnes proceeds to the contemplation of two stuffed parrots, each alleged to be the inspirations for Flaubert's short story "A Simple Heart." From the mystery surrounding the parrots, he moves toward the process of discovery he himself undergoes as he ponders how best to use his research about Flaubert. The creative process of the essay reflects the creative process of making the fiction resulting in Barnes' own novel, *Flaubert's Parrot*. At the essay's close, Barnes reminds us of his beginnings and anticipates what might lie ahead for one who indulges in "The Follies of Writer Worship":

> I no longer own my spar of Somerset Maugham's gate. It disappeared in a move, or was burned by mistake, or stolen to patch someone else's gate. Besides, I am no longer quite so keen on Maugham. But I have something else now, an odder and more poignant trophy—an unopened packet of Disque Bleu that was found at Arthur Koestler's elbow after his suicide two years ago. The cigarettes sit on a shelf a few feet from my desk. I look at them from time to time … (8)

Where might this reminder of the despair behind such an indictment of twentieth-century inhumanity as *Darkness at Noon* take Barnes next?

Just as Julian Barnes's essay illustrates, whenever we write we are engaged in making meanings out of the material world we inhabit that also contain the traces of others, but these meanings are never fixed or static on the page (or on the screen or the world, for that matter); these meanings shape texts constantly undergoing construction as readers read and remake them through the lenses of their own representations of reality. Writing through such awareness of what happens is akin to what Joan Didion describes in the opening lines of her essay, "Why I Write":

> Of course I stole the title for this talk from George Orwell. One reason I stole it was that I like the sound of the words: *Why I Write*. There you have three short unambiguous words that share a sound, and the sound they share is this:
> I
> I
> I (257).

Didion continues the exploration of her preoccupation with the sound of her own voice and its significance for her identity as a writer. By acknowledging her debt to Orwell's essay, she places herself in the company of those who see writing as a process of creating the "I."

Engaging the Creative Process

Another student took full advantage of this process of creating the "I" to shape an essay he called "Purgatory," in which he writes of his own life against reading Virginia Woolf's *A Room of One's Own* and Dante's *Divine Comedy*. Here is how Charles opens the piece: "Virginia Woolf—that was the name embossed on the tattered binder of the slim black book. It was strange the significance the name and the book had taken in my life."

Charles traces his memory of hearing about this book from earlier high school years when "I was excited to add her to my growing list of 'must reads.' She joined Milton, Melville, and Hemingway." In college, Hemingway remained prominent while Woolf remained unread, but Charles's involvement with women friends whose growing interests in feminist ideas and issues began to affect him as well—often in spite of himself: "A few months later Deidre took *A Room of One's Own* out [of the library] in my name, read it, and left it on my desk. I asked her about it. I wanted her to sum up the answers it contained and hand them to me ready for consumption." After a period of time had passed with the loss of Deidre as lover and friend, Virginia Woolf's book remained as yet unread until "I started to read" these words: "'But, you may say, we asked you to speak about women and fiction—what has that got to do with a room of one's own?' I nearly slammed the book shut in my shock. What was this woman doing—talking directly to me? I hadn't asked anything. Shouldn't she just leave me alone and let me read her story and take it as I wish? Something was obviously wrong here."

Charles examines his own troubling relationships with and attitudes toward women through his responses to the constant sound of Virginia Woolf's voice. The autobiographical essay takes on the shape of a dialogue between aspiring male writer and authoritative female writer—a twist on the usual gender roles, with Charles in the role of Dante and Virginia Woolf as Vergil:

```
Virginia Woolf, with her casual yet firm voice, seemed
to be offering her hand to anyone who was willing to under-
```

> take the journey. Convinced I would not reach the end without her as my guide, I took hold of her hand. Mine was sweaty.
>   No sooner had we begun than Virginia asserted, "Fiction here is likely to contain more truth than fact…. I need not say what I am about to describe has no existence."
>   I squeezed her hand tighter—no existence—for she deemed the earth below my feet to be imaginary, and it sank away. Before my vertigo subsided, I found we were walking along the venerable turf of Oxford University, surrounded by its ancient buildings, sacred churches, and revered libraries—this was something of a comfort.

In this excerpt, Charles makes use of the imagined experience to mingle with details of his reality and the language of Woolf's text to organize meaning into a text of his own.

Several features distinguish the textual form of "Purgatory" in addition to its literary allusions and resonances. First, the author keeps the piece firmly grounded in place. He describes his scene of reading as follows and keeps referring to that place until the end of reading *A Room of One's Own:*

> I picked it up one day, and lay beneath a tall, strong maple tree which was caressed by an unusually brilliant sun. Its leaves were just beginning to ignite; some on top were unusually bright red, and the rest were in various stages of combustion—orange, yellow, and green. I was as happy as I could hope, under the circumstances, under the tree on the thick grass on a fine September day.
>   I started to read.

The second most important feature of Charles's essay is the way he relies on dialogue to advance the narrative and its revelatory power. The central dialogue is the one he carries on with Virginia Woolf as his mentor, using her actual language in combination with his imagined (yet real!) language:

> All through lunch Virginia's insistent question, "why, why are men so angry?" rang in my head. It was driving me crazy. Meanwhile Virginia read the newspaper. Suddenly she announced, "The most transient visitor to this planet must see that England is under the rule of a patriarchy." I perked up. The ringing question stopped. This was common ground. I agreed enthusiastically, remembering my paper on Milton, "*Paradise Lost:* A Poetical Rationalization of Patriarchy." Yes, the domination of women is key to upholding social hierarchies, the state, and …

Charles constantly punctuates this dialogue with Virginia Woolf by references to other writers interspersed with dialogues with his sister, Deidre, and other women in his life. In these remembered conversations, Charles realizes the many connections between Woolf's words and his own relationships with women and his attitudes about male and female in art and as artists. Woolf's own metaphor of the mirror also inspires Charles's recognition of how that same image in his own relationships with the women in his life makes it a central metaphor of his essay as it is in Woolf's:

> Virginia returned to the question. Why are men angry? Her calm voice shattered my careful logical constructions. "Life for both sexes … is arduous, difficult, a perpetual struggle … it calls for confidence in oneself. And how can we generate this imponderable quality most quickly? By thinking that people are inferior to oneself?" I nearly choked…. "Women have served all these centuries as looking-glasses possessing the magic and the delicious power of reflecting the figure of man at twice the natural size."
>
> Sheri, my little sister, not yet five, sat across from me on the floor. She looked in a toy mirror and pretended to apply makeup. I sauntered over and knocked it out of her hands.

True to memory and true to the way memory operates in time, the third feature Charles's writing displays so vividly is that, although a narrative, his autobiographical essay moves around in time so that the contemporary consciousness becomes intrinsic to the development of the self. He writes:

> Virginia kept pushing further and further, memory after memory crowded my mind.
>
> "The looking-glass vision is of supreme importance because it changes the vitality; it stimulates the nervous system. Take it away and a man may die like a drug fiend deprived of his cocaine."
>
> Cocaine! cooo-caine….. Karla, my high school girl-friend, … sat on my bed….
>
> "Yeh, Karla, let's do another line—I still have to write that paper."
>
> "But I have to drive home, and the roads are terrible."

This mirrorlike scene also continues as Charles recognizes yet another painful instance of his exploitation of women, especially with regard to writing—a recurring theme in this self-examination.

Moving around in time and evoking many voices in literature and in his own life through full, developed scenes and settings enable Charles to create a textual form that, although clearly linked to what writers in the past from Dante to Woolf have done with the actual circumstances of their own lives, expresses what he sees himself as being at this time in his education. It's a marvelous blend of reader-response literary criticism and of autobiography that calls the self into being while making a text. Through writing "Purgatory," with its intertextual resonances of Dante and Woolf, Charles expands his knowledge of autobiography as literature, the lives of men and women as writers, and the emerging contours of his own capacity for creating voices through which to give voice to his world.

Open-Ended

While it may not be appropriate on all writing occasions to use "I" as personally as I have shown it being used in this chapter, knowing more ways to incorporate your own life experience into the life of what you read whenever you write about literature gives you more choices about which voice to select for expressing yourself. Much of what I've suggested is close to William Stephany's advice in Chapter 14, "Imaginative Writing and Risk Taking." Much of what I've suggested also has links to Toby Fulwiler's "Journal Writing" (Chapter 1) and Sarah Turner's "Writing Critical Essays" (Chapter 12). It's as if the personal response to literature falls somewhere between the informality of journal writing and the more formal structures of the critical essay, bringing it closer to the passionately personal essay Cynthia Ozick has written about what has happened to Anne Frank, "Who Owns Anne Frank?"—an essay in which the writer-reader's response shapes the writing and reaches out to the many readers of *The Diary of Anne Frank*.

Perhaps I've altered the way you will regard yourself as a writer about literature while you're reading literature. You are, after all, an author whenever you write, and just *who* you are signifies a great deal for your ongoing process of self-creation. The autobiographical element in all texts is what makes all of us anxious when we show what we have written to another reader, no matter how sympathetic that reader might be: It is always as if we are being judged along with our words—our words *are* us in an important way as we seek to join a community of readers and writers through literary study. Writing autobiographically is exploratory and, for that reason, risky. Writing personal essays in response to the study of literature does not create a closed world of known answers; rather, such writing opens the writer-reader to a new world of possibilities. You may often ask, as Charles does at the end of his essay, "But how, how, I wondered, would I squeeze this onto paper? Virginia Woolf had one more answer. 'So long as you write what you wish to write, that's all that matters, and whether it matters for ages or hours, nobody can say.' I walked on."

WORKS CITED

Barnes, Julian. "The Follies of Writer Worship." *The Best American Essays 1986*. Ed. Elizabeth Hardwick and Robert Atwan. New York: Ticknor & Fields, 1986.

Didion, Joan. "Why I Write." *Eight Modern Essayists*. Ed. William Smart. 4th ed. New York: St. Martin's, 1985.

Dillard, Annie. *Pilgrim at Tinker Creek*. New York: Harper & Row, 1974.

Dyson, Freeman. *Disturbing the Universe.* New York: Harper & Row, 1979.

Fowlie, Wallace. "On Writing Autobiography." *The Southern Review* 22(1986): 273–279.

Muschg, Adolf. "Staying Alive by Learning to Write." *New York Times Book Review* February 1, 1987: 1, 27–28.

Ozick, Cynthia. *Quarrel & Quandry.* New York: Alfred A. Knopf, 2000.

Wordsworth, William. *The Norton Anthology of English Literature.* Ed. M. H. Abrams et al. 7th ed. Vol. 2. New York: W. W. Norton & Co., 2000.

Tompkins, Jane. "An Introduction to Reader-Response Criticism." *Reader-Response Criticism from Formalism to Post-Structuralism.* Ed. Jane Tompkins. Baltimore: The Johns Hopkins University Press, 1980.

Woolf, Virginia. "A Sketch of the Past." *Eight Modern Essayists.* Ed. William Smart. 4th ed. New York: St. Martin's, 1985.

CHAPTER 14

Imaginative Writing and Risk Taking

William A. Stephany

In most cases, writing an analytical or interpretive paper will be the way you can best demonstrate the quality of your reading and thinking about a work of literature in an academic setting, but it need not be the only one. There may be times when the best way for you to respond to a work might be to write a parody or an imitation of it or to write some other form of imaginative or playful paper. Recently, when I assigned a paper in a survey of British literature, in addition to four traditional topics for analytical essays, I offered students the following option:

> Congratulations! You have just been awarded a one-month trial membership in the Scribler's Club. Now that you have read some of the works of your fellow club members Jonathan Swift and Alexander Pope, perhaps you would like to try your hand at a similar act of creation. Perhaps you would like to bring Lemuel Gulliver out of retirement and compose a portion of his fifth voyage, one which would reveal something about our world. Or perhaps you have found some of the lost couplets of Alexander Pope, originally intended for inclusion in *any* of his poems assigned for class.
>
> Or perhaps you'd like to try your hand at a parody of the conventions, style, or concerns of *any writer* or work covered this semester. Try your hand at a metaphysical conceit or Miltonic blank verse or heroic couplets. Remember that parodists often strive for a disparity between content and parodied form: part of the fun of the *Dunciad* and "Rape of the Lock" lies in the heroic treatment of inherently nonheroic subjects.

In response to this assignment, several students did write chapters from an imagined fifth book of *Gulliver's Travels,* and most of them did an excellent job of maintaining a tone akin to Swift's. For example, Swift uses gratuitous detail to imply, tongue-in-cheek, that these clearly fantastic voyages actually happened, and the following example catches this spirit:

```
… I left with a crew of sixty-five aboard the Devonshire
well equipped for most difficulties I would encounter. It
had been four years since my last voyage…. First mate Lou
Noonford spotted land at 3:15 on the twenty-second day,
```

> so we sailed south until we reached the rocky shore where
> we were met by what appeared to be a friendly fisherman.
> (Andy)

Only someone who had entered into the pleasure of reading *Gulliver's Travels* could emulate the style in this way. And because of the way it brings one element of the work to the foreground, Andy's imitation may itself be considered a form of interpretation.

An imaginative paper can also demonstrate an understanding of a work's thematic concerns. In his version of a fifth book, another student, Jim, extended one of the patterns through which Swift presents Gulliver's increasing misanthropy. In Book I, Gulliver is shipwrecked; in Book II, he is abandoned; in Book III, he is set adrift by pirates; in Book IV, he is the victim of mutiny. The motivation for his "journeys" gets worse and worse. In Jim's paper, Gulliver, whom we had left hating humans and loving horses at the end of Book IV, murders a man who is whipping a horse, and so begins his final adventure by fleeing in an open boat from a lynch mob.

A creative response to an assigned reading can also use the form of the original to comment on some aspect of our contemporary world. A third student wrote about Gulliver's journey to a fictional "land of excessive knowledge," where he encounters a native named Dalloway:

> The inhabitants are much like humans, but supposedly better because of their capacity to take in verbal and written knowledge … lessons are taught by educators who speak at sixty *words per ciab*. A *ciab* is almost equal to ten seconds. These people have existed for nearly two trillion years, so in each education period almost two thousand years are covered…. [Knowledge] is served to them at such a quick pace that they neither can retain, nor recall much of it. Dalloway also conveyed to me that the thirst for knowledge is so great that most pupils interpret it in the wrong way. (Phil)

Phil is here recalling Swift's own thematic concerns, especially in Book III, in which he satirizes inappropriate approaches to knowledge. His imagined world allows him to make his point about the frustrations of taking a lecture-format survey, one covering British literature from the seventh through the eighteenth centuries in one semester. Since his parody is true to the spirit and form of Swift's work (and elsewhere includes quotations from and mock scholarly annotations on Shakespeare), he also demonstrates how much he has learned from his reading, a technique that inherently confers credibility to his implied critique of the course format.

"RULES" FOR RISK TAKING

However attractive an option of this sort might seem, you need to acknowledge from the outset that novelty of approach is no guarantee that a paper will be writ-

Chapter 14 Imaginative Writing and Risk Taking   **185**

ten well, and if you've never tried this kind of writing before, you will probably welcome some guidelines before beginning. You will realize, I assume, that none of the suggestions I'm about to make should be regarded as hard-and-fast rules for writing this kind of paper. It would be ironic for me to propose in one paragraph that you expand the possibilities for writing about literature, only to begin limiting those possibilities in the next one. I would like to describe what some of my students have done, in order to suggest a range of what is possible and use those examples to generalize about why certain kinds of creative responses may have worked. There are, however, three principles that seem so universally applicable that I'd like to begin by suggesting that you violate them at your peril.

Read Carefully

Rule number one is important for any kind of writing about literature: *Know your subject matter.* To do a good job writing the kind of paper I am proposing, you need to have read the text closely, to have thought about it deeply, and to have internalized for yourself its form, its themes, its structure, its rhythms, both verbal and conceptual, and its relationship to the other readings in the course. If your paper is to be effective, it will be more than just a clever reaction to the text; it will be an indirect interpretation of it. Whether your purpose is to mimic a writer's stylistic quirks (as Andy does in his parody of Gulliver), or to cast light on an aspect of the text (as Jim does), or to illuminate our own world as mediated through the assigned text (as Phil does), you need a clear sense of your purpose as a writer and a solid understanding of the original text in order to write an effective paper.

Maintain a Consistent Voice

Rule number two is more specifically appropriate for an imaginative paper: *Maintain a consistent voice.* If your paper requires you to adopt a voice or a point of view, don't shift ground in the middle to explain what you're doing; allow the voice to develop. Swift himself provides an excellent model for this principle in his famous essay "A Modest Proposal." As an Irish patriot, he had already written a wide range of pamphlets protesting the economic abuses England had been inflicting on Ireland in the early eighteenth century. The suggestions he made in these "analytical essays" were all ignored, so he finally circulated anonymously a pamphlet written in the style of a "Projector," the term used in his day to describe people who proposed projects for implementation of economic or social policy. In this case, the project being advanced is one that would allegedly cure the country of its crippling poverty. Only after we've read several pages of cool, deadpan calculation about the scope of the problem does the full horror of the project become clear—that the infants of the poor be fattened for the first year of their lives and then slaughtered, their meat offered for sale to the wealthy. A bit later still, the pamphlet's underlying figure of speech becomes clear: Since the landlord class has been metaphorically consuming the parents, they may as well literally consume the children. The chilling effect of the whole piece depends on Swift's relentless consistency in maintaining the speaker's matter-of-fact voice. With his concentration on mathematical finesse and blind logic, the speaker implicitly condemns those like himself who would treat a human crisis as if it were a purely intellectual problem.

Revise and Edit

Rule number three also applies to any kind of writing, not just to writing about literature: *Revise and Edit.* Your paper will assume its final polish and its final point only as a result of several revisions as well as careful editing and proofreading. The point seems obvious but needs to be made, since a creative paper might often begin life as a journal entry or free writing. While this might be a thoroughly appropriate and normal way for the idea, or even for an entire draft, to be generated, such a draft, if left unrevised, will almost surely be inadequate as a final paper. Be prepared for the possibility that you may be too close to your original draft immediately after completing it to assume editorial objectivity toward it: It's difficult—indeed, for most of us, it's impossible—to be creative and critical at the same time. Let at least a day pass after you've written your draft before you return to it to revise it, and then try to read it objectively, as someone else will read it. Better still, find someone else to whom you can read your work, ideally a friend who is also in the course for which you're preparing the paper. Such a person has read the text you're writing about and shares with you a familiarity with the dynamics of the class and the concepts that have been considered. As you read your paper aloud to such an audience, you will hear the parts of the paper that work well or poorly; your friend will hear more.

CREATIVE CHOICES

There are several ways in which you might write creatively about a work of literature; descriptions of a few of them follow.

Imitation of Form: Close Parody

Parody is the term used for writing that imitates the style of another, usually famous, piece of work, and sometimes this imitation of form can be extremely close, maintaining the exact rhyme scheme of a poem, for example, or the syntax of the original's sentences.

The sixteenth-century writer Christopher Marlowe's poem, "The Passionate Shepherd to his Love," inspired two well-known parodies of this sort. Marlowe begins his poem:

> Come live with me and be my love,
> And we will all the pleasures prove

> That valleys, groves, hills, and fields,
> Woods, or sleepy mountain yields. (989)

In this famous pastoral poem, Marlowe's shepherd invites his beloved nymph to live with him a simple life of uncomplicated pleasure. Several of his contemporaries wrote poems in response to Marlowe's, two of which are themselves quite famous. Walter Raleigh's "The Nymph's Reply to the Shepherd" repeats many of the same words and deals with many of the same concepts, but to make the opposite point. For Raleigh's nymph, time and deception make it impossible to accept the offer of a world without responsibilities. He begins:

> If all the world and love were young,
> And truth in every shepherd's tongue,
> These pretty pleasures might me move
> To live with thee and be thy love. (879)

If Raleigh's response is serious, John Donne's is comic. He begins his poem, "The Bait," by inviting his love to live with him so they can go fishing together:

> Come live with me and be my love,
> And we will some new pleasures prove,
> Of golden sands and crystal brooks,
> With silken lines and silver hooks. (1247)

Both parodies closely imitate Marlowe's verse form—both its meter and its rhyme scheme.

In response to the assignment reproduced near the beginning of this chapter, some students wrote similar close parodies of poems studied during the semester, and, as with Raleigh's and Donne's, some were serious, some comic. As an example, Shakespeare's Sonnet 73 appears on the next page with Melissa's parody below it.

The rhyme schemes of the two poems are the same (although the logical structure of Shakespeare's first twelve lines consist of three groups of four lines, and Melissa's consists of four groups of three). As in Shakespeare's poem, Melissa's speaker is conscious of aging and speaks of what one can see "in her," but in contrast to the relatively tranquil resolution in Shakespeare's poem, where advancing age increases the intensity of love, Melissa's sonnet presents a terrifying view of aging. "In me thou seest what soon shall be thy fate," says her speaker, and the result is a rejection that isolates the elderly from loved ones.

Original

> That time of year thou mayst in me behold
> When yellow leaves, or none, or few, do hang
> Upon those boughs which shake against the cold,
> Bare ruined choirs, where late the sweet birds sang.
> In me thou seest the twilight of such day
> As after sunset fadeth in the west;

Which by and by black night doth take away,
Death's second self that seals up all in rest.
In me thou seest the glowing of such fire,
That on the ashes of his youth doth lie,
As the deathbed whereon it must expire,
Consumed with that which it was nourished by.
This thou perceiv'st, which makes thy love more strong,
To love that well, which thou must leave ere long. (1035)

Shakespeare

Parody

That time of year thou mayst in me behold
When yellow teeth, or none, or few do stay
In softened gums which chatter gainst the cold.
A halo of hair, yet sparse and bristly grey
In me thou seest, and yet thou failst to see
My heart, that hasn't changed inside.
Inside I'm more than how I look to thee
My body's weak, but my soul shall never die.
In me thou seest what soon shall be thy fate.
My mind a mix of thoughts half done,
Cherished loves shriveled to bitter hate,
Awaiting friends who oft forget to come.
This thou perceiv'st, which keeps thee from my side
And chokes thy love until the day I've died.

Melissa

More General Parodies

Parodies of specific works need not follow the form of the originals as closely as the previous examples do. Students of mine have written a wide range of imitations that have in various ways illuminated either the original text, our modern world, or both. They have written modern versions of Old English riddles, dramatic monologues imagined to have been spoken by Beowulf, and a "boasting speech" by a contemporary boxer at a prematch weigh-in in the style of Beowulf on the eve of his battle with Grendel, all following the conventions of Old English poetry. Several students in my Chaucer courses have written imitations of "The General Prologue" to *The Canterbury Tales,* usually in iambic pentameter couplets, sometimes even attempting to use Chaucer's Middle English.

If you do attempt a parody of this sort, try to be as faithful as you can to the style of the original. Show your reader how thoroughly you have interiorized its poetic conventions and "intellectual tics." At its best, writing of this sort is not only elegant and fun, but incisive literary criticism: You teach your reader to see the work, at least the parts you parody, as you do. The boxer's boast, for example, even while it showed a familiarity with the forms and conventions of Old English poetry, suggested something about the survival in an analogous modern context of the Anglo-Saxon warrior's spirit of assertiveness on the brink of battle. I've had students write mock cantos of Dante's *Divine Comedy*. Dante presents his journey as a "moral geography" of hell, purgatory, and paradise: A soul's location in the afterlife defines the moral values by which the person lived. Two of my students wrote cantos in which they imagined encountering Dante's own spirit on a journey through the otherworld. One found Dante in hell among the Blasphemers; the other in Purgatory among the Proud. In both cases he was being punished for his arrogance in presuming to pass judgment upon the lives of his contemporaries. What made the students' poems so successful was the way they imitated Dante's stylistic and conceptual habits: Filled with telling allusions to various different parts of the Comedy, they could have been written only by people who had assimilated Dante's poem in great detail and with great sensitivity. Successful parodies, by the way, are usually acts of love; people rarely devote this much time and effort to a work unless they feel some affection or admiration for it.

Imitation of Modern Literary or Cultural Forms

I have also had students devise modern versions of Chaucer's "General Prologue" to explore alternative ways of presenting characters in a quasi-encyclopedic format. One wrote about arriving in Canterbury with Chaucer's group of Pilgrims in the style of an article for the *New York Times* travel section. Another wrote a mock yearbook with invented biographies, student activities, and quotations, imagining for each pilgrim the high school characteristics that would develop into the characters as Chaucer presents them. In both cases, the fun and value came from the writer's ability to invent specific details that recalled and responded to details from Chaucer's text. The intent was not to escape from, but rather to illuminate, the literary work dealt with. One student imagined the sexually aggressive Wife of Bath on a television talk show; another, in a Playboy interview. Another dealt with "The Clerk's Tale," in which the improbably patient Griselda endures one affront after another from her increasingly obsessive husband, as an episode in the soap opera "Patience Place." All found ways of illuminating both Chaucer's text and our own cultural forms.

Finally, several students have written modern variants of Chaucer's *Troilus and Criseyde*, a romance about two young lovers in the doomed city of ancient Troy. Jennifer rewrote the story as a modern "romance" of the type you'd find on the shelves near a supermarket checkout, beginning her version as follows:

```
The tall and glamorous Criseyde glided into the fashionable
hall, located in the exciting Greenwich Village section of
New York City. Her flowing black gown enhanced the shim-
mering clear blue of her electric eyes. She slid into an
elegant mahogany chair, the color of which contrasted
darkly with her golden tresses. Crossing her shapely legs,
she glanced across the Palladium, the most popular club
```

> in the Big Apple. Criseyde, the young and beautiful widow, glistened like a brilliant diamond among rough stones ...

In Chaucer's romance, the Palladion is the name of the annual celebration of Pallas Athena, goddess of Wisdom, at which Troilus first sees Criseyde and falls in love with her. In reconceiving the encounter as taking place in a singles' bar, and the form as the modern "romance" of soft-core sexploitation, Jennifer is able to suggest something about the diminution of the term "romance" in our own culture, while simultaneously suggesting a sinister dimension to what is going on in Chaucer's poem as well.

Greg's response to the Troilus was a made-for-television movie called "Trevor and Chrissie" as seen through the eager eyes of Randall, Jr., an eleven-year-old who "has seen previews for it throughout the week and also read the *TV Guide* review that called it 'a hot and steamy romance.'" What Greg presents is both a send-up of modern advertising hype and an indirect commentary on Chaucer's technique of having an intrusive narrator interrupt his story, particularly at moments of sexual interest, in a way that breaks the emotional spell he is creating. Greg approaches his conclusion in the following passage:

> Chrissie rolls her black silk stocking off of her well-formed calves. Trevor kisses her neck. "I'm crazy about you!" he says. He kisses her shoulder and reaches for the tassled silk strap that holds on her nightgown. He begins to pull it below her shoulder. Randall, Jr., has stopped breathing. He sits trembling, his eyes focused on the screen. Trevor pulls the strap even lower and starts on the other. Chrissie arches her back and licks her lips.
> The screen goes blank for a half second.
> "NEW CHEESE WIZ, NOW IN MICROWAVABLE CONTAINER!"

Both the intrusion of the commercial and the eleven-year-old's voyeurism create effects analogous to those of the *Troilus*'s narrator, making the parody itself an act of interpretive analysis.

Changing the Form

You might rewrite a passage from a piece of fiction from an alternative point of view. If it is written in the third person, for example, rewrite it as if it were narrated by one of the characters. This would require you to be confident about the limits of the character's knowledge and about the peculiar qualities that would affect how this character would serve as a filter or center of consciousness through which the story could be told. Recent published examples include *Ahab's Wife*, an alternate view of *Moby Dick* and *The Wind Done Gone*, a retelling of *Gone with the Wind* from a slave's perspective.

You might also rewrite a work in a different genre: If it's a narrative, rewrite it as dialogue; if it's a play, retell it through a narrator. With any of these topics, what you would probably discover and should be sure to demonstrate is the way in which fundamental artistic choices limit subsequent decisions and predetermine the range of esthetic effects.

In a wonderful example of what this approach can achieve, Margaret rewrote Chaucer's "Knight's Tale" as a fifteen-page first-person narrative by Emily, the young woman fought over as a prize by two young suitors. She never speaks a word in Chaucer's poem, this despite the fact (introduced at the beginning of the poem and immediately disregarded) that she is sister of the conquered queen of the Amazons. Margaret's narrative not only invents a voice for her, it reconceives Chaucer's poem from the point of view of the captive warrior-woman. In the process, she was able to cast light on some of the hidden gender assumptions of the poem, but also, indirectly, on the kinds of accommodations young women continue to be asked to make to conform to gendered expectations about power.

Rewriting the Ending

One day in a recent semester, a student came up to me after class and said in an offhanded way, "You know, I really don't like the way Sir Gawain and the Green Knight ends." I was a bit distracted at the time and let the remark pass. Only later did I realize that I'd missed an opportunity. I should have said, "If you don't like the ending, rewrite it." The student would then have had to engage questions of structure, of theme, of closure. To figure out why he didn't like the ending, he'd first have had to figure out very carefully just why the poem does end as it does and how that ending affects him. Next time I'll be ready!

One student, for example, Paul, took up Chaucer's abandoned "Tale of Sir Thopas" and brought it to conclusion. Chaucer's poem is intentionally "bad," itself a parody of popular romances written in a doggerel verse form about an inane subject with clichéd formulas placed in rime positions, and in the fiction of *The Canterbury Tales*, it's abandoned because the Host of the pilgrimage can't stand any more of it. Paul's ending catches the rhyme scheme and the tone just right, beginning where Chaucer left off:

> Til on a day, in quite a fit,
> Our hero rose, to finish it,
> He felt no sense of dread.
> A knight must have his armor clean,
> And when he goes looking for his queen,
> This Thopas know so well.
> He quickly caused his shield to shine
> Then donned his boots and clothes most fine
> And set out for that dell.

Through eight more stanzas, Paul sustains the tone and form in what stands ultimately as a tribute to his skill, but also to his understanding of the "point" of Chaucer's own playful parody.

Creating Dialogues

One way to demonstrate your mastery of the subject matter in a course is to create imagined discussions. For example, imagine an encounter between two or more of the writers whose works you're reading in a course. Or between two or more characters, perhaps from different works. Or between a writer and one or more of his or her characters.

Some Final Examples

For her paper on *Troilus and Criseyde,* Lisa wrote an imagined letter from Criseyde to Helen of Troy, composed after the fall of the city. When she and Helen at that point are both safely back in Greece, Lisa has her present her side of the story, which Chaucer has his narrator tell about her. Since Helen puts in a cameo appearance in Chaucer's romance, Lisa's premise is not really far-fetched, especially since Troilus and Criseyde exchange letters both before they become lovers and after they are separated, and these letters become one of the ways in which Chaucer himself presents their characters. Lisa's letter, in fact, filled with specific references to episodes in Chaucer's romance—all as perceived by Criseyde—is really a creative variant of the traditional paper analyzing a character. In a similar way, Robin's contemporary retelling of the *Troilus* narrative is filled with the pricey consumer goods of the upper class "good life," underscoring the largely invisible class assumptions of Chaucer's poem, and her lovers' epistolary exchange—in modern fashion—takes place on e-mail:

To criseyde@greekstown.com
From: troilus@troy.com
Subject: Where the hell are you?

    I'll end with two more examples from the Survey course. One student transformed the quarreling of Adam and Eve, a moment of epic grandeur in Book IX of *Paradise Lost,* into a dispute among the actors on the set of the fictional soap opera, "Paradise Tossed." In this imagined dialogue, the actress, Eve, protests the role that the creator (presumably God) and the writer of the series (Milton) had conspired for her to play. Another student wrote a poem in blank verse—imitating Milton's form—with the capitalized first words of each line forming an acrostic, spelling out vertically down the left margin the words "of Paradise Lost and Regained." (This imitates a technique we had seen Milton use on one occasion in his poem.) The subject matter of the student's poem, however, was not adapted from Milton, but from Chaucer: It imagined the emotional reaction of the maiden who is raped in the initial episode of "The Wife of Bath's Tale." Either of these students might have written about the cultural basis of gender roles or about the cultural distortion inherent in the canon of predominantly male-authored texts enshrined in the traditional Beowulf to 1800 survey course. In a way, both did.

Chapter 14   Imaginative Writing and Risk Taking   **193**

THE EXPERIMENTAL TRADITION

Some of the student papers I've been discussing in this chapter are in many ways similar to some works we normally think of as "great" literature. When works become accepted as influential or significant within our cultural tradition, it is easy for us to forget that often they were originally daring. Perhaps you have recognized this playful quality in some of the works I've mentioned already in this chapter: Swift's "Modest Proposal" and *Gulliver's Travels* and Donne's "The Bait" come readily to mind. But did you think of how outrageous Dante was in the *Divine Comedy* in claiming that he's telling us about a journey he took through hell, purgatory, and heaven, conducted at first by the ancient Roman poet Virgil, then by a woman he had once loved, and finally by St. Bernard? Does Chaucer's conceptual daring occur to you when he insists that he was only a reporter traveling on the pilgrimage to Canterbury Cathedral, thereby denying authorial responsibility for the tales he narrates? His lesser-known *Troilus and Criseyde* is equally daring in its insistence that the narrator is a pedantic scholar, innocent of sexual intimacy, who is translating from Latin into English a lost history of the Trojan War at the center of which is a story of passionate love. When the story he is translating turns erotic, he becomes alternately flustered and voyeuristic; when it turns tragic, he feels dread at his obligation to be true to a "history" he can't alter.

What all these texts share is their fundamental "bookishness." They are incorporating, reacting against, even rewriting earlier works from the culture in which they share, and in so doing they are contributing to a tradition that goes back to antiquity. The first-century Roman poet Ovid, in his *Heroides,* presents a series of fictional letters, supposedly written by famous heroines, in which they present revisionist versions of the stories about them which literary tradition had perpetuated. As we get closer to our own time, we sometimes lose sight of the fact that authors commonly rework the literary past. Mark Twain, for example, is so much of an American institution that we might overlook his brilliance in putting his Connecticut Yankee into King Arthur's court, thereby intersecting the worlds of modern scientific skepticism and medieval magic, the technological horrors of American Civil War weapons and the traditional concepts of military courtesy and chivalry found in Arthurian romance. Closer to our own time, John Gardner's novel *Grendel* presents a book-long stream-of-consciousness monologue of the thoughts of the monster from Beowulf. Grendel's mind is filled with specific echoes from the Anglo-Saxon epic as re-imagined from his point of view, but the book's real focus seems to be to provide a commentary on certain twentieth-century philosophical and political ideologies to which the monster's ideas bear a disquieting similarity.

What all of these writers are doing is playing with and interpreting their inherited literary tradition, while finding ways to let it speak to their own worlds. There are times when you might choose to do the same. In fairness to you and your teachers, however, you need to remember that kind of paper I've been talking about is not always appropriate. Be sure to ascertain whether such an approach would be acceptable before submitting such a paper. But even when it's not appropriate for a course assignment, if you're keeping a course-related journal, either as a requirement or on your own, it would be perfectly natural for you to explore this kind of writing there. Moreover, remember that writing about literature need not always be a command performance and that your teacher need not be your only audience. Why not write something like this to show to your friends? And if the paper works, consider showing it to your teacher even if it doesn't count as part of a grade. Writing for an audience rather than for a grade might be an important step in your development as a writer.

I'll tell you what I tell my students. As a teacher, when I approach a stack of student papers, I want to be taught. As a result of your paper, I want to read the work you're writing about in a new way. The kind of paper I've been discussing in this chapter can have the effect of "de-familiarizing" a work of literature. Works that were starting when they were originally written—and startling for me when I originally read them—can come to seem normal, tame, familiar after they've been processed through the forms and formulas of academia year after year. Your paper can help make the work's original lightning visible, both for you and for me.

WORKS CITED

Donne, John. "The Bait" and "The Good Morrow." *The Norton Anthology of English Literature*. Gen. Ed. M. H. Abrams. 7th ed. New York: Norton, 2000.

Marlowe, Christopher. "The Passionate Shepherd to His Love." *The Norton Anthology of English Literature*. Gen. Ed. M. H. Abrams. 7th ed. New York: Norton, 2000.

Raleigh, Walter. "The Nymph's Reply to the Shepherd." *The Norton Anthology of English Literature*. Gen. Ed. M. H. Abrams. 7th ed. New York: Norton, 2000.

Shakespeare, William. "That Time of Year Thou Mayst in Me Behold." *The Norton Anthology of English Literature*. Gen. Ed. M. H. Abrams. 7th ed. New York: Norton, 2000

CHAPTER 15

Writing with Research

Richard Sweterlitsch

I recently asked students in my nineteenth-century American humor senior seminar to tell me what "research paper" means to them. Among their responses were "a research paper can't be written in the first person," "long nights in the library and on the Internet," and "stress and anxiety." A few had more positive replies: "investigating a subject about which I'd like to or need to know more," and "combining knowledge one already has with other information gathered from other sources." Jeff wrote: "A research paper is a way for a student to learn a topic independently. It helps give students self-learning skills. Teaches them how to use different research methods. Teaches students how to work alone. Builds writing and problem-solving skills and develops decision-making skills." That's a lot of meaning wrapped into "research paper."

Several years ago, Ken Macrorie wrote in his book *Searching Writing:* "Most research papers written in high school and college are bad jokes. They're funny because they pretend to be so much and actually are so little" (116). Jeff might disagree, because he saw some benefit in the research-based assignment. But unfortunately Macrorie is probably right in many cases. I recall teaching a number of years ago an American literature class geared for first-years students. I asked that they come up with their own topics for a research paper. One student, whom I'll call Marsha, remembered her high school teacher discussing how F. Scott Fitzgerald's relationship with Zelda Sayre influenced his novel *The Great Gatsby*. So, she checked out several books that delved into the matter: Arthur Mizener's *The Far Side of Paradise,* Sara Mayfield's *Exiles from Paradise: Zelda and F. Scott Fitzgerald*, and *Zelda: A Biography* by Nancy Milford. By skimming a few chapters in each book, Marsha found enough material about the lovers' stormy relationship in order to fill a dozen or so index cards. Thus far, she had done exactly what she learned in high school about finding sources and taking notes. A few days later, she spent part of an afternoon arranging her cards into a chronology that sequenced events of the affair. Her writing task was simple and mechanical: provide links or transitions between the quotes she had arranged; add an introduction and a conclusion; then complete the endnotes and the bibliography. Finally, Marsha typed her final draft and submitted it to me.

Her work was simple, to the point, and, for the most part, a waste of time. It was nothing more than a summary of selected existing sources. She already knew from high school about the Fitzgerald-Sayre relationship and its impact on *The Great Gatsby*, and her hours of work added nothing significant to what she already knew. Technically she completed the assignment, but educationally, it was mostly a bust.

I am convinced that writing with research does not mean a mindless series of tasks, of collecting, documenting, organizing, and regurgitating a variety of existing sources. It can be personal writing with a fresh twist. The voice of the writer—"I"—should come through loudly and clearly expressing "I's" personal insights. "I think" and "I believe" have a place in a humanities research paper, along with "I read." In fact, while this entire book examines different writing strategies and situations, research is handmaid to many of them, or at least it can be. A critical essay becomes more convincing because its author considered the opinions of other writers. Different perspectives on a topic infuse an analytic paper with dialogue and debate. A personal essay gathers strength through the writer's awareness of what others have witnessed. Sometimes an idea for a paper begs its author to venture into arenas beyond the most obvious, there to gather new insights and different viewpoints. An analysis of setting in a Jane Austen novel gains greater breadth and depth if the author is aware of the architectural and horticultural norms of nineteenth-century manor house gardens. A colleague of mine, Philip Baruth, published a novel a year or two ago. He set it in Burlington, Vermont, where he currently lives. In the novel, he sought to catch the characters of the city and of particular residential neighborhoods. Therefore, he did some research, looking closely at the community, noting its people and its physical layout. His research informed *The Dream of the White Village: A Novel in Stories* with a vibrant dose of realism that could only come from the author's familiarity with Burlington.

Much of what you write for a literature class is, broadly speaking, literary criticism. It has three main goals: to describe, to interpret, and to evaluate a literary text. Writing with research enhances these objectives by drawing upon a network of scholars whose insights help to spur you to original insights. Writers who research what others before them have already learned advance, sometimes in concert and sometimes in opposition, the opinions and judgments of a scholarly community. Writing with research means involving the ideas of others in order to learn and move in fresh directions.

In my Survey of Folklore course, I ask students to consider writing an essay on some contemporary retellings of traditional folktales. Bonnie spoke to me right after class one day and asked if I had seen the film *Pretty Woman*, starring Julia Roberts. I hadn't at the time. She was sure that it was a retelling of "Cinderella," a tale she had known from childhood. "Go with it," I told her. She began, naturally enough, by renting the film at a local video outlet. She viewed it several times, pausing the tape in order to write down notes. She turned to *The Types of the Folktale*, a reference guide that I had discussed in class, and found a structural skeleton of the tale and a listing of the folk motifs generally found in the Cinderella story. Via the university's online library catalogue she discovered Alan Dundes's *Cinderella: A Casebook,* which contained twenty-one essays and seven pages of bibliographic material. Because the film appeared after the publication of the Dundes book, Bonnie turned to the online MLA bibliography and to several film journals in order to track down extended reviews of *Pretty Woman.* The latter resources she learned about by asking the reference librarian for the names of film journals with bibliographies in them. After she completed her library research, she viewed the film again. Well-equipped with a familiarity of the film and with her secondary sources, Bonnie analyzed the Julia Robert's film by contrasting its innovations that broke from folk traditions with its retention of traditional structures and motifs. Bonnie learned through her own efforts an immense amount about folklore, film, and popular culture. Her final paper was not one of Macrorie's bad jokes.

Writing an intelligent, perceptive research paper that utilizes the resources of a community of critics and scholars marks a crucial phase of a personal inquiry into a topic that evolved from a nagging curiosity, from a personal opinion, or from a flash of insight, which necessitated explorations beyond the writer's own personal knowledge. I want to simplify the whole process of writing with research by describing five steps in writing a college-level research essay. I can't say "five easy steps," because none of them is easy, but they work for me and for students and have actually made writing with research an intellectually empowering and gratifying experience. The steps are

1. **Getting started,** or testing ideas, posing questions and doing a little inquiring.
2. **Gathering information first-hand,** or creating your own resources.
3. **Seeking second-hand sources,** or learning what others have written.
4. **Pulling the paper together,** or using sources as informing voices.
5. **Giving credit,** or citing your sources.

GETTING STARTED

What holds true for any kind of essay your instructor may ask you to write—finding a subject to write about, narrowing it down to a specific topic, and then generating an appropriate thesis—is fitting for the research-informed essay as well. Oftentimes, your instructor assigns a topic or suggests a general plan for it. Perhaps there is something in your class lecture notes or a comment made in class discussion that you think is worth pursuing. Maybe you can turn to your course journal where a question you had or a passage you wrote about suggests possibilities worth exploring. After Sandra reread in her journal, her complaint that William Faulkner made the history of the McCaslin lineage in "The Bear" too difficult to follow, she figured that the assignment to write a research-oriented paper offered the prospect of developing and maybe resolving her gripe.

I once assigned a research paper on Faulkner's *As I Lay Dying,* requiring students to come up with their own topic and thesis. Tom, a junior English major, was curious about Darl, a central figure in the novel. The year before he took my course, Tom had taken an introductory psychology course, and he remembered that schizophrenia was discussed in it. From what Tom could recall about the illness, Darl seemed to exhibit some of its symptoms. Initially, Tom put up a trial balloon: In class discussion, he posed the proposition that Darl was a schizophrenic. Some agreed with his diagnosis; others disagreed, saying that Darl was the sanest one of the whole Bundren clan. After class he said to me that he might pursue the topic. I told him that I liked his idea, but frankly I couldn't offer much specific help other than suggesting he look at some bibliographies on Faulkner's works in order to see what has been written about Darl. At this point, Tom began seriously researching sources that might prove or disprove his proposition. He looked over his notes from the psychology class, talked with his psychology professor, and read more about schizophrenia in books he located in the library. All of this he completed before he was ready to write about Darl's condition. In all, Tom might have spent eight to ten hours boning up on schizophrenia and rereading key passages in the novel, looking for connections. The fellow was learning and getting ready to think on his informed own.

Tom might have lucked out on this topic, but the point is, he began by asking himself some questions about Darl and drawing upon some sketchy information he knew from another class. He brought that background and some newly found information to bear on his topic.

The advice that others in this book give about coming up with a topic is equally applicable to papers in which research will play a part. But before formulating a final thesis that you wish to support and defend, spend time consulting with others who have already looked at the subject. Maybe you will find an essay that addresses exactly what you want to explore as you might have done on your own. There is, then, no need for you to restate what has already been stated to your satisfaction.

GATHERING INFORMATION FIRST-HAND

Okay, so you know what you want to write about. Now, begin the research. For most students the campus or community library and the Internet are the most obvious sources. Nevertheless, these may not always be the best sources. Libraries and the Internet are fabulous resources of secondary material—that is, what other people have written about a topic. Good stuff is packed away in those buildings and in cyberspace, and you should not ignore either. Nevertheless, consider the following scenarios that happened to three students.

In a course on Vermont literature, Martha decided to research the background of "Marjorie Grey," a poem accredited to a nineteenth-century local-color writer, Julia Dorr. Set in the early 1800s, the poem depicts the hardships suffered by a Rockingham, Vermont, woman who lost her way in the forests and wandered for several months before she stumbled into a New Hampshire settlement. Wanting to visit the setting for the poem and hoping to meet someone there who might tell her some more information, Martha drove one afternoon to Rockingham, where she, in fact, found a distant relative of Marjorie Grey. She learned

Chapter 15   Writing with Research   **199**

about this person by stopping to chat with the manager of the general store. The poem, she learned, depicted a real event. Moreover, her informant said that the story of Marjorie Grey had been set to music sometime in the nineteenth century by an unknown balladeer and had been in oral circulation ever since. Suddenly Martha faced some important questions: Had Dorr written the poem herself, or had she based it on a ballad with a life of its own? Why did Dorr not include the poem in her volume of complete works, although she had published it under her own name earlier? These questions Martha initially sought to answer. After weighing the information she had accumulated, she realized that there simply was not enough available information in order to reach any definitive answers. She eventually wrote an essay that presented what she had found and then compared oral texts of the ballad to Dorr's published poem. A little curiosity, an afternoon trip to Rockingham, and a chance meeting marked the beginning of some truly original research.

Linda, in another course, did not need to venture far from the campus. She literally found herself crying as she read passages in *Uncle Tom's Cabin* and thought that her reaction might be worth exploring. She wanted to know why she was so moved, and whether she was alone in her reaction. To gather some information, she decided to create a questionnaire based on qualitative research methods she had learned in a sociology class and took it, along with a particularly emotionally moving passage from the novel, to a class of first-year students. They read the passage and then filled out the questionnaire, which asked about how the text affected them. Linda was generating her own data. Using her findings, she wrote a very intriguing paper about gender identification with characters and how this affects responsive sentiments to a text.

Bart, a folklore student, was interested in superstitions among college students. He placed a ladder outside the door of a friend's fraternity house in such a way that one could go easily under the ladder and into the house or struggle around some shrubs in order to avoid going under the ladder. He stood inconspicuously nearby and kept count of those entering and leaving the building and the path they chose. He then randomly questioned several of his subjects. The data he gathered played an integral part in his paper's thesis that a college education and traditional superstitions are not necessarily exclusive.

All three of these students engaged in primary research; that is, they gathered data first-hand, through interviews, questionnaires, and observations. Each went beyond the library and into the field, so to speak, and ended up bagging significant information that enlivened their papers significantly.

Interviews give you the opportunity to talk with people who have information you may need. Too often students forget that their own college campus has faculty members who are experts in various fields. You can talk to your professors about your topic, and you can interview them. As we will see, there is a difference. Poets and novelists visit schools, and you can always check with their on-site sponsor, usually the person or organization that brings them to campus, in order to see if you may interview them. Often, as in Martha's case, there is someone beyond the campus who has valuable information. Tom, who wanted to write about Darl, pursued his ideas in some depth when he interviewed his psychology professor and a social worker about schizophrenia; their knowledge provided him with more information that reshaped his thinking and, eventually, his essay on Darl.

Interviewing is one of the most common and intriguing devices for gathering in-depth information. Careful preparation can make a gigantic difference on the final product. Here's a simple checklist of tips worth keeping in mind as you plan your interview:

1. Once you are sure that your potential interviewees can speak with some authority on the subject you are investigating, contact them several days in advance. A phone call or e-mail is all it usually takes. Explain specifically what you are doing and why you wish to interview them. If you plan to tape-record the interview, ask for approval ahead of time.
2. Prepare yourself for the interview. Do some research, and based on what you find and on your interest, create an extended list of questions that will elicit both general and specific information. Phrase questions to avoid yes or no answers. If you plan on interviewing campus professors, ask them if you may have a copy of their curriculum vitae—a statement of their scholarly activity and interests. If you get one, locate and read relevant material that they have published. As a folklorist, I am often interviewed by students regarding various local legends, particularly those about the Lake Champlain monster. Both the student and I find the interview frustrating when the interviewer has not prepared some well-conceived questions. Two or three questions are nowhere near enough. Remember that an interview is not a conversation, an informal bull session, or a fishing expedition. Don't expect your experts to lead the interview. You want particular information. Go prepared with a list of specific questions. In fact, you might even want to send or e-mail your interviewees in advance the questions you plan to ask.
3. If your interviewees are agreeable and you are planning to use a tape recorder, know your equipment—especially the quirks of microphones—before you walk into the interview. Spend time learning how well the microphone picks up voices at various distances and how well it ignores background noises. Avoid using batteries because they seemed to be programmed to fail when needed. Remember that a thirty-minute tape records fifteen minutes to a side.
4. Be on time for the interview, and don't forget paper and a pencil. If the recording equipment becomes a distraction or does not function properly, put it aside at once and be thankful you can write. Taping or not, take notes. Write down unusual terms and the spelling of names and places. At the very beginning of your notes and on the tape, state the time, date, and place the interview is conducted, and the names of those present. You will need this information when you write your "Endnotes" and "Sources Cited." Then begin by asking your questions and listening carefully to the responses. Don't interrupt your interviewees, even if they aren't directly answering your question. If you talk over their voice, the tape will record gibberish

because the machine cannot distinguish between voices speaking at the same time as well as the human ear can. So, wait until they are done, and rephrase your question. Ask the questions you have prepared, but always be ready to follow another line of questioning if something worth pursuing comes up. Then return to the next question on your list. But remember, no matter how famous or intimidating your interviewees are, you are in charge of the interview. Ask questions forthrightly. Don't hesitate to ask how to spell unusual terms and proper names. If your interviewees start using "they" or "it," ask them to clarify to what "they" or "it" refers. And before you leave, get your interviewees' permission to quote them. Get it on tape, or, better yet, take a release form with you that simply states that by their signing it, the interviewees give you permission to quote them in your essay. Your library might have sample forms available.

5. A word about silence. In the course of an interview, your interviewees might pause to ponder a point or to recall a detail. Give them time, a little silence, to think. Sometimes, particularly after a very short response or a very long one, allowing for some silence will prompt the interviewees to elaborate on what they have just said. Silence is a time for reflection. Use it well. Some of the best information I have received in an interview came after a period of silence when both the interviewee and I had the chance to think about what had been said.

6. Immediately after the interview, sit down with your notes and tape, if you have one, and review everything about the event. Put your notes into accurate sentences. Link answers with the questions you asked. Does what you heard or wrote down an hour ago still make sense? Do you have the correct spelling of proper names and unusual terms? Once again, check that the "they's" and "she's" and "here's" and "then's" are clear. If you are missing information, contact your interviewees and get the information straight. Maybe you might even want to make a followup visit to clarify obscure points. It is good advice to write down the salient points of your interview within a few hours of completing it.

Attending public readings and lectures is another research method. Poets sometimes field questions during or after their presentations. Guest scholars present public lectures on campus. Even class lectures are contexts for doing research. Go, listen, take notes, and ask questions directly related to your interest. If you want to tape a lecture or poetry reading, or any public presentation, get permission from the speaker and the sponsor beforehand. And always note the date and place of the event and always make handwritten notes, independent of whatever you might record on tape.

If you see value in questionnaires, create one that is clear and will provide you with the information that you seek. Many of my students have discovered that getting others to fill out a form and to return it is next to impossible, particularly if they canvas people randomly and anonymously. Your best bet is to have folks complete a questionnaire immediately and in your presence. I have on occasion allowed students to pass out questionnaires in my classes, provided that filling them out will only take a few minutes of class time and that the students have made appropriate arrangements with me a few days before the class meeting.

SEEKING SECOND-HAND SOURCES

When I asked my students what "research paper" means to them, almost every one of them mentioned the library and the Internet as the resources they typically use for their research. Moreover, the majority of my respondents talked about using books rather than scholarly articles. Newspapers and popular journals received some mention, but chiefly it was books.

Once upon a time, before the Internet, libraries were the most obvious wellspring for humanities students and scholars. Plays, poems, novels, photographs, audio and video recordings, pieces of art, maps, manuscripts of private letters and diaries, microforms, and CD and DVD disks are held in libraries along side an endless number of the secondary texts, quantitatively the largest holdings in most college libraries. Libraries were once rated according to the number of volumes they held, but with the introduction of the Internet and the other electronic databases, the number of volumes that a library holds becomes less significant to the average researcher, but access to all possible sources has become more important. Learning to use a library and all the resources it offers is one of the most crucial skills you need to develop. Almost every library publishes a guide to its resources and explains the various ways of locating material you may need. Pick up a copy of it and look it over. Usually a reference librarian or someone at an information desk can give you advice and directions about specific issues.

The library is fundamentally a research facility at the service of students and faculty. The primary research tools include various bibliographies (lists of primary and secondary resources), checklists (resources listed according to specific topics), indices (a sequential list of resources), and most obviously, the catalogue of holdings (listing of titles and authors and subject matters housed in a library) and access to various forms of electronic storage data. Approaching these resources may seem intimidating. Nonetheless, an hour spent learning how to access available resources eradicates drudgery, relieves anxiety, and reduces stress. Familiarity with them can cut hours of late-evening toil into minutes of well-spent research. Unfortunately, many literature programs do not specifically teach their majors how to handle the library, and so students tackle the challenge in other ways, perhaps with mini-courses offered by library staff or on their own by using locally available published guides.

There are particular general research tools in print that can point toward specific sources for literary research. For example, if you want to know where to turn to get some information about studies on Alexander Pope or Michael Dorris, a number of guides can help. Nancy L. Baker's *A Research Guide for Undergraduate Students: English and American Literature* (New York: MLA, 1995) and James L. Harner's *Literary Research Guide* (3rd ed. New York: MLA, 1998) provide excellent entry into literary research. I am sure that your library has both books.

Chapter 15   Writing with Research   **203**

    I find that many students begin their research by looking up the name of an author in the library catalogue. Such a search produces a list of book titles. Books have the advantage of presenting general ideas that can be developed in considerable depth, and a book dealing specifically with your topic should be read thoroughly. Unfortunately students may not have the time in a semester to read several entire books. Develop the skill of using a book's table of contents, bibliography, and index to decide whether you should peruse or skim a book.

    While book-length studies cannot be ignored, most of my students are served well by journal articles. Locating them can be more of a challenge because library catalogues do not list articles as they do books. To find articles in print, one turns to other sources, namely bibliographies and checklists.

    For students of language and literature, the most formidable and fortunately accessible bibliography is *The MLA International Bibliography of Books and Articles on the Modern Languages and Literature*, published annually since 1963 by the Modern Language Association. It is the successor to the Association's *Annual Bibliography* (1956–1962), which was preceded by *American Bibliography* (1921–1953). The *International* is an extremely comprehensive bibliography arranged according to national literatures and subdivided into literary periods. You could, for example, look up American literature, subsection nineteenth century, sub-subsection Henry David Thoreau, and find a list of the many articles and fewer books published each year regarding Thoreau. The last twenty-five years or so of the *MLA Bibliography* is available on CD-ROM, and is probably one of your library's databases available through its Website.

    Various scholarly periodicals specialize in a particular area, genre (type of literature), or national literature. Many may publish annual bibliographies appropriate to specific fields of interest. For example, from 1917 to 1969, *Studies in Philology* published each year a bibliography listing scholarly publications about Renaissance literature. From 1926 through 1974, *Philological Quarterly* published its annual bibliography on English literature written between 1660 and 1800. Since then, Robert Allen has edited *The Eighteenth Century: A Current Bibliography* (New York: AMS Press, 1979–).

    You will discover esoteric journals and newsletters devoted to particular fields and authors, such as the *Eudora Welty Newsletter*, founded in 1977, and the *Keats-Shelley Journal*, begun in 1952. All these resources, as with any bibliography or index, are only helpful when the researcher understands how to locate them and how to use them. Although you need not master every resource in the library, you should discover what aids are available for the project at hand.

    Discovering that a source exists is fine and it is excellent if your library has the material you want. If not, you might have to go through interlibrary loan or to one of the online businesses that specialize in photocopying and sending articles from journals. If you need a source your library does not have, go to the reference librarian for directions.

    Of course, there is the Internet. I direct you to read Kate Hoffman's essay "A Web of One's Own: Electronic Texts in the College Classroom" (Chapter 16, found immediately after this essay). It is about using the Internet and other electronic resources. I want to reiterate her observations about evaluating Internet sources and extend her *caveat emptor* to include all sources you might consider using. No matter whose work you are reading, question the credentials of the author. Unsigned articles on the Web or in publications (the latter case is rare) might read well and support what you think, but avoid using them simply in order to build your own argument. Evaluate any idea you want to include in your paper. At the time I am writing this essay, The Wolfgram Memorial Library at Widener University offers online a useful bibliography of resources for evaluating Websites: **http://ww2.widener.edu/Wolfgram-Memorial-Library/webstrbib.htm.** Or try **http://milton.mse.jhu.edu:8001/research/education/net.html** for a discussion on how to evaluate Web sources.

Books printed by university presses and major publishers and essays appearing in scholarly journals have been read and reviewed by other scholars. Although they may not agree with the author's findings, the readers believe nonetheless that the scholarship on which the books or essays are based is sound. Tabloids bought at the grocery checkout counter might be useful for discussing popular legends about space aliens, but they are not reliable sources for verifying that spacefolk actually exist. Treat these sources (*Globe, Star, National Examiner,* and their kin) and popular magazines (*Time, Reader's Digest, Cosmopolitan,* and the like) for what they are; consider scholarly journals (*PMLA, Proverbium, Western Folklore,* and their peers) and serious publications (*The Wall Street Journal, Atlantic Monthly, National Review,* and their ilk) for what they can offer. For general advice about evaluating printed sources, look at **http://www/library.cornell.edu/okuref/research/skill26.htm.**

Encyclopedias and similar compendiums provide useful summaries of various topics, but they are opening statements and not the final word. They are useful for specific bits of data, but useless for critical analyses and interpretations. Use them wisely, and only for what they are.

Regardless of what source you use, copy material accurately. Photocopying is the most accurate way of collecting material from printed sources. But why copy a whole article when all you want is a short passage out of it? Copy that page and mark it. Otherwise take notes that summarize material, or paraphrase it. But be sure to do either accurately. Whichever path you choose to take, accurately identify your sources and where they can be found. Authors, titles, editors, volume numbers, dates of publication, place of publication, and page number are important. This is equally true for the Internet and electronic sources, as Kate Hoffman points out. Think of the identification material as an address that you will be giving your readers when you write the paper. It is not much help simply to provide your reader with a name or a title and give no directions on how to reach that source.

PULLING THE PAPER TOGETHER

Now that you have most of your research completed and have your topic and thesis clearly in mind, you want to use your sources as effectively as possible. Your task is to integrate your sources—the voices of others—into your argument and paper.

Erika-Beth wrote a paper about the nineteenth-century author Frances Whitcher. In part of it, she discussed Whitcher's humor within a broader context of women's culture. Her research drew her to Nancy Walker's essay "Women's Humor in America," published in *What's So Funny? Humor in American Culture*. When she went to write her paper, Erika-Beth wanted to use not only Walker's ideas, but also Walker's voice because she found that what Walker wrote was very succinctly stated. It was a matter of incorporating Walker's insight and voice into her own paper. Here's how she did it:

```
As a writer of humor, Whitcher, like other woman humorists,
produced a different kind of humor than her male counter-
parts. According to Nancy Walker, a scholar of women's
humor, "while America's female humorists have often writ-
ten in the same modes as their male counterparts, used
many of the same devices, and followed similar trends in
humor, their work has been neither imitative nor deriva-
tive" ("Women's Humor" 171).
```

Later in the same paper, Erika-Beth cited Linda Morris as the source for the idea that Whitcher saw her audience as essentially female. Since Morris did not say this in so few words, Erika-Beth summarized Morris's longer statement, putting the idea into her own words. Nonetheless, she needed to cite Morris as the source for the idea:

```
It was clear from her first published work in Neal's Sat-
urday Gazette in 1846 that Whitcher was writing for a female
audience (Morris 49).
```

Here an idea of Morris and not her voice informs the paper.

As a writer, you need to consider the least distracting and most effective way of incorporating sources into your paper. By and large, the most desirable is to summarize them, that is, accurately putting the ideas of others into your own words. Of course, there are times when you will sense that the voice of your source is more effective, not necessarily for what the voice says, but for how the voice says it. If your are quoting from a literary text or in cases where the original voice adds a nice variety to your own, quote your source directly. Nevertheless, quote no more than what you need in order to make your point.

Stylistically, more and more writers prefer to integrate authors' names and titles of works into their own text. Subsequently, if the author's name is repeated elsewhere in the text there is no need to repeat the title every time you quote the same source, if by omitting it there is no confusing it with other works by the same author. If you are using more than one source by the same author, you might have to make a short reference to the title the second time you use it.

Poetry is quoted differently because of its structure. Like a prose quote, try to weave the author and title into your text, at least the first time you quote from a particular poem. One line of poetry is simply written with quotation marks without any indentation:

> Shelley begins his elegiac poem "Adonais" with a force unmatched in literature: "I weep for Adonais—he is dead!" (1)

Two or three lines are incorporated into your text with a "space-slash-space" separating the lines:

> Shelley' elegiac poem "Adonais" begins with the poet expressing his intense grief for the fallen god: "I weep for Adonais—he is dead! / Oh, weep for Adonais—though our tear / Thaw not the frost which binds so dear a head!" (1–3)

For more than three lines, indent the entire poem ten spaces from the left and begin each verse on a new line:

> In "Adonais," Shelley expressed his grief for the fallen god and invites all to weep for him:
>
>   I weep for Adonais—he is dead!
>   Oh, weep for Adonais! though our tears
>   Thaw not the frost which binds so dear a head!
>   And thou, sad Hour, selected from all years
>   To mourn our loss, rouse thy obscure compeers,
>   And teach them thine own sorrow! (1–6)

The author, of course, did not summarize the sentiment Shelley expressed in these lines because the context in which the author was using the poem required reproducing the verses as originally written. Unless this was needed, the author might have summarized the idea behind the lines. Unnecessarily extensive quotes distract your reader. Draw other voices into your paper when necessary—content-wise or for stylistic benefits. Otherwise, stick with your own because it provides a unifying tone to the whole essay and be sure to give credit to your sources.

GIVING CREDIT

Imagine that you are at a big party. You meet some interesting, new people with great ideas, great bodies, and great personalities. As the party winds down, you casually ask a friend for some names and phone numbers of two or three of the invited guests. What if your friend said, "Oh, that was a woman. She lives in an apartment somewhere in the county. And him? He's a student at some school and lives somewhere in the state. And that brunette is a person from somewhere"? You didn't get a lot of helpful information, and you'll have a very rough time trying to set up a doubles tennis match with those three guests.

This situation is similar to the one you face when it comes to documenting sources. As a writer, consider yourself like the host. Be ready to give your readers-guests information they may want about the interesting ideas and voices you invited into your paper. Citing your source is giving your readers enough information so that they can get further acquainted with interesting material that they

Chapter 15   Writing with Research   **207**

met in your paper. Readers need names, addresses, and other specific details that allow them quickly and accurately to contact any source that you invited into your paper. "Tell me," asks the reader, "who came up with that idea? Give a name and an address—title of the article or book, where and who published it, when it was published—because I want to know more about the source."

Besides providing your reader with access to your sources, everything you draw from another source—regardless of whether you summarized the ideas in your own words, paraphrased your source, or quoted your source directly—needs to be noted ethically and legally. Common sense and ethics urge us to cite accurately and completely any material—words and ideas—that is not general knowledge and that we drew from other sources. Ethically we do not present points that our reader might mistake as our own. It is simply professional—and legal—to give credit where credit is due.

The various formats for citing sources can pose hassles, I know. On my office shelves and beside my computer at home, I have several books that provide examples of various citations styles and examples of various kinds of notations. While I might wish to handle citations in my own way, I am expected, as part of my membership in my profession, to follow the rules set down by my profession. Most English programs want students to follow the documentation style set by the Modern Language Association. It's all in the fifth edition of Joseph Gibaldi's *MLA Handbook for Writers of Research Papers*, published by the Modern Language Association, and your library probably has several copies of it in its reference section. It is the authoritative resource for all citation formats that a student of literature might need. Purdue University provides help based on the MLA guidelines online at **http://owl.english.purdue.edu/Files/33.html**. The Writer's Workshop at the University of Illinois at Urbana-Champaign is also very helpful. You can find it at **http://www.english.uiuc.edu/cws/wworkshop**. If you face a difficulty citing an electronic source, look at **http://www.uvm.edu/~ncrane/estyles**. Kate Hoffman gives more information about citing electronic sources in her essay.

Social scientists follow the rules prescribed in the *Publication Manual of the American Psychological Association*. The fourth edition appeared in 1994. Occasionally, you may be encouraged to follow the advice in the *Chicago Manual of Style*, the fourteenth edition appearing in 1993. If you don't know which style to follow, ask your instructor, or if the matter never comes up, use for your English classes the MLA style.

Every college writing handbook worth the paper it's printed on provides sample citations for books with one, two, or more authors, for essays in journals, and for electronic sources. If you are incorporating your own research into the paper, all of the sources I have mentioned supply specific guidelines for citing your self-created data.

At the end of every paper that uses research, you should list sources that you actually cited in your paper. There is no need to list sources you looked at but did not use, unless you may want to mention these in some broad way because you want your reader to know that you at least looked at them. Consider putting these unused but consulted sources in a separate list at the end of your paper, identifying them as "Works Consulted," apart from "Works Cited." Once again, the various formats for the list of different kinds of works cited are exemplified in writing handbooks and in the MLA, the APA, or Chicago Style guides.

As students of literature, we do not learn alone in some quiet corner all of the time. We read novels, poems, essays, dramas, philosophical tracts, critical essays, and maybe even papers written by colleagues or classmates; we watch motion pictures and videos; we listen to songs; but most of all we talk to one another about our mutual interests. This is what writing a paper—research based or not—is all about: sharing ideas with a community of like-minded people. Engaged in literary studies, we are constantly listening to and reading other voices, and in the process, consciously or unconsciously, learning, thinking, and rethinking. The research paper is a very natural outcome of communing with thinker-writers. When it is completed, ideas, supported by those of others, are merged into a persuasive essay. Nevertheless, through our research and recognition of that research we introduce our ideas into a community of scholars and admit our debt to it.

PUBLISHED WORKS CITED

Gibaldi, Joseph. *MLA Handbook for Writers of Research Papers.* 5th ed. New York: Modern Language Association, 1999.

Macrorie, Ken. *Searching Writing.* Upper Montclair, NJ: Boynton/Cook, 1984.

Publication Manual of the American Psychological Association. 4th ed. Washington, DC: American Psychological Association, 1994.

Shelley, Percy Bysshe. "Adonais." *How Does a Poem Mean?* Ed. John Ciardi and Miller Williams. 2nd ed. Boston: Houghton Mifflin, 1975. 176–87.

University of Chicago Press. *Chicago Manual of Style.* 14th ed. Chicago: University of Chicago Press, 1993.

CHAPTER 16

A Web of One's Own: Electronic Texts in the College English Course

Katherine Anne Hoffman

I teach my first year writing course in a computer room, and halfway through the semester, I often poll students about their initial reactions to having an English class in a computer lab. Their responses are often similar:

```
I was surprised and a little intimidated. (Matt A.)

I walked in the first day and I thought I was in the wrong
class, I was like could someone tell me where English 1
is? When I was told I was in the right room I was a lit-
tle surprised. (Andrew S.)

What the hell do we need on computers for? It's English.
(Adam W.)
```

However, others are more positive:

```
I thought it would be more convenient for writing papers
and maybe a more interactive class. (Michelle A.)

When I first learned that this class would be held in a com-
puter room I was excited because our whole world is on
computers now. (Andrew F.)

Yeah! (Steve P.)
```

Although feelings are mixed when it comes to using computers to teach English, it is increasingly difficult to avoid using them. Computers can make the learning of English both more lively and more efficient. Most important for student writers, computers allow for the storage, retrieval, and editing of electronic texts. This chapter explores how electronic texts can be used both in and out of the college English class to advance research, writing, and publishing.

209

RESEARCH

Research helps you write credible texts. Without research, you would not have enough information to formulate a strong argument for your opinions. However, the introduction of newer technologies has revolutionized the research process. The increasing availability of networked computers allows us access to startlingly vast amounts of information—or at least, networked computers provide a doorway to such information.

Are you writing a research article about snowmobiling? You can e-mail questions to **snow@snowmobile.org** and get first-hand answers from a national organization dedicated to the sport. Are you against your school's parking policy? You can send off one e-mail to 100 students and get survey results to support your claims within a day. Are you curious about how to start a small business? Go to Magic Hat's Web page **http://www.magichat.net/** and look up the history of how this small brewer got started. By incorporating the electronic resources, your research essay will have current information to complement the additional wealth of knowledge found in research libraries.

The four major online research tools include search engines, newspapers, magazines, and journals. Search engines give you a sense of the kind and amount of information available on your topic. Using a search engine might also help you make connections you might not have previously made. Some of the most popular search engines include **http://www.google.com** or **http://www.metacrawler.com**. News services such as CNN (**http://www.cnn.com**) and the AP wire (**http://wire.ap.org/**) allow you instantaneous access to breaking news. Magazines and journals are catalogued online in searchable databases such as Lexis-Nexis Academic Universe (**https://web.lexis-nexis.com/universe/**), for which you may need a university password for, or Findarticles (**http://www.findarticles.com**), which searches more than 300 magazines and journals for free and provides the full text for many articles.

Computers make the retrieval of certain kinds of data more interesting. The two main paths for data retrieval with the Internet: e-mail and the World Wide Web. E-mail gives you access to teachers, to other students, as well as to experts in the field you are researching. Being able to send off a quick note to your professor allows you to interact and get feedback about any assignment you might have. Also, if your class is on a listserv (an electronic mailing list that simultaneously sends mail to all subscribers), you can survey classmates about research topics.

Finally, you can complete some of your field research online, either by e-mailing a list of questions to a source or by using interactive software to communicate with an expert in the field you are researching. Instant Messenger, for instance, allows you and your interviewee to complete question-and-answer sessions simultaneously, allowing you to change your questions based on the responses you get, and you can go off on appropriate tangents if the opportunity presents itself. If you want to contact the creator of a Web page, that information is usually linked on their Website.

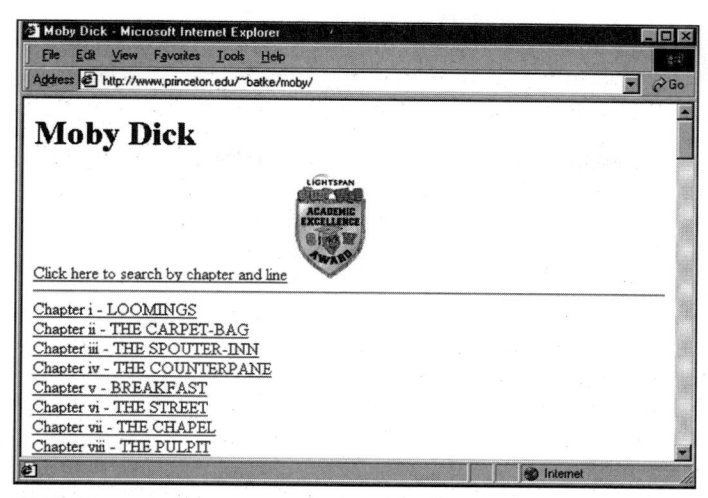

Chapter 16   A Web of One's Own: Electronic Texts in the College English Course   **211**

FIGURE 16-1 Screen Shot of Search Results

Computers can also help you develop more sophisticated interpretive papers. For example, you can use quantitative research to identify and locate symbolic patterns in literary texts. Perhaps you are writing about white imagery in Herman Melville's *Moby Dick*. You've already marked several passages in the book about the whiteness of the whale, and you understand the importance of the symbolism, but now you want some hard evidence about the use of the word "white." After conducting a general search on a web search engine such as **http://www.metacrawler.com,** for the words 'Moby Dick white' you would find 57 hits. If you clicked on the link **http://www.princeton.edu/~batke/moby/,** (see Figure 16-1) you would find the entire text of *Moby Dick* is online for you to search. You can look for occurrences of the word "white" throughout the book or in specific chapters. For instance, in Chapter 42 "The Whiteness of the Whale," there are 73 uses of "white" or a derivative of the word. Now your numerical count of the frequency of this word supports your claims about its importance. The ability to calculate the occurrences of the word "white" within seconds gives you more time to concentrate on the meanings of whiteness instead of constantly flipping the pages of your book, looking for, and possibly missing, all those "white" words.

Many times in interpretive or critical essays you will need to use a secondary critical source. The Internet might help you in this project by pointing you toward valuable resources. For instance, you might find the Melville Organization's Website (**http://www.melville.org**) has multiple pages listing criticism of Melville's work, which you could then locate in your school's library.

Don't forget that the Internet can also help you with personal essays as well. One student writes: "Sometimes I use the Internet for ideas. I'll type in a word and see what it connects to." Another student explains: "When writing, should

I need to look up a fact or e-mail my essays to a classmate for revision—both are just two clicks away."

EVALUATING INTERNET SOURCES

The key to using the Internet and e-mail for research is being able to recognize what's worthwhile, and what isn't. The main things to consider are the author and the purpose: Who put this together and why? It is important to consider the creator when viewing Web pages because you want to know why the information is there.

Questions to ask yourself include: Did an individual or a corporation post this information? Are they trying to make a profit from the information posted? Some basic clues about accuracy of information come from the Website address itself. The last segment of the URL, or Web page address, will indicate what kind of server the information is located on (see Figure 16-2). In the instance of the *Moby Dick* page, we know it is a site affiliated with a university because it is Princeton.edu, but we also know it is a personal Web page because of the ~batke after the .edu.

To find out exactly who the author of the Web page is, you may need to go into the page source and look at the html code. In Netscape you can go to "View" and then select "Page Source," causing a window to open with the page's html code, and possibly, the author's name. For instance, *Moby Dick* was put on the web by Peter Batke, the Humanities Consultant for Computer and Information Technology at Princeton University. On the surface, one would surmise that his motives are purely academic, as he's also uploaded a number of other texts to the Web. To find this out, I had to delete the last part of the URL (/moby/) and ended up at Peter's index page, which showed me the other pages he has done. Among other links, electronic texts for the following are also accessible from Peter's page: *The Collected Works* by George Eliot, *Leaves of Grass* by Walt Whitman, and *Walden* by Henry David Thoreau. By being able to see the full

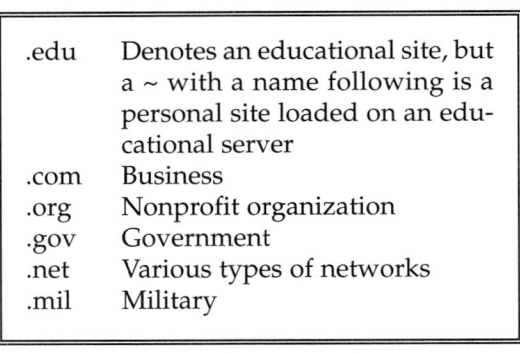

.edu	Denotes an educational site, but a ~ with a name following is a personal site loaded on an educational server
.com	Business
.org	Nonprofit organization
.gov	Government
.net	Various types of networks
.mil	Military

FIGURE 16-2 Website Server Information

extent of material on his page, including the background of its creator, I was able to conclude he was a reliable source affiliated with a well-known university, with a background in Humanities.

If you found a Website where an individual not affiliated with an organization posted their claims about *Moby Dick* (based, for instance, on the TV miniseries) you might consider their input in a very critical manner: Is it endorsed by anyone? Are there advertisements on the page (that is, is somebody trying to make a profit from this page)? Has the page been given any legitimate awards or recognition? Often a site can be months or years out of date, so if that information is available, it helps to check the date the page was last updated.

There is no one rule to go by when evaluating Web sources, so keep asking yourself about author and purpose. You can also verify information by checking other sites; however, sometimes people just copy information from one incorrect source to their own site. Always try to double-check your Internet sources with information from books or other reputable Websites (see Figure 16-3). Keep in mind that the depth of information in carefully researched books remains indispensable in any serious research; computers only make your time spent with books more efficient.

Sometimes even off-the-wall Websites can serve your purpose. If you want to get radical opinions or information that is usually censored, your research on the Web can be invaluable. Many organizations have Web pages that give you ideas and information that will allow you to portray both sides of an argument. You can access Websites for black power and white supremacist groups; pro-environment and pro-corporation groups; pro-drug and anti-drug use. This information is usually posted on the Web for a purpose, and you need to keep in mind the rules for evaluation when viewing these sites, as many are not only uncensored, but unedited, and may have inaccurate or skewed information.

For instance, perhaps you are researching a political event—reactionary groups have Websites you can use as resources. There's the Green Party

---

Helpful Websites for Evaluating Sources:
- The Good, The Bad and The Ugly, or Why It's a Good Idea to Evaluate Web Sources
  http://lib.nmsu.edu/instruction/eval.html
- How to Critically Analyze Information Sources
  http://www.library.cornell.edu/okuref/research/skill26.htm
- Ten C's for Evaluating Internet Resources
  http://www.uwec.edu/Admin/Library/Guides/tencs.html

FIGURE 16-3

(**http://www.greenparties.org/**), an organization devoted to changing the way the current government operates while maintaining a strong environmental stand. Or maybe Vermont's Grassroots Party might be helpful in showing an alternative (**http://www.vermontel.net/~epgorge/vgrp.htm**), as they are an organization devoted to among other things, the legalization of marijuana.

The Internet has also proved to be a lively place to learn about the economic battles between large corporations and individuals. Many people now use the Web as a way to fight large corporations. For instance, Infact, at **http://www.infact.org** is a national corporate watchdog organization. A site with an interesting perspective is **http://www.ihatestarbucks.com,** where people can post their opinions about the corporate coffeehouse. The nonrestrictive nature of the Internet means you'll get info that would normally never get past a publisher or a newspaper editor.

Besides giving you access to uncensored information, the Web also provides you with information on a 24-hour basis. If you needed to look up the definition and history of a word, such as "gam," you could easily go to the Internet Public Library **http://www.dictionary.com** and find out that gam means "1. A social visit or friendly interchange, especially between whalers or seafarers; 2. A herd of whales or a social congregation of whalers, especially at sea." The usefulness of the Internet is apparent, but you must know how to use the tool properly. Obviously if it took me 20 minutes to find an answer via computers that would have taken me 5 without, I am not being efficient.

One way to increase efficiency when using the Internet is to create a list of useful, reliable, and often-used Websites. I suggest using Bookmarks when online to mark useful pages or ones you frequently visit (see Figure 16-4). In Netscape Navigator you would merely click the Bookmark button on your toolbar, and select Add Bookmark. It makes your time online less frantic and

---

Some Useful Websites to Bookmark:

- http://www.bartleby.com/
  Bartleby.com Great Books Online: full text of numerous well-known authors and poets.
- http://owl.english.purdue.edu/
  Purdue's Online Writing Lab: helpful resource for writing, editing, and revising.
- http://www.imdb.com
  Internet Movie Database: a massive index of movies, actors, directors, and plots.
- http://www.ipl.org/
  Internet Public Library: great for quick queries and general information.

FIGURE 16-4

more efficient by creating a shortcut to a favorite site without having to type in an address.

A caveat is in order. Although the Web can save you time, it can also eat away your time. Sierra, a student in my intermediate composition class pointed out, "It wastes hours on end" and Arianna agrees, "When I am writing a paper and looking things up, I get sidetracked and start surfing the Web. This gets me in trouble because it then takes me twice as long to write the paper." If you are going online, make a list of what you need to know, and you won't waste time surfing from site to site trying to figure out what exactly you need. By figuring out what information you need before you even log on, you will be more efficient and it will be clear when you have completed your research.

WRITING AND COMPOSING

Once you've gathered research from a variety of reliable sources, you still need to compose an academic essay. Writing down carefully gathered information into a cohesive whole demonstrates your knowledge—which makes your audience believe you. In many ways, the ability to compose electronically has changed the way we write. The benefits of revising on screen are numerous: As a computer file, a text is never finished because you can always open that file and make changes; the text is less permanent on the screen, making revision less of a chore than if you had to retype a paper; the revision process is less overwhelming—seeing only a half a page at a time helps writers focus on a paragraph at a time; cutting and pasting allows different documents, like interview transcripts, to be easily integrated; most of all, with electronic texts there is mobility—you can save your document on a disk and work on it anywhere on campus. More than that, computers allow more freedom for students to experiment. Brian, a student in my intermediate composition class, writes: "I feel like I can play more, that is to say I can try something, scrap it, and not feel bad about killing a tree." That students are able to take more risks and play with their writing seems a valuable asset of computers.

Additionally, when writing, the computer can prove an invaluable communication tool. Instant Messenger, e-mail, or chat rooms provide outlets for peer input and teacher suggestion. Jen, a sophomore, explains: "If I get stuck—or can't decide if a sentence sounds right or works—I can just IM anyone on my buddy list."

However, there are also limitations—with revision on the computer screen it is difficult to revise at the theme level because you can't see the entire document as you might if you laid it all out on a table in front of you. Electronic texts can also slow you down, as you may never seem finished with the infinite possibilities of revision. And you may not have a computer at home that has Internet access, or your school's server may be down when you are trying to write your paper. All of these limitations do not mean you should avoid computers; they just serve as a warning to not rely too heavily on these tools, but to use them as best benefits you and your writing.

Beyond the capacity to communicate as you write, computer word processors allow you to transform your text by using columns, adding pictures and graphs, or changing font size and style. By making your essay more visually appealing, you invest yourself more, produce better work, and increase reader interest. Do not add pictures or graphs to generate space fillers; rather, add only what will enhance your work. For instance, an image of a whale capsizing a boat could visually emphasize your points about the devastation a whale could inflict on a small boat—and also save you the space of explaining an image you can just as easily include in your paper. It may be more useful, however, to include a bar graph of the occurrences of the word "white" in each chapter.

One of the best reasons behind the inclusion of graphics is to complement the genre you are writing in. If you are writing a feature-style article, by making it appear as it would in a magazine, you will be more inclined to work hard to capture a style particular to a magazine. Your words become the glue that holds these multiple images together on the page and should, in fact, include a critical reason for why the specific images you have chosen appear within your text. The step beyond this is the Web page—allowing your multimedia text to be accessible to the rest of the world. (And Web pages are made or broken by how effectively they use visual layout.)

PUBLISHING

For many students, the Internet is a new realm for publishing. You have access to a massive new audience. Not only can you post your *Moby Dick* essay online, you could mail it to the Melville society's listserv Ishmail, devoted to the discussion and exploration of all Melville-related subjects (**http://www.melville.org/ishmail.htm**), and ask the members of the list for their opinions on it. More importantly, you could create a Web page that included your original work and add to the growing number of Web pages devoted to *Moby Dick,* therefore coming full circle and making your own text a research source for others.

Having a Web page of your own provides you with opportunities for personal and scholarly import. When my students created Web pages for their research essays, the rest of the students were able to read each other's work and discuss it during class—allowing everyone access to the information gathered by the individual students.

The research assignment had only two requirements for topics: first, it had to be based on something the student was passionately interested in; second, it had to have a local slant, because one of the sources had to be an interview with a local expert. Jaret, a first year student who wanted to get involved in the University of Vermont's Creamer program, wrote about his experiences working at the school's dairy farm and researched the qualifications he needed to become a member of the UVM Creamers. Most of the class had not realized UVM even had a dairy farm, nor did many of them realize the amount of dedication and hard work it took to be a part of that farm. Besides creating a well-written essay and attractive Web-

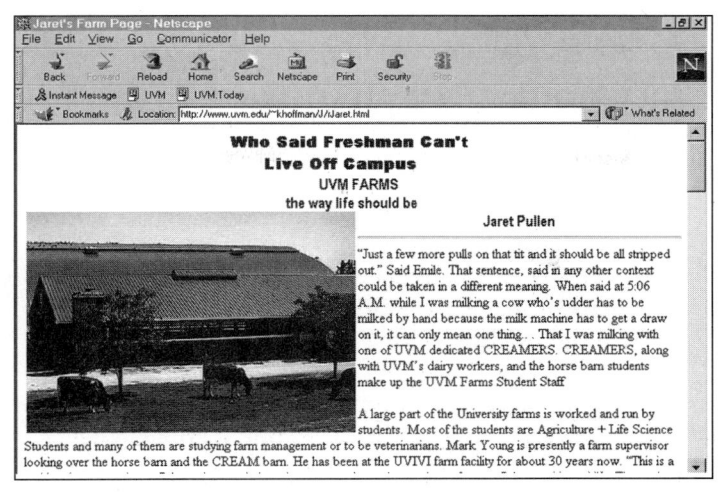

Chapter 16   A Web of One's Own: Electronic Texts in the College English Course   217

FIGURE 16-5   Jaret's Web Page

site, Jaret was able to introduce his classmates to an aspect of their school they had not previously been aware of (See Figure 16-5).

The creation of the visual text of the Website enables students to educate and engage their professors, their peers, and the world as well. Any Website a student creates becomes a part of the World Wide Web, it becomes a part of the information network of the WWW and perpetuates the model of engaged learning, and becomes more than just a four- to six-page essay that is written, handed in, graded, and filed in a student's folder or wastebasket.

Many of my students e-mailed their parents the Web address for our class, creating an even larger audience for their work. Having a Web page allows you to distribute information to thousands of people simultaneously, and the Internet allows your information to include multimedia aspects such as sound and image. By creating a Web page of your own, based on your research and interpretation of that research, you will be adding to the numerous sources on the Internet, making your work a resource for others who are concerned with the information you have gathered (See Figure 16-6).

Most importantly, Web publishing and research is useful in enhancing learning, not inflating poor work with flashy pictures. I've had students ask me why their final projects, littered with glamorous pictures and snazzy fonts, had earned them "only a C." My response is always the same—substance is the first priority of a paper, and pictures and fonts should serve only to enhance what is already there.

For instance, one student had researched local clubs to find out what types of live music were played in the Burlington area. While his work was superficial (it was obvious he had not visited these places recently and his interview transcripts had only three or four superficial questions and answers), his Web page was filled with irrelevant images of hot dogs, lava lamps, and

> **Four Sites on Web Publishing and Design:**
>
> - http://www.ncsa.uiuc.edu/General/Internet/WWW/HTMLPrimer.html
>   Beginner's Guide to HTML: this resource clearly explains html for any beginner.
> - http://home.netscape.com/browsers/createsites/index.html
>   Netscape's resources for creating Websites: a useful wizard that walks you through the process slowly.
> - http://www.iso.gmu.edu/~montecin/web-page-create.htm
>   Considerations When Creating a Web Page: Virginia Montecino's list of questions is useful in determining Website effectiveness.
> - http://www.wpdfd.com/wpdhome.htm
>   Web page design for Designers: This e-zine contains editorials, reviews, tips, and tricks.

FIGURE 16-6

animated pictures that served no apparent purpose in illuminating the reader about local music.

By making the graphics and colors work with the essay topic, the reader's experience is enriched. A great example of this came from a student's personal essay about a quilt her aunt had made for her while another aunt had been very sick. She wrote in snapshot style (like quilt blocks) and formatted the paper with text boxes that had different-colored patterns for each snapshot image, creating a quiltlike effect. The radically different colors and styles of each segment reminded the reader of the quilt image throughout the essay.

As you decide what you should add to your essay to enhance it, consider the two main questions used for evaluating sources: Who is the audience, and what is the purpose? If you find yourself unable to see a purpose for adding an image, clearly you can do without it.

While technology is rapidly changing, the use of computers in the classroom will probably increase. While this will be useful for research, writing, and publishing, remember that computers will not do the work for you—but they can make your work more efficient.

CHAPTER 17

Examining the Essay Examination

Tony Magistrale

Please write on two of the following topics. You will have 50 minutes to complete this examination. Write only in the examination book provided.

1. Define Wordsworth's attitude toward childhood as it is expressed in *The Prelude*. (25 minutes)
2. Discuss the importance of the urban environment in two of Dostoevski's novels. (25 minutes)
3. Compare Emily Dickinson's view on immortality in the poem "I've known a Heaven, like a Tent" to her perspective on this subject in any of her other poems studied this semester. (25 minutes)

When I showed these exam topics to several of the authors of the other chapters in this book, all veterans of many essay examination campaigns, each one gave me a similar response: relief at not having to answer any of the questions. If English professors are glad to be free of such an ordeal, why do they put their students through it? Is the essay examination an educational rite of passage? A traditional testing routine teachers are reluctant to give up? A fundamental illustration of the profession's tendency toward sadistic behavior? Maybe a little of each. But it is also something more.

Sid Poger, author of the poetry chapter, told me that he assigns essay examinations out of a desire to "help the student discover for him- or herself the major themes of the course throughout the term. These ideas are what the essays will address, and I hope the student who has been in class, in mind as well as body, will come to recognize what's been going on." Another author included in this book, Tom Simone, feels that an essay exam is "the place for a student to shine. If he or she has been paying attention and has been thinking about the class material, my essays are always open-ended enough to allow him or her to show off." Bill Stephany, co-editor of this volume and our department's medievalist, reminded me that he looks for "connections that surprise the teacher ... giving information on topics I want to know more about." Toby Fulwiler, the book's other editor and author of the journal chapter, often sees essay exams as more like "free writes" than methodically structured prose. If you look carefully at the reasons each of these professors gives for assigning essay questions, it is clear that exams are always more than a means for establishing a grade.

Each of these teachers seeks to test your ability to interpret aspects of specific literary works or to synthesize disparate material covered in class into a more comprehensive whole. Sometimes, as in the Dickinson question above, a writing task may also ask you to recognize similarities and differences between two or more characters, themes, symbols, or individual texts. In any event, the most challenging essay topics appear to center not only around how much you know about a particular subject, but also about the course as a whole. The kind of surprise Bill Stephany encourages gets a teacher excited about what you have to say; it demonstrates not only a solid understanding of a poem, or a novel, or a core concept, but also shows that you have spent some time considering its larger connections to the course and to your own life. In contrast, a student who disagrees with me without much thought and merely for the sake of saying something different or who goes off into a new interpretation without adequate support for the position is surely going to give me a surprise, but it will be one I will probably not enjoy.

WRITING UNDER PRESSURE

Composing answers to an essay examination may appear difficult enough when you are given several days to construct responses, as in a take-home exam. The assignment becomes all the more challenging, however, when you must write in a short, predetermined period of time, usually surrounded by other students who seem to possess magical pens that seldom rise from the exam book's page. Writing under a time constraint demands even more concision and discipline than ordinarily employed in producing a research paper or a critical essay over an extended period of days or weeks. Time restraints preclude the luxury of multiple drafts or the leisure of returning to your answer after an elapsed length of time. Perhaps this is one reason so many teachers continue to assign in-class essay exams and believe they are important: As is often the case in contexts outside the classroom, we do not always have the opportunity to polish language until it says exactly what we want it to. We are often required to think quickly, to use words spontaneously yet accurately. And although this is a difficult activity, there are a few tricks you might learn to get better at it.

PRELIMINARY STEPS AND A CHECKLIST OF PRACTICAL ADVICE

An essay exam is first and foremost an essay. As such, it is important to decide what to include, what to exclude, how to arrange, and what to emphasize.

1. Before beginning any writing, you should read the entire test. What choices, if any, does the exam allow? What specific kinds of information will each essay require?

Chapter 17   Examining the Essay Examination   **221**

2. Which of the questions do you feel most comfortable answering? (It might help to start with the easiest and work your way to the most difficult.)
3. What types of information is the exam question asking for? Does it ask you to evaluate or argue, analyze or discuss, compare or contrast?
4. Without rewriting the entire exam request, can you highlight the most important concepts of what you are being asked in the opening sentence of your answer?
5. Keep your eye on the clock. Allot yourself a certain period of time per answer and hold yourself to it. Instructors seldom sympathize with an indication you have run out of time.
6. Finally, when you feel ready to begin the actual writing, keep the following points in mind to help in organizing and presenting the essay: (a) circle core issues, concepts, and requests in the exam question itself; (b) use frequent paragraph breaks to capture a tired professor's attention; (c) leave space on the left side of your paper or exam book for second thoughts and revisions; (d) write on every other line, as this will make it easier for your professor to read and for you to make changes directly into the text of your answer.
7. Plan on building in enough time to read the exam over before handing it in. Simple qualifications to central arguments as well as mistakes in diction are hard to recognize in a first draft, but may be captured in revision. (This is why you will want to leave room on the left side of your paper or exam booklet.)

TYPES OF INFORMATION REQUESTS

The key to performing well on an essay examination is to understand completely what the questions are asking. The language of a given assignment will often contain hidden clues that reveal potential directions for composing an answer. Consider, for example, this examination question from a recent American literature midterm:

> The general tone of Crevecoeur's *Letters of an American Farmer* presents an image of America that finds restatement in the work of Emerson and the transcendentalists: It is that of a young, beautiful, optimistic, and enduring country that is destined to complete the cycle of history begun in Europe. Compare this version of America to that found in Twain's *Huckleberry Finn*.

First, notice how much information is already supplied in the topic itself: an implied chronology, that Emerson and the transcendentalists are coming out of an American literary tradition that was shaped by earlier writers such as Crevecoeur. Moreover, the exam also supplies you with a solid definition of what Crevecoeur and the transcendentalists generally felt about America. Lastly, the topic also suggests that these are your starting points, and perhaps the easiest way to begin composing a response would be to assemble evidence from *Huckleberry Finn* that either agrees or disagrees with the Crevecoeur-transcendentalist assessment.

In other words, to answer this particular information request, I would start at the ending and work my way back to its beginning. However, it is quite possible to argue that Twain's novel presents at the same time both a negative portrait of America's social institutions and a positive example of American individualism in the survivalist instincts of Huck. Another way to answer this question, then, would be to refrain from making the distinction regarding whether *Huck Finn* is essentially an optimistic or pessimistic work, and instead to demonstrate where the novel both disagrees and concurs with the perspective associated with Crevecoeur and the transcendentalists. The word "compare" in the exam question allows you this flexibility. The term "comparison" usually means a larger, more inclusive approach to the topic that may include both similarities and differences. But if you were asked instead to contrast Twain's book with these earlier writers, you would want to emphasize the differences only.

Therefore, any question that asks you to compare or contrast may be requesting

- The differences between two or more things.
- The similarities between generally dissimilar things.
- A combination of both the differences and similarities.
- An explanation of one thing in relation to something else.
- A basis for evaluation and/or argument.

All comparisons and contrasts require you to go beyond individual positions, theses, or texts—to think about the interrelationships between characteristics of two or more concepts or texts. Ascertain and note well the operative verb in the exam request. The direction word is usually an imperative verb—for example, compare/contrast, discuss, trace, respond, support. Some of these words give you more flexibility than others. For example, compare/contrast strongly limits the potential shape of your response, while the words "discuss" and "respond" imply greater freedom.

PLANNING

Once you understand the type of information the exam requests, you should plan a response to it. First, make a simple list of main ideas. This will generate new concepts at the same time as it will help in formulating the language you will need to construct a coherent argument. Second, use a written plan to keep your writing focused on the subject. After you have composed such a plan, check it against the examination request. Are the topics you intend to discuss in your answer relevant to what is being asked?

Here is an outline Nancy used to help her address the midterm examination topic raised at the beginning of this chapter, "Compare Emily Dickinson's view on immortality in the poem 'I've known a Heaven, like a Tent' to her perspective on this subject in any one of her other poems studied this semester." Nancy's

American literature class had not studied this poem prior to the test, so it was reproduced on the exam itself:

Nancy's Plan:

Interpret Poem:
   —"heaven" as circus tent
   —circus tent as symbol of afterlife
   —circus as non-permanent, already gone

Compare To:
   "I heard a Fly buzz—when I died"
   —human isolation
   —lost vision, taken away
   —same conclusion: no hope/light

Looking at Nancy's plan, it becomes clear that she has constructed a solid framework for composing an essay answer. She chooses first to analyze the poem cited in the exam, "I've known a Heaven, like a Tent," emphasizing the use of a departed circus as a simile for describing the loss of heaven. (Pay particular attention to the manner in which she will blend her reading of the poem with specific excerpts from the poem itself, thereby making her interpretation all the more persuasive.) From there, she then seeks to complete the assignment by comparing it to another Dickinson poem, "I heard a Fly buzz." Because the exam asked for a comparison, Nancy elected to work with a poem that has a perspective similar to that in "I've known a Heaven, like a Tent." She could just as well have gone in the opposite direction, choosing a poem to contrast with the poem cited in the exam (the operative verb—*compare*—in the exam question gives her this freedom). Finally, note that in both the plan and the essay that emerge, Nancy maintains her critical attention on the unifying thesis of the issue at hand: how each of these poems reflects a comparable attitude toward the theme of immortality:

> In the poem "I've known a Heaven, like a Tent," Emily Dickinson in her own way is describing her idea of heaven. It seems as though she breaks a childhood myth with this poem. The myth being that heaven is a visible place that awaits us with its great pearly gates and its angels waiting to take you in and check your name off this great ledger that some old white-haired man is seated in front of. This "Heaven" she has "known," may refer to a glimpse of God's happy place, or perhaps she is recalling a special "heavenly" moment or event that profoundly touched her life. In either event, myth or reality, this recollected image of heaven is now gone, and it is significant that she ties its departure to a circus show "That dazzled, Yesterday." The carnival is a visual image from childhood (perhaps invoking the poet's earlier innocent perception is unfulfilled and betrayed), as the tent "wrap[s] its shining Yards— / Pluck[s] up its stakes, and disappear[s]—." What

was here yesterday, her heaven or hope of attaining swallowed up, of "View." Dickinson now interprets heaven as a vast emptiness, just a "View." She discovers that heaven cannot be traced with empirical evidence, that it is just an eternity: "No Trace—no Figment of the Thing," leaving only "just the miles of Stare." This theme of disillusionment with heaven, of eternal loneliness and emptiness, can be traced throughout her poetry.

In "I heard a Fly buzz—when I died," when the speaker began the poem in the process of dying, she rose above herself and was aware of everything going on around her: the "Breaths gathering firm," the "Eyes wrung dry," and the "Keepsakes—Signed away." But when she finally dies, at the moment of death, "the windows failed—and then / I could not see to see," meaning that she could no longer see anything ahead of her. Just as in the exam poem, the afterlife portrayed in "I heard a Fly buzz" is unattainable, the "Heaven" remains unseen, a mere suffocating darkness. As her "Heaven" in the circus poem just dissolves, in "I heard a Fly buzz" there is no hope for a beautiful or fulfilling afterlife. Her view in both these poems is filled with the dark despair of a Melville or a Hawthorne, rather than the unqualified faith in the future of a transcendentalist.

Nancy's analysis is a good illustration of how the act of writing helps the mind not only to clarify concepts, but also to develop new insights and parallels. Her answer is a study in the art of discovery. It starts by working through the complex details of a poem she has never seen before and concludes by reconnecting to information in "I heard a Fly buzz," which is a work she knows quite well. On the other hand, since the last three sentences of her final paragraph are crucial to answering the exam assignment, perhaps Nancy should highlight them in some way. Putting them in a separate paragraph (note how desperately her answer needs additional paragraph breaks) or even switching them to the opening of her answer are potential ways to underscore their importance.

Note also that in writing about both of these poems Nancy not only discovers some similarities they share, but also goes on to enlarge her understanding of Dickinson as a nineteenth-century American poet. The concluding sentence of her essay is different—in diction and scope—from the rest of her response. Here is evidence of the "surprise" William Stephany mentioned earlier when explaining his reason for assigning essay topics. Nancy's final sentence jumps at the reader because it extends her analysis of these two Dickinson poems to include an important assertion about the poet's relationship to her literary contemporaries. If Nancy were able to revise this essay, or if it were a take-home examination, this final sentence might well become her first sentence, as it is a large thesis statement that is supported in the act of interpreting the two poems. In any event, as this concluding sentence represents the culmination of Nancy's effort to understand the poetry of Emily Dickinson, she might highlight it in a new paragraph or by somehow distinguishing it from the rest of the essay.

Nancy saved the actual comparison the exam topic requested until the end of her writing, after she had focused individual attention on each of the Dickinson poems. On the one hand, I think her essay is organized in such a way that the material is presented clearly and concisely (and organization is one of the most difficult accomplishments in writing an essay exam, since good insights may occur late in the writing). On the other hand, Nancy could have structured things differently and still achieved similar results. Employing the same ideas listed under her plan, the major points of the essay could easily be reorganized to introduce the comparison between the two poems at the beginning (and perhaps throughout the course of the essay), rather than saving it for the end.

STRUCTURING ESSAY ANSWERS

Under the tense and circumscribed conditions of a timed examination, some students spill out a torrent of information: By saying as much as they can about a particular text or a writer, they trust that the torrent of information they provide will sufficiently impress the teacher or somehow manage to strike upon a response relevant to the question. Consider, for example, Ken's response to a midterm examination question asking him to discuss the significance of Madeline Usher's role in Poe's tale "The Fall of the House of Usher":

> Poe's tales have no apparent logic to them. He was a writer from the period of dark romanticism and his stories often show a person's inability to control experiences that exist psychologically and from his personal negative motivations. Poe hated women, or at least he didn't trust them very far, so all his male characters rebel against them. Poe's own relationship to women was influenced by his mother's rejection of him at an early age and he spent the rest of his life trying to find someone to take her place. The male characters in his stories take drugs and use exotic settings to forget tragic love affairs that are similar to the ones Poe himself experienced with women in his own life. For them, time is always an enemy—it is there as a reminder of frustration and ultimate death. Madeline Usher is a symbol of Poe's women. She is all the things her brother hates, all the things out of his control. She suffers from the same kind of illness that is killing Usher.

What can we say is strong in this essay? Ken demonstrates a wide-ranging understanding of Poe. Many of the points he makes in this essay are valid. He knows, for instance, that Poe was a dark romantic, that the writer's feelings toward women were ambivalent, that his male protagonists are deeply disturbed individuals subject to compulsive and aberrant behavior, that time is a symbol of human destruction throughout Poe's stories, and finally, that Madeline is a constant source of irritation for her brother.

What could Ken have done differently? A central problem in this response is within its organization or structure; Ken wanders around the subjects of Poe's fiction in a manner painfully reminiscent of Roderick himself wandering the corridors of the Usher mansion. His writing has neither direction nor thesis; he never really comes to terms with Madeline's role in the story, and thus produces more of a collection of assertions rather than a cohesive essay. Instead of pursuing only material relevant to answering the exam question, Ken tries to impart everything he knows about Poe's fiction. He doesn't really begin to answer the question until the last two sentences of his response.

There are several places in this answer where the writer might have "turned the corner" in order to commence a more focused analysis of "The Fall of the House of Usher," and Madeline's character specifically. What, for instance, are "all the things her brother hates, all the things out of his control"? If Madeline is symbolic of these restrictive elements, a more detailed explanation of (1) exactly what these elements are and (2) how they are embodied in Madeline would help the reader to see the connection between her character and the rest of the story. Once Madeline's relationship to Roderick is ascertained and clarified, then a discussion of the larger issue of Poe's general attitude toward women—either in other stories or as biographical criticism—makes more sense. A general discussion of Poe and women might occur in the beginning or at the end of this answer, but in either case this discussion must be relevant to what the exam writer has to say about Madeline herself. Unless these issues are tied directly to the discussion of Madeline's relationship with her brother, the examination question remains essentially unanswered.

Rather than simply "leaping into" an essay answer on an exam, and thereby encouraging your thoughts to wander in a number of directions, as in Ken's example, it is better to keep your writing focused. Here's where some sort of writing plan can prove particularly useful, as with Nancy's response to the Dickinson question, since long, meandering responses suggest imprecise, fuzzy thinking, even if relevant information is embedded somewhere in your response. Once you have decided exactly what the exam question requires and the plan is completed, you are ready to begin writing.

But how? Your written plan contains pertinent information for developing an essay, but in what order should these points be presented? What form should the answer take? What should come first?

In discussing strategies for structuring essay exams, several of my English department colleagues suggested that the strongest part of any essay should be its beginning. Because professors read hundreds of essays in a rush, students should give them what they want up front, and certainly within the first paragraph. Consequently, Nancy might have inverted the form of her essay—starting with a few sentences to introduce the most important points of comparison between the two poems, then a paragraph or two describing how each poem connects to the theme of immortality, and concluding with a summary that brings the two poems together again. Nancy's comparison/contrast example supplied earlier illustrates that the form an essay takes is often less important

Chapter 17   Examining the Essay Examination   **227**

than the information it provides and the degree to which that information responds accurately to what the examination question asks.

Other instructors may feel differently. It would be well within the province of a teacher to argue that Nancy's answer does not confront the issue of an actual comparison between two of Dickinson's poems until the final paragraph, and as a consequence her response is not as complete as it should be. Some instructors might feel that since the request for a comparison is at the heart of the examination question, language directly addressing this issue should appear within the essay's opening paragraph.

Thus, the standard advice in structuring essays is to create some version of a "funnel" shape: start broadly by stating and defining the most important elements, or thesis, of your argument. Then, gradually narrow or specify your main argument through examples and illustrations of the points raised initially in the broad thesis statement. In this way, your examples and analyses will refer to concepts you have established, and your supporting evidence can be tailored to fit the major points that began the essay. Sometimes finding a way to transpose the exam question into a thesis is one of the safest ways to put the teacher on your side. Moreover, getting the most important points of the answer upfront early on is a confidence booster; as time narrows in your effort to deepen your answer, you know that at least some important information has already been presented. This principle can be illustrated in the paragraphs that follow, taken from a midterm examination in which Susan was asked to relate the theme of Walt Whitman's short poem "A noiseless patient spider" to his larger poetic vision:

> Walt Whitman was a poet who wrote about the unity of all things. He took Emerson's doctrines to their furthest extremes, believing that not only were the diverse and individual elements of the universe related to one another but, in fact, that they were reflective of the same identical thing.
>
> Whitman's themes were about everything—a blade of grass, a prostitute, a dying man alone on a battlefield—and he believed sincerely that no one thing was better, or worse, than another. A spider (which before this class I would probably squash) is only a small part of the "whole," yet is still connected to the "whole," just as one human being is representative of a larger humanity.
>
> Whitman's verse accomplishes the same sort of connecting. He unifies everything and everybody in poetic song. In the first half of "Song of Myself" the poet takes all of life's experiences and makes them his own—he observes and studies them—and then seeks to understand how they are connected to one another.
>
> In "A noiseless patient spider" he asks his soul the same question: "Where do I stand? / Surrounded, detached, seeking spheres to connect them." Only by "connecting" himself to everything and everyone he observes can the poet,

```
like the spider's web, "form a bridge" that will link him
to the rest of the world.
```

In the opening paragraph, Susan begins her analysis with a broad assessment of Whitman's poetry; she even includes a mention of Emerson's influence on his work. After establishing the unity theme in Whitman's poetry, she ends her first paragraph by tying this concept to "A noiseless patient spider": "A spider (which before this class I would probably squash) is only a small part of the 'whole,' just as one human being is representative of a larger humanity." For me, as the professor evaluating this response, the "unsquashed" spider that is now included as part of the cosmic whole for Susan as a result of her reading Whitman is a memorable moment, as the writer makes an honest and spontaneous connection between literature and her life.

In the second paragraph, however, Susan's analysis becomes even more specific, centering on the relationship between the metaphor of the spider's web and Whitman's broader poetic principles: "... the spider creates a web which 'connects' things together. Whitman's verse accomplishes the same sort of connecting. He unifies everything and everybody in poetic song." The connection between "A noiseless patient spider" and Whitman's canon is made explicit in her reference to one of his major poems, "Song of Myself," and here she is careful to stress common themes found in both poems. The use of the "funnel" structure as an organizing metaphor in this essay aids Susan in gradually developing her analysis from the general to the specific, so that by the conclusion Whitman's poetic vision and the symbolic spider web have become synonymous in purpose: "Only by 'connecting' himself to everything and everyone he observes can the poet, like the spider's web, 'form the bridge' that will link him to the rest of the world."

THE TAKE-HOME EXAMINATION

A well-written essay—whether composed during a timed in-class examination or in response to a take-home assignment—reflects the strengths described in this chapter: It is organized and focused; it demonstrates the ability to analyze and/or engage comparative thought; it shows the capacity to assemble, evaluate, explicate, and argue information; and it indicates an understanding of course material and the capability to shape this understanding into writing appropriate to the exam topic. The take-home essay is closely related to its in-class brethren in form, content, and purpose. However, since they are each composed under different circumstances, there are some slight variations in their manner of production. Primarily, a take-home examination affords the chance to edit, to revise, and to rethink what you have composed. Furthermore, the take-home exam provides the opportunity to incorporate research—class notes, quotes, journals, and (sometimes) published scholarship—directly into the composition. It is, of course, a fatal mistake not to acknowledge citations used in a take-home exam. Richard Sweterlitsch provides assistance in his research chapter for avoiding plagiarism, and his advice should be applied to take-home exams as well as to the composition of more formal research projects.

Using Class Notes and Journals

As Toby Fulwiler suggests in his chapter, journals are an excellent source for helping you to study for examinations, to assemble information for conducting research, and as a place to generate ideas through informal prose. Before composing an essay assignment, read through your journal entries, class notes, notes you may have written in the margins of texts, and e-mail correspondence with your instructor and classmates on areas germane to the topic. Sometimes you may discover whole sections or passages that require only slight modification for inclusion into the essay. Often a sentence or two, even the seed of an idea currently in undeveloped form, can point you in the direction for further writing. Aside from generating ideas to use in composing a response, the journal is also the place to begin the actual writing of the essay itself. Because a take-home exam affords you a certain amount of flexible time, use the journal to free write about your subject. The journal will not only help to start the flow of writing itself, but a couple of good entries may become the basis for your essay.

Revising and Editing

The take-home examination typically allows you several days to produce an essay, so the sooner you get started writing, the more chance you will have to polish and improve its contents. Once a first draft of the essay is complete, reread it from start to finish, paying particular attention to logic and overall organization. Is your thesis clear, and is it developed throughout the length of the essay? Does it answer the question? Do individual paragraphs fit together, or would the thesis be more coherent if the order of presentation were rearranged? What about the element of "surprise"? Is there a place in your writing where you make a particularly original and provocative connection or insight? Is this moment sufficiently highlighted—that is, does it stand out in its own paragraph, is it developed sufficiently, and do you use it early enough in the essay? When the revisions are completed, read the work aloud to a friend. The very act of reading an essay aloud can often reveal places where language might be improved, or where the logic of the argument needs to be strengthened. I often dictate my own prose into a tape recorder; the act of hearing my thoughts forces me to concentrate on how the writing sounds, from the overall development of a thesis to the way in which individual words work (or do not work) harmoniously with one another.

BEGINNING AT THE END: ENDING AT THE BEGINNING

A few years ago, I returned to my undergraduate alma mater, Allegheny College, for the first time since graduation. I arrived on campus on a day late in May, one of those glorious spring afternoons filled with promise when even the earth of the western Pennsylvania snow belt is refreshed in light. It was warm and final examinations were in session, so all the windows of Arter Hall, home of the English Department, were open to the afternoon. As I strolled alongside the building, bemused by the torrent of recollections each step seemed to summon, a series of bells sounded from inside indicating the start of a final exam. All the old feelings returned—the nervous fingers, the twitch somewhere near the base of my stomach. The exam bell removed the brightness of that May afternoon. I was back in the dim and musty gray air of ancient Arter Hall, blue book open on the desk in front of me, three exam topics measuring the distance between my pen and the onset of summer vacation. I may well have decided at that very moment to write the chapter you have just finished reading.

APPENDIX

MLA Documentation

Modern Language Association (MLA) is the standard form for documenting sources in research-based English papers. The fundamental point of this system is to avoid the need for footnotes or endnotes simply to identify source information. The basic MLA system is simple:

1. In the text of your paper, all sources are briefly mentioned by author name.
2. At the end of your paper, on a separate page called Works Cited, the publication data for each source is listed.
3. Additional explanatory information is included in footnotes or endnotes. (The MLA system is explained in authoritative detail in the *MLA Handbook for Writers of Research Papers*, 5th ed. (New York: MLA, 1999) or on their Website **http://www.mla.org**.

GUIDELINES FOR FORMATTING MLA MANUSCRIPTS

The MLA guidelines for submitting English papers are fairly conservative and do not reflect the wealth of visually interesting options in font, point sizes, visual insertions, and other options available on most modern word processors. If your instructor requests MLA format, follow the guidelines below. If your instructor encourages more open journalistic formats, use good judgment in displaying the information in your text.

Paper and Printing

Print all academic assignments on 8½ × 11 clean white paper in a standard font (e.g., Times New Roman, Courier) and point size (11 or 12) using a good quality printer.

Margins and Spacing

Allow margins of one inch all around. Justify left margin only. Double space everything, including headings, quoted material, and Works Cited page. Indent five spaces for paragraphs. Indent ten spaces for prose quotations of five or more lines or poetry of more than three lines (do not use quotation marks when indenting ten spaces).

Identification

On page one, include your name, course title, instructor's name, and the date on separate lines, double spaced, flush with the upper left margin.

Title

Center the title on the first page using conventional title case punctuation (capitalizing key words only). If your instructor asks for strict MLA style, avoid using italics, underlining, quotation marks, boldface, unusual font, or enlarged point size for the title. (MLA does not require a title page or an outline.) Double space to first paragraph.

Page Numbers

Set page numbers to print in upper right margin of all pages, one-half inch below top of paper. If following strict MLA form, include your last name before each page number to guarantee correct identification of stray pages (Turner 1, Turner 2, etc.).

Punctuation

One space is required after commas, semicolons, colons, periods, question marks, exclamation points, and between the periods in an ellipsis. (Double spacing is optional after end punctuation.) Dashes are formed by two hyphens, with no extra spacing on either side.

Visual Information

Label each table or chart as Table 1, Table 2, etc. Label each drawing or photograph as Figure 1 or Fig. 2, etc. Include a clear caption for each, and place in the text as near as possible to the passage that refers to it.

GUIDELINES FOR IN-TEXT CITATIONS

The following guidelines explain how to include research sources in the main body of your text following MLA style.

Each source mentioned in your paper needs to be accompanied by a brief citation including author's last name and page number. These are placed either in the text itself or parentheses following. This *in-text citation* refers readers to the alphabetical list of Works Cited at paper's end, listing full publication information about each source. The following examples illustrate the most common in-text citations.

Author Identified in a Signal Phrase

When you include the source author's name in the sentence introducing the source, add only the specific page on which the material appeared in parentheses following the information:

```
Carol Lea Clark explains the basic necessities for creating a
page on the World Wide Web (77).
```

Do not include the word *page* or the abbreviation *p.* before the number; the parenthetical reference comes before the period.
For a work by **two or three authors,** include all authors' names:

```
Clark and Jones explain …
```

For works with **more than three authors,** list all authors or use the first author's name and add *"et al."* (Latin abbreviation for "and others") without a comma:

```
Britton et al. suggest …
```

Author Not Identified in a Signal Phrase

When you do not include the author's name in your text, add it following the information in parentheses along with the source page number:

```
Provided one has certain "basic ingredients," the Web offers
potential worldwide publication (Clark 77).
```

For a work by two or three authors, include all authors' last names:

```
(Clark and Jones 15) (Smith, Web, and Beck 210).
```

For works with more than three authors, list all authors' last names or list the first author only, adding et al.:

```
(White et al. 95).
```

Do not punctuate between the author's name and the page number(s).

Two or More Works by the Same Author

If your paper refers to two or more works by the same author, each citation needs to identify the specific work. Either mention the title of the work in the text or include a shortened version of the title (usually the first one or two important words) in the parenthetical citation. Three correct ways to do this:

```
According to Peter Elbow in Writing Without Teachers, the best
way to overcome writer's block is to write (5).

According to Peter Elbow, the best way to overcome writer's block
is to write (Writing 5).

The best way to overcome writer's block is to write (Elbow, Writing 5).
```

Identify the shortened title by underlining (e.g., published titles) or quotation marks (e.g., articles) as appropriate. Put a comma between the author's last name and title.

Unknown Author

When the author of a work is unknown, either give the complete title in the text or a shortened version in the parenthetical citation, along with the page number.

```
According to Statistical Abstracts, in 1990 the literacy rate for
Mexico stood at 75 percent (374).

In 1990 the literacy rate for Mexico stood at 75 percent
(Statistical 374).
```

Corporate or Organizational Author

When no author is listed for a work published by a corporation, foundation, organization, or association, indicate the group's full name in either text or parentheses:

```
(The Modern Language Association 3)
```

If the name is long, it is best to cite it in the sentence and put only the page number in parentheses.

Authors with the Same Last Name

When you cite works by two or more different authors with the same last name, include the first initial of each author's name in the parenthetical citation:

```
(C. Miller 63; S. Miller 101-04).
```

Works in More Than One Volume

Indicate the pertinent volume number for each citation before the page number, and follow it with a colon and one space:

```
(Hill 2: 70)
```

If your source is one volume of a multivolume work, do not specify the volume number in your text, but specify it in the Works Cited list.

One-Page Works

When you refer to a work one-page long, do not include the page number since that will appear in the Works Cited list.

Quotation from a Secondary Source

When a quotation or any information in your source is originally from another source, use the abbreviation "qtd. in":

```
Lester Brown of Worldwatch feels that international agricultural
production has reached its limit (qtd. in Mann 51).
```

Poem or Play

In citing poems, name part (if divided into parts) and line numbers; include the word line or lines in the first such reference. This information will help your audience find the passages in any source where those works are reprinted, which page references alone cannot provide:

```
In "The Mother," Gwendolyn Brooks remembers "the children you got
that you did not get" (line 1).
```

When you cite up to three lines from a poem in your text, separate the lines with slash marks:

```
Emily Dickinson describes being alive in a New England summer:
"Inebriate of air am I / And debauchee of dew / Reeling through
endless summer days" (lines 6-8).
```

When you cite more than three lines, indent ten spaces.
    Cite verse plays using act, scene, and line numbers, separated by periods. For major works such as Hamlet, use identifiable abbreviations:

```
(Ham 4.4.31-39).
```

More Than One Work in a Citation

To cite two or more works, separate them with semicolons.

```
(Aronson, Golden Shore 177; Didion 49-50)
```

Long Quotation Set Off from Text

Set off quoted passages of five or more lines, by indenting one inch or ten spaces from the left-hand margin of the text (not from the paper's edge); double-space, and omit quotation marks. The parenthetical citation *follows* end punctuation (unlike citations for shorter, integrated quotations) and is not followed by a period:

```
Fellow author W. Somerset Maugham had this to say about Austen's
dialogue:
        No one has ever looked upon Jane Austen as a great
        stylist. Her spelling was peculiar and her grammar
        often shaky, but she had a good ear. Her dialogue is
        probably as natural as dialogue can ever be. To set
        down on paper speech as it is spoken would be very
        tedious, and some arrangement of it is necessary. (434)
```

Electronic Texts

The MLA guidelines on documenting online sources are explained in detail online at **http://www.mla.org/set_stl.htm**.

Electronic sources are cited in the body of the text the same as print sources by author, title of text, or title of Website and page numbers. If no page numbers appear on the source, include section (sec.) number or title and/or paragraph (par.) numbers.

```
The Wizard of Oz "was nominated for six Academy Awards, including
Best Picture" (Wizard par. 3).
```

However, Web pages commonly omit page and section numbers and are not organized by paragraphs. In such cases, omit numbers from your parenthetical references. (For a document downloaded from the Web, the page numbers of a printout should normally not be cited since pagination may vary in different printouts.)

NOTES TO PROVIDE ADDITIONAL INFORMATION

MLA style uses notes primarily to offer comments, explanations, or additional information (especially source-related information) that cannot be smoothly or easily accommodated in the text of the paper. In general, however, you should omit additional information, outside the main body of your paper, unless it is necessary for clarification or justification. If a note is necessary, insert a raised (superscript) numeral at the reference point in the text. Introduce the note itself with a corresponding raised numeral, and indent it.

Appendix

Text with Superscript

Louise Erdrich's Love Medicine is good example of the contemporary story cycle.[1]

Note

[1] For further studies of story cycles, see Forrest Ingram, "Representative Short Story Cycles of the Twentieth Century;" and Maggie Dunn and Ann Morris, "The Composite Novel: The Short Story Cycle in Transition."

Any published references listed in the notes also appears in the Works Cited list.

Notes may come at the bottom of the page (paragraph indentation) on which the citation appears as footnotes or may be included as endnotes, double spaced on a separate page at the end of your paper. Endnote pages should be placed between the body of the paper and the Works Cited list, with the title Note or Notes.

SAMPLE PAGE MLA STYLE

Turner 1

Andrew Turner

English 2

Professor McIntosh

3 October 2002

The Freedom of Henry David Thoreau

Henry David Thoreau led millions of people throughout the world to think about individual freedom in a new way. During his lifetime, he attempted to live free of unjust governmental constraints as well as conventional social expectations. In his 1849 essay "On the Duty of Civil Disobedience," he makes his strongest case against governmental interference in the lives of citizens.

Thoreau opens "Civil Disobedience" stating "that government is best which governs not at all" (222). Because Thoreau did not want his freedom overshadowed by governmental regulations, he tried to ignore them. However, he was arrested and put in the Concord jail for failing to pay his poll tax—a tax he believed unjust because it supported the government's war with Mexico as well as the immoral institution of slavery. Thus the doctrine of passive resistance was formed:

> How does it become a man to behave toward this American government today? I answer that he cannot without disgrace be associated with it. I cannot for an instant recognize that political organization as my government which is the <u>slave's</u> government also. (224)

According to Charles R. Anderson, Thoreau's other writings, such as "Slavery in Massachusetts" and "A Plea for Captain John Brown," show his disdain of the "northerners for their cowardice on conniving with such an institution" (28). He wanted all free American citizens, north and south, to follow their consciences.

GUIDELINES FOR THE WORKS CITED PAGE

Every source mentioned in the body of your paper should be identified in a Works Cited list attached to the end of the paper using the following format.

- Center the title *Works Cited*, with no quotation marks, underlining, or boldface one inch from the top of a separate page following the final page of the paper. (If asked to include works read but not cited, attach an additional page titled Works Consulted.)
- Number this page, following in sequence from the last text page of your paper. If the list runs more than a page, continue the page numbering in sequence, but do not repeat the Works Cited title.
- Double space between the title and first entry and within and between entries.
- Begin each entry at the left-hand margin, and indent subsequent lines the equivalent of a paragraph indention (five spaces or one-half inch).

ORDER OF ENTRIES

Alphabetize entries according to authors' last names. If an author is unknown, alphabetize according to the first word of the title (but do not use an initial A, An, or The).

ENTRY FORMATS

Each item in the entry begins with a capital letter and is followed by a period. Each period is followed by one space. Capitalize all major words in the book and article titles. Underline published titles (books, periodicals); put quotation marks around chapters, articles, stories, and poems within published works. Do not underline volume and issue numbers or end punctuation. The four most common variations on general formats are the following:

```
Books
Author(s). Book Title. Place of publication: Publisher, year of
publication.

Journal Articles
Author(s). "Article Title." Journal Title volume, (year of
publication): inclusive page numbers.

Magazine and Newspaper Articles
Author(s). "Article Title." Publication Title date of
publication: inclusive page numbers.

Electronic Sources
Author(s). "Document title." Published source title. Date of
publication: number of pages, sections, or paragraphs. Sponsoring
organization. Date of access <electronic address>.
```

Authors

- List the author's last name first, followed by a comma and then the rest of the name as it appears on the publication, followed by a period. Never alter an author's name by replacing full spellings with initials or by dropping middle initials.
- For more than one author, use a comma rather than a period after the first author; list the other authors full names, first name first, separated by commas. Do not use an ampersand (&). Put a period at the end.

- For more than one work by the same author, use three hyphens for the name after the first entry.

Titles

- List full titles and subtitles as they appear on the title page of a book or in the credits for a film, video, or recording. Separate titles and subtitles with colons (followed by one space).
- Underline titles of entire books and periodicals.
- Use quotation marks around the titles of essays, poems, songs, short stories, and other parts of a larger work.
- Put a period after a book or article title. Use no punctuation after a journal, magazine, or newspaper title.

Places of Publication

- Places of publication are given for books and pamphlets, not for journals or magazines.
- Give the city of publication from the title page or copyright page. If several cities are given, use only the first.
- If the city could be unfamiliar or if there are several cities with the same name, abbreviate the state or country, preceded by a comma.
- Use a colon to separate the place of publication from the publisher.
- For electronic sources, include Internet address at end of entry in angle brackets.

Publishers

- The name of the publisher is given for books and pamphlets.
- Shorten the publisher's name as described below under Abbreviations. If a title page indicates both an imprint and a publisher (for example, Arbor House, an imprint of William Morrow), list both shortened names, separated by a hyphen (Arbor-Morrow).
- Use a comma to separate the publisher from the publication date.

Date

- For books, give the year of publication followed by a period.
- For other publications, give the year of publication within parentheses followed by a colon.
- For newspapers, put the day before the month and year (25 May 1954) with no commas separating the elements.
- For magazines and newspapers, put a colon after the date.
- For electronic sources, include the date the site was accessed.

Page Numbers

- Page numbers are included for all publications other than books.
- Use a hyphen, not a dash, between inclusive page numbers, with no extra space on either side.

Appendix

- Use all digits for ending page numbers up to 99 and the last two digits only for numbers above 99 (130–38) unless the full number is needed for clarity (198–210).
- If subsequent pages do not follow consecutively, use a plus sign after the last consecutive page number (39; 52–55).
- If no page numbers are available for electronic sources, include paragraph or section numbers.

Abbreviations

- Use standard postal abbreviations (NY, VT, FL) to identify the state after the city of publication.
- To shorten a publisher's name, drop the words Press, Company, and so forth in the publisher's name (Blair for Blair Press). Use the abbreviation UP for University Press (Columbia UP; U of Chicago P).
- Use only the first name if the publisher's name is a series of names (Farrar for Farrar, Straus & Giroux). Use only the last name if the publisher's name is a person's name (Abrams for Harry N. Abrams).
- If no publisher or date of publication is given for a source, use the abbreviations n.p. (no publisher) or n.d. (no date).
- For periodicals, abbreviate months using the first three letters followed by a period (Apr.; Dec.) except for May, June, and July. If an issue covers two months, use a hyphen to connect the months (Apr.–May and June–Aug.).

DOCUMENTING BOOKS

Book by One Author

Thomas, Lewis. Lives of a Cell: Notes of a Biology Watcher. New York: Viking, 1974.

Book by Two or Three Authors

Fulwiler, Toby, and Alan R. Hayakawa. The Blair Handbook. Boston: Blair-Prentice, 2002.

Second and third authors are listed first name first. Do not alphabetize the author's names within an individual Works Cited entry. The final author's name is preceded by "and". Do not use an ampersand (&). A comma always follows the inverted ordering of the author's first name.

Book by More Than Three Authors

Britton, James, et al. The Development of Writing Abilities (1–18). London: Macmillan Education, 1975.

With more than three authors, you have the option of using the abbreviation et al. (and others) or listing all the authors' names in full as they appear on the title page of the book. Do not alphabetize the names within the Works Cited entry.

Book by a Corporation, Organization, or Association

> U.S. Coast Guard Auxiliary. <u>Boating Skills and Seamanship.</u> Washington: Coast Guard Auxiliary National Board, 1997.

Alphabetize by the name of the organization.

Revised Edition of a Book

> Hayakawa, S. I. <u>Language in Thought and Action.</u> 4th ed. New York: Harcourt, 1978.

Edited Book

> Hoy, Pat C., II, Esther H. Shor, and Robert DiYanni, eds. <u>Women's Voices: Visions and Perspectives.</u> New York: McGraw, 1990.

Book with an Editor and Author

> Britton, James. <u>Prospect and Retrospect.</u> Ed. Gordon Pradl. Upper Montclair: Boynton, 1982.

The abbreviation Ed. when followed by a name replaces the phrase "edited by" and cannot be made plural.

Book in More Than One Volume

> Waldrep, Tom, ed. <u>Writers on Writing.</u> 2 vols. New York: Random, 1985-88.

When separate volumes were published in different years, use inclusive dates.

One Volume of a Multivolume Book

> Waldrep, Tom, ed. <u>Writers on Writing.</u> Vol. 2. New York: Random, 1988.

When each volume has its own title, list the full publication information for the volume you have used first, followed by information on the series (number of volumes, dates).

>Churchill, Winston S. Triumph and Tragedy. Boston: Houghton, 1953. Vol. 6 of The Second World War. 6 vols. 1948-53.

Translated Book

>Camus, Albert. The Stranger. Trans. Stuart Gilbert. New York: Random, 1946.

Book in a Series

>Magistrate, Anthony. Stephen King, The Second Decade: Danse Macabre to The Dark Half. Twayne American Authors Series 599. New York: Twayne, 1992.

A book title appearing in a book's title is not underlined (or italicized). Add series information just before city of publication.

Reprinted Book

>Hurston, Zora Neale. Their Eyes Were Watching God. 1937. New York: Perennial-Harper, 1990.

Add the original publication date after the title, then cite current edition information.

Introduction, Preface, Foreword, or Afterword in a Book

>Atwell, Nancie. Introduction. Coming to Know: Writing to Learn in the Intermediate Grades. Ed. Nancie Atwell. Portsmouth, NH: Heinemann, 1990. xi-xxiii.

Work in an Anthology or Chapter in an Edited Collection

>Donne, John. "The Canonization." The Metaphysical Poets. Ed. Helen Gardner. Baltimore: Penguin, 1957. 61-62.

Gay, John. The Beggar's Opera. 1728. British Dramatists from Dryden to Sheridan. Ed. George H. Nettleton and Arthur E. Case. Carbondale: Southern Illinois UP, 1975. 530-65.

Use quotation marks around the title of the work (poem, short story, essay, chapter) unless the work was originally published as a book. In that case, underline (or italicize) the title. Add inclusive page numbers for the selection at the end of the entry.

When citing two or more selections from one anthology, you may list the anthology separately under the editor's name.

Gardner, Helen, ed. The Metaphysical Poets. Baltimore: Penguin, 1957.

All entries within that anthology will then include only a cross reference to the anthology entry.

Donne, John. "The Canonization." Gardner 61-62.

Essay or Periodical Article Reprinted in a Collection

Gannet, Lewis. Introduction. The Portable Steinbeck. New York: Viking, 1946. 1-12. Rpt. as "John Steinbeck's Way of Writing" in Steinbeck and His Critics: A Record of Twenty-five Years. Ed. E. W. Tedlock, Jr., and C. V. Wicker. Albuquerque: U of New Mexico P, 1957. 23-37.

Include the full citation for the original publication, followed by Rpt. in (*Reprinted in*) and the publication information for the book. Include inclusive page numbers for the article or essay found in the collection; include inclusive page numbers for the original source when available.

Articles in a Reference Book

"Behn, Aphra." The Concise Columbia Encyclopedia. 1998 ed.

Miller, Peter L.

For a signed article, begin with the author's name. For commonly known reference works, full publication information and editor's names are not necessary. For entries arranged alphabetically, page and volume numbers are not necessary.

Anonymous Book

> The <u>World Almanac and Book of Facts.</u> New York: World Almanac-Funk, 2000.

Alphabetize by title, excluding an initial A, An, or The.

Dissertation

> Kitzhaber, Albert R. "Rhetoric in American Colleges." Diss. U of Washington, 1953.

Use quotation marks for the title of an unpublished dissertation. Include the university name and the year. For a published dissertation, underline (or italicize) the title and give publication information as you would for a book, including the order number if the publisher is University Microfilms International (UMI).

DOCUMENTING PERIODICALS

Article, Story, or Poem in a Monthly or Bimonthly Magazine

> Linn, Robert L., and Stephen B. Dunbar. "The Nation's Report Card Goes Home." <u>Phi Delta Kappan</u> Jan. 2000: 127-43.

Abbreviate all months except May, June, and July. Hyphenate months for bimonthlies (July–Aug. 1993). Do not list volume or issue numbers. If unsigned article, alphabetize by title.

Article, Story, or Poem in a Weekly Magazine

> Ross, Alex. "The Wanderer." <u>New Yorker</u> 10 May 1999: 56-63.

Note that when day of week is specified, publication date is inverted.

Article in a Daily Newspaper

> Brody, Jane E. "Doctors Get Poor Marks for Nutrition Knowledge." <u>New York Times</u> 10 Feb. 1992, B7.

For an unsigned article, alphabetize by the title. Give the full name of the newspaper as it appears on the masthead, but drop any introductory A, An, or The.

```
"Redistricting Reconsidered." Washington Post 12 May 2001: B2.
```

If the city is not in the name, it should follow in brackets: El Diario [Los Angeles].

With the page number, include the letter that designates any separately numbered sections. If sections are numbered consecutively, list the section number (sec. 2) before the colon, preceded by a comma.

Article in a Journal Paginated by Volume

```
Harris, Joseph. "The Other Reader." Journal of Advanced
Composition 12 (1992): 34-36.
```

If the page numbers are continuous from one issue to the next throughout the year, include only the volume number (always in Arabic numerals) and year. Do not give the issue number or month or season. Note that there is no space between the end parenthesis and the colon.

Article in a Journal Paginated by Issue

```
Tiffin, Helen. "Post-Colonialism, Post-Modernism, and the
Rehabilitation of Post-Colonial History." Journal of Commonwealth
Literature 23.1 (1998): 169-81.
```

If each issue begins with page 1, include the volume number followed by a period and then the issue number (both in Arabic numerals, even if the journal uses Roman). Do not give the month of publication.

Editorial

```
"Gay Partnership Legislation a Mixed Bag." Editorial. Burlington
Free Press 5 April 2000: A10.
```

If signed, list the author's name first.

Letter to the Editor and Reply

```
Kempthorne, Charles. Letter. Kansas City Star 26 July 1999: A16.
Massing, Michael. Reply to letter of Peter Dale Scott. New York
Review of Books 4 Mar. 993: 57.
```

Review

    Kramer, Mimi. "Victims: Rev. of "Tis Pity She's a Whore." New

    York Shakespeare Festival. New Yorker 20 Apr. 1992: 78-79.

DOCUMENTING ELECTRONIC SOURCES

Electronic sources include both **databases,** available as CD-ROM, diskette, or magnetic tape, and **online sources** accessed with a computer connected to the Internet.

DATABASES

The Works Cited entries for electronic databases (newsletters, journals, and conferences) are similar to entries for articles in printed periodicals: cite the author's name; the article or document title in quotation marks; the newsletter, journal, or conference title; the number of the volume or issue; and the year or date of publication (in parentheses); the number of pages, if available.

Periodically Updated CD-ROM Database

    James, Edgar. "A Novel as Strong as Its Weakest Link." New York

    Times Book Review 16 Sep. 2000: New York Times Ondisc. CD-ROM.

    UMI-Proquest. Oct. 2001.

If a database comes from a printed source such as a book, periodical, or collection of bibliographies or abstracts, cite this information first, followed by the title of the database (underlined), the medium of publication, the vendor name (if applicable), and the date of electronic publication. If no printed source is available, include the title of the material accessed (in quotation marks), the date of the material if given, the underlined title of the database, the medium of publication, the vendor name, and the date of electronic publication.

Portable databases are much like books and periodicals. Their entries in Works Cited lists are similar to those for printed material except that you must also include the following items:

- The medium of publication (CD-ROM, diskette, magnetic tape).
- The name of the vendor, if known (this may be different from the name of the organization that compiled the information, which must also be included).
- The date of electronic publication, in addition to the date the material originally may have been published (as for a reprinted book or article).

Nonperiodical CD-ROM Publication

    "Rhetoric." The Oxford English Dictionary. 2nd ed. CD-ROM.

    Oxford: Oxford UP, 1992.

List a nonperiodical CD-ROM as you would a book, adding the medium of publication and information about the source, if applicable. If citing only part of a work, underline the title of the selected portion or place it within quotation marks, as appropriate (as you would the title of a printed short story, poem, article, essay, or similar source).

Diskette or Magnetic Tape Publication

```
Lanham, Richard D. The Electronic Word: Democracy, Technology,
and the Arts. Diskette. Chicago: U of Chicago P, 1993.
```

List these in the Works Cited section as you would a book, adding the medium of publication (e.g., Diskette or Magnetic tape).

ONLINE SOURCES

Documenting a World Wide Web (WWW) or other Internet source follows the same basic guidelines as documenting other texts: *who said what, where, and when*. However, important differences need to be noted. In citing online sources from the World Wide Web or electronic mail (e-mail), two dates are important: the date the text was created (published) and the date you found the information (accessed the site). When both publication and access dates are available, provide both.

However, many WWW sources are often updated or changed, leaving no trace of the original version, so always provide the access date, which documents that this information was available on that particular date. Thus, most electronic source entries will end with an access date immediately followed by the electronic address: 23 Dec. 2001 <http://www.cas.usf.edu/english>. The angle brackets <> identify the source as Internet.

The following guidelines are derived from the MLA Website <http://www.mla.org>. To identify a WWW or Internet source, include, if available, the following items in the following order, each punctuated by a period, except date of access:

- **Author** (or editor, compiler, or translator). If known, full name, last name first (if unknown, include alias).
- **Title.** Include title of poems, short stories, articles in quotation marks. Include title of posting to discussion list or forum in quotation marks followed by Online posting. Underline the titles of published sources (books, magzines, films, recordings).
- **Editor, compiler, or translator.** Include name, if not cited earlier, followed by appropriate abbreviation, Ed., Com., Tran.
- **Print source.** Include the same information as in a printed citation.
- **Title** of scholarly project, database, personal, or professional site (underlined); if no title, include description such as Home page. Include name of editor if available.
- **Identifying number.** For a journal, include volume and issue number.
- **Date of electronic publication.**
- **Discussion list** information. Include full name or title of list or forum.
- **Page, paragraph, or section numbers.**
- **Sponsorship or affiliation.** Include the name of any organization sponsoring this site.

Appendix

- **Date of access.** Include date you visited this site.
- **Electronic address.** Include within angle brackets <> .

Published Website

Beller, Jonathon L. "What's Inside the Insider?" <u>Pop Matters Film.</u> 1999. 21 May 2000 <http://popmatters.com/film/insider.html>.

Personal Website

Fulwiler, Toby. Home page. 2 Apr. 2000 <http://www.uvm.edu/~tfulwile>.

Professional Website

<u>Yellow Wall-Paper Site.</u> U. of Texas. 1995. 4 Mar. 1998 <http://www.cwrl.utexas.edu,daniel/amlit/wallpaper/>.

Book

Twain, Mark. <u>The Adventures of Tom Sawyer.</u> Internet Wiretap Online Library. 4 Jan. 1998. Carnegie-Mellon U. 4 Oct. 1998 <http://www.cs.cmu.edu/Web/People/rgs/sawyrtable.html>.

To interrupt an electronic address at the end of a line, hit return, but do not hyphenate.

Poem

Poe, Edgar Allan. "The Raven." <u>American Review,</u> 1845. <u>Poetry Archives,</u> 8 Sep. 1998. <http://tqd.advanced.org/3247/cgi-bin/dispoem.cgi?poet=poe.edgar&poem>.

Article in a Journal

Erkkila, Betsy. "The Emily Dickinson Wars." <u>Emily Dickinson Journal</u> 5.2 (1996): 14 pars. 8 Nov. 1988. <http://www.colorado.edu/EDIS/journal/index.html>.

Article in a Reference Database

"Victorian." <u>Britannica Online.</u> Vers. 97.1.1 Mar. 1997. <u>Encyclopedia Britannica.</u> 2 Dec. 1998 <http://www.eb.com>180.

Posting to a Discussion List

Beja, Morris. "New Virginia Woolf Discussion List." Online posting. 22 Feb. 1996. <u>The Virginia Woolf Society,</u> Ohio State U. 24 Mar. 1996 <gopher://dept.English.upenn.edu:70/0r0-1858-?Lists/20th/vwoolf>.

E-Mail or Listserv

Fulwiler, Toby. "A question about electronic sources." 23 May 2000. E-mail to the author. U. Vermont.

Robert Harley. "Writing Committee meeting." 24 Jan. 1999. Distribution list. UCLA. 25 June 2001.

Newsgroup (USENET) Message

Answerman (Mathes, Robert). "Revising the Atom." 2 Mar. 1997. 4 July 1997 <alt.books.digest>.

If you quote a personal message sent by somebody else, be sure to get permission before including his or her address on the Works Cited page.

DOCUMENTING OTHER SOURCES

Cartoon, Titled or Untitled

Davis, Jim. "Garfield." Cartoon. <u>Courier</u> [Findlay, OH] 17 Feb. 1996: E4.

Roberts, Victoria. Cartoon. <u>New Yorker</u> 13 July 2000: 34.

Film or Videocassette

Casablanca. Dir. Michael Curtiz. Perf. Humphrey Bogart and Ingrid Bergman. Warner Bros., 1942.

Fast Food: What's in It for You. Prod. Center for Science. Videocassette. Los Angeles: Churchill, 1988.

Begin with the title, followed by the director, the studio, and the year released. You may also include the names of lead actors, producer, and the like between the title and the distribution information. If your essay is concerned with a particular person's work on a film, lead with that person's name, arranging all other information accordingly.

Lewis, Joseph H., dir. Gun Crazy. Screenplay by Dalton Trumbo. King Bros., 1950.

Personal Interview

Holden, James. Personal interview. 12 Jan. 2000.

Begin with the interviewee's name and specify the kind of interview and the date. You may identify the interviewee's position if relevant to the purpose of the interview.

Morser, John. Professor of Political Science, U of Wisconsin-Stevens Point. Telephone interview. 15 Dec. 2001.

Published or Broadcast Interview

Sowell, Thomas. "Affirmative Action Programs." Interview. All Things Considered. Natl. Public Radio. WGTE, Toledo. 5 June 1990.

For published or broadcast interviews, begin with the interviewee's name. Include appropriate publication information for a periodical or book and appropriate broadcast information for a radio or television program.

Print Advertisement

Cadillac DeVille. Advertisement. New York Times 21 Feb. 1996, natl. ed.: A20.

Begin with the name of the product, followed by the description Advertisement and publication information for the source.

Unpublished Lecture, Public Address, or Speech

```
Graves, Donald. "When Bad Things Happen to Good Ideas." National
Council of Teachers of English Convention. St. Louis, 21 Nov.
1989.
```

Begin with the speaker, followed by the title (if any), the meeting (and sponsoring organization, if needed), the location, and the date. If there is no title, use a descriptive label (such as Speech) with no quotation marks.

Personal or Unpublished Letter

```
Friedman, Paul. Letter to the author. 18 Mar. 2000.
```

Personal letters and e-mail messages are handled nearly identically in Works Cited entries. Begin with the name of the writer, identify the type of communication (e.g., Letter), and specify the audience. Include the date written, if known, or the date received.

To cite an unpublished letter from an archive or private collection, include information that locates the holding (for example, Quinn-Adams Papers. Lexington Historical Society. Lexington, KY.).

Published Letter

```
King, Jr., Martin Luther. "Letter from Birmingham Jail." 28 Aug.
1963 Civil Disobedience in Focus. Ed. Hugo Adam Bedau. New York:
Routledge, 1991. 68-84.
```

Cite published letters as you would a selection from an anthology. Specify the audience in the letter title (if known). Include the date of the letter immediately after its title. Place the page number(s) after the publisher information. If you cite more than one letter from a collection, cite the entire collection in the Works Cited list, and indicate individual dates and page numbers in your text.

Map

```
Ohio River: Foster, KY, to New Martinsville, WV. Map. Huntington:
U.S. Corps of Engineers, 1985.
```

Appendix

Cite a map as you would a book by an unknown author. Underline the title and identify the source as a map or chart.

Performance

> Bissex, Rachel. Folk Songs. Flynn Theater. Burlington, VT. 14 May 1990.

Identify the pertinent details such as title, place, and date of performance. If you focus on a particular person in your essay, such as the director or conductor, lead with that person's name. For a recital or individual concert, lead with the performer's name.

Audio Recording

> Young, Neil, comp., perf. <u>Mirror Ball.</u> CD. In part accompanied by members of Pearl Jam. Burbank: Reprise, 1995.

Depending on the focus of your essay, begin with the artist, composer, or conductor. Enclose song titles in quotation marks, followed by the recording title, underlined. Do not underline musical compositions identified only by form, number, and key. If you are not citing a compact disc, specify the recording format. End with the company label, the catalog number (if known), and the date of issue.

Television or Radio Broadcast

> "Emissary." <u>Star Trek: Deep Space Nine.</u> Teleplay by Michael Pillar. Story by Rick Berman and Michael Pillar. Dir. David Carson. Fox. WFLX, West Palm Beach. 9 Jan. 1993.

If the broadcast is not an episode of a series or the episode is untitled, begin with the program title. Include the network, the station and city, and the date of broadcast. The inclusion of other information such as narrator, writer, director, or performers' depends on the purpose of your citation.

Work of Art

> Holbein, Hans. <u>Portrait of Erasmus.</u> The Louvre, Paris. <u>The Louvre Museum.</u> By Germain Bazin. New York: Abrams, n.d., 148.

Begin with the artist's name. Follow with the title, and conclude with the location. If your source is a book, also give pertinent publication information.

GUIDELINES FOR A WORKS CITED PAGE

Center the title Works Cited on a separate last page of your paper. Alphabetize each entry by author's or editor's last name; if no author, alphabetize by title (omitting the words A, and, and the).

When two or more works appear by the same author, include full name only for the first listing; for subsequent entries, instead of typing the name, use three hyphens followed by a period, following alphabetical order of each work's title.

Type the first line of each entry flush with left margin; indent second and following lines five spaces (i.e., a hanging indent). Double space the entire page.

SAMPLE WORKS CITED PAGE

Turner 9

Works Cited

Anderson, Charles Roberts, ed. *Thoreau's Vision: The Major Essays.* Englewood Cliffs: Prentice, 1993.

"Ghandi." *Britannica Online.* Vers. 97.1.1 Mar. 1997. *Encyclopedia Britannica.* 2 Mar. 1998 <http://www.eb.com:180>.

King, Jr., Martin Luther. "Letter from Birmingham Jail." 28 Aug. 1963 *Civil Disobedience in Focus.* Ed. Hugo Adam Bedau. New York: Routledge, 1991. 68-84.

Poger, Ralph. "A Postmodern Dissent." Home page. 2 Apr. 2000 <http://www.scu.edu/~rpoger>.

Franklin, George. Professor of American Literature, Northfield College. Interview. 5 Apr. 2000.

Spiller, Robert E., et al. *Literary History of the United States: History.* 3rd ed. New York: Macmillan, 1963.

Thoreau, Henry David. "On the Duty of Civil Disobedience." *Walden* and "Civil Disobedience." New York: Signet-NAL, 1995. 222-240.

Walden: or, Life in the Woods. New York: Harcourt, 1987. 6-187.

Glossary

Action   A series of events that moves the work from one point to the next.

Alliteration   The repetition of initial consonant sounds, as "On the bald street breaks the blank day."

Antagonist   A character or force that opposes the main character, or protagonist, in a plot.

Atmosphere   A mood or emotional aura.

Audience   Those to whom writing is directed.

Black-and-white, color   Major elements of film stock and the ways they are used. While color images are standard now, most films before 1950 and television before 1962 used black-and-white images.

Camera angle   The slant of the camera as it photographs the subject. A camera angle looking down at a character can diminish that figure's stature; an upward angle can add to the figure's stature.

Characters   The people in fictional narratives.

Climax   (a) A moment of emotional or intellectual intensity; (b) a point in the plot at which one opposing force overcomes another and the conflict is resolved.

Close-up, medium shot, long shot   Indications of the relative distance of the camera from the subject.

Conflict   A struggle between opposing forces or characters.

Connotation   What a word suggests, beyond its dictionary meaning.

Conventions   The familiar structures that literary texts use to create meaning, as the dramatic aside or the Shakespearean soliloquy.

Denotation   The dictionary definition of what a word means.

Diction   The choice of particular words whose educational, social, and situational levels help create meaning.

Documentation   The form by which one gives credit for materials taken from other sources.

Editing, montage   The joining together of individual shots to create a visual continuity.

Epiphany   A flash of intuitive understanding.

Figurative language   Language that deviates from the literal in order to suggest special meanings or effects. Metaphors and similes are examples of figurative language.

Film acting   Because the camera and microphone can amplify image and sound, film acting can range from extremely minimal to purposefully exaggerated.

Focalization   The use of a character's perspective to tell part, or all, of a story.

Frame   A single image in a video stream. While it can be looked at like a still photograph, the frame is part of the sequence of images that becomes movement in presentation.

Genre   A literary form, such as poetry, fiction, drama, autobiography, or essay.

Imagery   Language that appeals directly to one of the five senses.

Literary criticism   The practice of posing and answering interpretive questions about literary texts.

Literary theory   The practice of posing and answering interpretive questions about competing critical forms.

Lyric   A fairly short, concentrated, and songlike poem (originally sung to a lyre).

Metadrama   A drama that calls attention to its form as a drama, as when a drama has, as part of its setting, a poster for the play that is being performed.

Metaphor   A comparison between two things; a direct comparison as opposed to the indirect comparison of the simile. "He is a lion in the field" is a metaphor.

Mise-en-scéne   Staging for the camera. From the French for "place in the scene," but used to cover how actors and scenes are manipulated to provide the intended effect for a filmed shot.

Moving camera   Reference to the camera's mobility as it photographs a scene.

Narrator   Someone who tells a story. A character narrator tells a story in which he or she is involved; an omniscient narrator tells a story about other people.

Parody   Writing that imitates the style, form, or theme of another work.

Pathos   The evocation of the feelings of tenderness, pity, or sympathetic sorrow.

Persona   A self invented by the author to present a poem, story, essay, or other piece of writing.

Plagiarism   Deliberately presenting the words or ideas of another writer as if they were one's own.

Plot   The events that happen and why they happen.

Poetics   The study of the codes and conventions that give literary texts meaning.

Point of view   (a) The narrative vantage point from which a literary work is told; (b) the position from which one sees a drama.

Protagonist   The main character, or "hero/heroine," of a plot.

Rhyme   The repetition of sounds, usually at the ends of lines of poems, but often recurring at regular places in the line, as in "moon," "June," and "spittoon."

Rhythm   The rise and fall of stress, within single words or in larger units such as sentences, paragraphs, speeches, and poems, as in "With a leap and a bound the swift Anapests throng."

Setting   The general locale in which the action occurs.

Shot The single continuous recording of a scene. The joining of separate shots into a sequence is one of the primary elements of visual media.

Simile An indirect comparison that uses the words "like" and "as"; distinguished from metaphor. "He is like a lion in the field" is a simile.

Sound The aural accompaniment to the visual image. Dialogue, sound of physical events, music, and voiceover are all part of the aural components of a film or video.

Style The particular way in which a writer uses words, including diction, sentence length, degree of formality and complexity, etc.

Symbol An object that represents itself and, through association, something else of an abstract nature, such as the white whale in *Moby Dick*.

Theme The meaning or meanings embodied in a work of literature.

Thesis The essential argument of a piece of nonfiction writing, such as a critical paper.

Tone The attitude toward self, subject, and audience contained in a piece of writing.

Transitions Words, scenes, or actions that show the relationship between the preceding and the ensuing sections of a work.

Voice An individual style or point of view through which a writer may be identified.

Index

A
Abbreviations, and MLA entry formats, 241
Academic journals, 13–14
Achebe, Chinua, 126
Action, 23
 and drama, 54
Adorno, Theodor, 95
Adventures of Huckleberry Finn (Twain), 119, 162, 166
Adventures of Tom Sawyer (Twain), 119
Affective fallacy, 92
Alcott, Louisa May, 112, 115
Allen, Robert, 203
Alliteration, 46–47
Ally McBeal, 82
The Ambassadors (James), 114
The American (James), 26
American Beauty, 82
American Bibliography, 203
American Graffiti, 84
The American Scholar, 172
Annual Bibliography, of the Modern Language Association, 203
Answers, and the writer, 8
Anzaldúa, Gloria, 163, 164
Apocalypse Now, 142
Aristotle, 62, 82
As I Lay Dying (Faulkner), 197
Atlantic Monthly, 204
Atmosphere, 27
Atwan, Robert, 70
Atwood, Margaret, 65
Austen, Jane, 122, 141, 142, 151, 152
Authors
 citing in MLA style, 232–236
 and documenting books, 241–242
 and MLA entry formats, 239–240
Autobiographical questionnaire, 172–174

Autobiography, 172

B
Baker, Nancy L., 202
Bakhtin, Mikhail, 133
Baldwin, James, 126
Barnaby, Andrew, 97, 139
Barry, Dave, 65
Baruth, Philip, 196
Batke, Peter, 212
Beardsley, Monroe, 132, 137
Benjamin, Walter, 95
Bennett, Alan, 125
Bennett, Arnold, 26
Bennett, William, 120
Bercovitch, Sacvan, 96
Best American Essays, 70
Blake, William, 120, 122
Bloom, Allan, 120
Bohannan, Laura, 117, 127
Books, documenting, 241–245
Bradford, William, 15
Bright Lights, Big City (McInerney), 26
Brooks, Cleanth, 93
Browning, Robert, 51
Bunyan, John, 121
Burroway, Janet, 31, 33
Byrd, William, 15

C
Canon, 117–127
 and the culture wars, 120–122
 and eurocentrism, 117–119
 postcolonial literature, 122–126
 toward a global culture, 126–127
The Canterbury Tales (Chaucer), 191, 193
Carver, Raymond, 140, 148
The Catcher in the Rye (Salinger), 25, 26

Central consciousness, 27
Character, 22, 23
　and drama, 54
　interpretation of, 58–59
　writing about, 57–58
Chaucer, Geoffrey, 188, 189, 190, 191, 192, 193
Chicago Manual of Style, 207, 208
Chodorow, Nancy, 95
Churchill, Winston, 73
Cinderella: A Casebook (Dundes), 197
Class notebooks, 14
Climax, 24
　and drama, 54
The Closing of the American Mind, 120
CNN, 210
"Coda," 38–39
Coleridge, Samuel Taylor, 44
The Collected Works (Eliot), 212
The Color Purple, 141
The Communist Manifesto (Marx), 102
Comparison, 47–48
Composition, and the writer, 9
Comprehension, and journal writing, 18–19
Conflict, 24
　and drama, 54
Connecting, and journal writing, 18
Conrad, Joseph, 142
Conventions, 9
　of written English, 152–153
Cooper, James Fenimore, 114
Coppola, Francis Ford, 142
Cosmopolitan, 204
Course in General Linguistics (Saussure), 95
Creative choices, in writing, 186–190
Crevecoeur, J. Hector St. John de, 221, 222
Critical essays, 157–167; *See also* Essays
　describing the text, 158–159
　establishing a dialogue, 163–166
　pulling it all together, 162
　questioning the text, 159–161
　suggestions for writing, 166–167
Culler, Jonathan, 95, 130
Cummins, Maria, 115

D

Dancing at the Edge of the World, 69
Dante Alighieri, 46, 189, 193
Databases, and MLA documentation, 247–248
Date, and MLA entry formats, 240
Day of the Locust (West), 161
Decolonizing the Mind (Ngugi), 124
Deconstruction, 96
DeMan, Paul, 96
Derrida, Jacques, 96, 102
Dialogue, creating, 192

Diaries, 13, 14
　vs. journals, 15
Dickens, Charles, 51, 68, 122, 125
Dickerson, Mary Jane, 11, 155, 168
Dickinson, Emily, 8, 18, 48, 158, 159, 165, 219, 220, 222, 224, 225, 227
Diction, 48–49
Didion, Joan, 65, 70
Dillard, Annie, 72
Dissent voices, 74–75
Disturbing the Universe (Dyson), 168
The Divine Comedy (Dante), 46, 193
Documentation, and writing, 153–154
Document design, and writing, 154
Donne, John, 93, 187, 193
Dorr, Julia, 198, 199
Dorris, Michael, 202
Dostoevsky, Fyodor, 219
The Double Life of Veronique (Kiéslowski), 103, 104
Drama, 54–64
　and character interpretation, 58–59
　conventions of, 61–62
　and language, 59–61
　metadrama, 62–64
　as performance, 54–56
　reading, 56
　television and film, 64
　writing about, 57–58
The Dream of the White Village: A Novel in Stories (Baruth), 196
Dryden, John, 93
Dumb and Dumber, 82
Dundes, Alan, 197
The Dynamics of Literary Response (Holland), 95
Dyson, Freeman, 168

E

The Eighteenth Century: A Current Bibliography, 203
Eisenstaedt, Alfred, 81
Electronic sources, documenting, 247
Electronic texts, 209–218
　evaluating Internet sources, 212–215
　and MLA style, 236
　publishing, 216–218
　and research, 210–212
　writing and composing, 215–216
Eliot, George, 212
Eliot, T. S., 51, 106, 127, 151, 152, 164
Emerson, Ralph Waldo, 15, 50, 70
Emma, 142
The Empire Strikes Back, 84
Endings, rewriting, 191

Index

The English Patient, 141
Epiphany, 24
Equiano, Olaudah, 119, 120
Essay examination, 219–230
  information requests, 221–222
  planning, 222–225
  steps and advice, 220–221
  structuring essay answers, 225–228
  the take-home examination, 228–229
  writing under pressure, 220
Essays, 65–79; *See also* Critical essays
  as conversation, 66
  conversations with others, 68–70
  conversations with self, 66–68
  critical, 157–167
  finding your voice, 78–79
  personal, 168–181
  voices that shape, 70–78
Eudora Welty Newsletter, 203
Evidence, and writing, 153
Exiles from Paradise: Zelda and F. Scott Fitzgerald (Mayfield), 195
Existentialism, 153
Explanation, and writing, 153
Explanation voices, 75–76
Extending, and journal writing, 18

F
Fallacy; *See* Affective fallacy; Intentional fallacy
The Far Side of Paradise (Mizener), 195
Faulkner, William, 7, 26, 27, 158, 170, 171, 197
Feminist readings, 108–115
Fetterley, Judith, 131
Fiction, 21–36
  and character, 23
  judging, 34–36
  nature of, 21–23
  and plot, 24
  and point of view, 25–27
  and setting, 27–28
  and style, 29–30
  and symbolism, 28–29
  and theme, 30–31
Film, 64, 139–149
  comparing to books, 148–149
  listening and seeing vs. reading, 146–148
  and revisionary reading, 141–142
  A River Runs Through It, 142–146
  writers and readers of, 139–141
Findarticles, 210
The Fisher King, 164
The Fisherman (Yeats), 45
Fitzgerald, F. Scott, 195
Fleming, Ian, 22

Focalization, 27
Foucault, Michel, 96
Four Quartets (Eliot), 51
Franklin, Benjamin, 70
Freud, Sigmund, 94
Frost, David, 51
Frost, Robert, 41, 48, 76
Fuller, Margaret, 70
Fulwiler, Toby, 10, 11, 219, 229

G
Gardner, John, 193
The Georgia Review, 172
Gesture, 23
Gibaldi, Joseph, 207
Gladiator, 157
Globe, 204
The Godfather, 141
The God of Small Things (Roy), 126
Golberg, Natalie, 16
Of Grammatology (Derrida), 96
Grangerford, Emmeline, 25
The Great Gatsby (Fitzgerald), 195, 196
Grendel (Gardner), 193
Grisham, John, 22
Gulliver's Travels (Swift), 183, 184, 193

H
Hall, Donald, 66, 67, 68
Hamlet (Shakespeare), 102, 103, 117, 127, 141
Hannah, Barry, 22
Hansberry, Lorraine, 59
Hansberry, William Leo, 118
Hardwick, Elizabeth, 70
Harner, James L., 202
Harper, Frances, 115
Hartman, Geoffrey, 96
Hawthorne, Nathaniel, 114, 125
Headings, and writing, 154
Heart of Darkness (Conrad), 142
Heckerling, Amy, 141
Hemingway, Ernest, 29, 30
Henry IV (Shakespeare), 142
Herrick, Robert, 51
Hitchcock, Alfred, 85
Hodge, Merle, 124, 125
Hoffman, Katherine Anne, 155, 207, 209
Holland, Norman, 95, 131
The House of Seven Gables (Hawthorne), 114
Housman, A. E., 49
Howard, Maureen, 78
Howe, James, 11, 54
Howell, William Dean, 114
Huckleberry Finn (Twain), 114, 221, 222
Huddle, David, 38–40, 45, 46, 48, 49, 50

Humanity, and the writer, 7
Hunt, Leigh, 48
Hurston, Zora, 173

I
Illinois at Urbana-Champaign, University of, 207
Image, and visual texts, 86–88
Imagery, 47
Incidents in the Life of a Slave Girl (Jacobs), 119
Information, and writing, 153
Intellectual excitement, 101
Intentional fallacy, 92
The Interesting Narrative Life of Olaudah Equiano (Equiano), 119
Internet sources, evaluating, 212–215
The Interpretation of Dreams (Freud), 94
Introductory Lectures on Psychoanalysis (Freud), 94
Iola Leroy (Harper), 115
Ironic point of view, 26
Iser, Wolfgang, 129, 130, 135

J
James, Henry, 9, 22, 26, 27, 114
Jameson, Frederic, 95
Jarrell, Randall, 76
Jefferson, Thomas, 70
Journal writing, 13–20
    academic, 13–14
    and comprehension, 18–19
    and connecting and extending, 18
    defined, 13
    vs. diaries, 15
    personal journals, 14–19
    and questions, 15–16
    suggestions for, 19–20
Joyce, James, 9, 24, 27

K
Kaplan, Justin, 119
Keats, John, 9, 47
Keats-Shelley Journal, 203
Kerouac, Jack, 34
Kete, Mary Louise, 97, 108
Kiéslowski, Krzysztof, 103
Kincaid, Jamaica, 123, 124, 127
King Lear (Shakespeare), 48
Kingston, Maxine Hong, 70
Kisonak, Rick, 157

L
Lacan, Jacques, 95
The Lamplighter (Cummins), 115
Language, 23

and writing, 153
Last of the Mohicans (Cooper), 114, 135
Leaves of Grass (Whitman), 212
Le Guin, Ursula, 69
Leith, David, 77, 78
Letters of an American Farmer (Crevecoeur), 221
Levi-Strauss, Claude, 95
Lexis-Nexis Academic Universe, 210
Life, 81
Limited omniscience, 26
Literary Research Guide (Harner), 202
Literary theory, 99–106
    and English major as anthropologist, 99–101
    expanding our field of view, 101–103
    moral conversation, 104–106
    pleasure of the text, 103–104
Little Women (Alcott), 112, 115
London Journal (Boswell), 15
Look Homeward, Angel (Wolfe), 34
Lucács, Georg, 95
Lucas, George, 83, 84
Lyric, 51

M
Macbeth (Shakespeare), 55
Maclean, Norman, 142–148
The Magic City (Nesbit), 168
Magistrale, Tony, 155, 219
Mahfouz, Naguib, 123
Manchester, William, 73
Marie de France, 129, 130
Marlowe, Christopher, 186–187
Marquez, Gabriel Garcia, 122, 123
Marvell, Andrew, 49
Marx, Karl, 102
Marxism, 95
Marxism and Literature (Williams), 95
The Matrix, 82
Mayfield, Sara, 195
Meditation voices, 71–73
Melville, Herman, 9, 14, 29, 114, 125, 211
Merchant of Venice (Shakespeare), 61–62
Metadrama, 62–64
Metaphor, understanding, 9
Meter, 43–45
Midnight's Children (Rushdie), 123
Milford, Nancy, 195
Miller, J. Rillis, 96
Milton, John, 44, 48, 50
Mise en scéne, 85
Mistral, Gabriela, 122
Mizener, Arthur, 195
MLA, 203, 207

Index

MLA Documentation, 231–254
  and databases, 247–248
  documenting books, 241–245
  documenting electronic sources, 247
  documenting periodicals, 245–247
  entry formats, 239–241
  guidelines for formatting manuscripts, 231–232
  guidelines for in-text citations, 232–236
  and online sources, 248–250
  order of entries, 239
  and other sources, 250–253
  providing additional information, 236–237
  sample page, 237–238
  works cited page, 238, 254
The MLA Handbook for Writers of Research Papers, 154, 167, 207, 208, 231
The MLA International Bibliography of Books and Articles on the Modern Languages and Literature, 203
Moby Dick (Melville), 29, 114, 211, 212, 213, 216
A Modern Instance (Howell), 114
Modern Language Association; *See* MLA
Montaigne, Michel, 65, 71, 72
Morris, Linda, 205
Morrison, Toni, 9, 35
Muschg, Adolf, 172
My Own Private Idaho, 142

N
The Name of the Rose, 141
Narrative film, as extension of literature, 82–83
Narrative of the Life of Frederick Douglass, 119
Narrator, 25
Nash, Robert, 104
National Examiner, 204
National Review, 204
Neruda, Pablo, 122
Nesbit, Edith, 168
New Criticism, 92–94, 96, 132, 136, 137
New Historicism, 96–97
New Webster's dictionary, 165
The New Yorker, 74, 172
The New York Review of Books, 172
New York Times, 189
New York Times Book Review, 69, 172
Ngugi Wa Thiong'o, 124
Nonce symbol, 28

O
Oates, Joyce Carol, 66, 67, 68
O'Brian, Tim, 70
O'Connor, Flannery, 7, 140, 142
The Old Wives' Tale (Bennett), 26

One Hundred Years of Solitude (Marquez), 123
Online sources, and MLA documentation, 248–250
On the Road (Kerouac), 34
Orientalism (Said), 96
Orth, Ghita, 10, 21
Orwell, George, 70, 77, 78
Othello (Shakespeare), 55
Outside Magazine, 157
Owen, Wilfred, 122
Ozeki, Ruth, 166

P
Page numbers, and MLA entry formats, 240–241
Paine, Thomas, 70
Paradise Lost (Milton), 50
Parody, 186–189
Particular symbol, 28
Paz, Ocatavio, 123
Pepys, Samuel, 15
Periodicals, documenting, 245–247
Personal essays, 168–181
  creating a new text, 169–170
Personal journals, 14–19
Persuasion (Austen), 122
Philological Quarterly, 203
Physical description, 23
Pilgrim's Progress (Bunyan), 121
Pirandello, Luigi, 62
Places of publication, and MLA entry formats, 240
Plath, Sylvia, 9
Plot, 22, 24
  and drama, 54
PMLA, 204
Poe, Edgar Allan, 17, 42, 51, 225, 226
Poetics (Aristotle), 82
Poetry, 38–52
  nature of, 41–43
  responding to, 52
  rewriting, 39–41
  techniques of, 43–52
Poetry techniques, 43–52
  alliteration, 46–47
  comparison, 47–48
  diction, 48–49
  imagery, 47
  point of view, 50–52
  rhyme, 45–46
  rhythm and meter, 43–45
  structure, 49–50
Poger, Sydney, 10, 38
Point of view, 25–27, 50–52, 153
  and drama, 55

The Political Unconscious (Jameson), 95
Pope, Alexander, 101, 202
Porter, Katherine Anne, 68
Pound, Ezra, 9
The Prelude, 219
Pretty Woman, 196, 197
Princeton University, 212
Proverbium, 204
Psychological criticism, 94–95
Publication Manual of the American Psychological Association, 207, 208
Publishers, and MLA entry formats, 240
Purdue University, 207

Q
Questions
  asking and answering, 16–17
  and the writer, 8

R
A Raisin in the Sun (Hansberry), 59–61
Ralegh, Walter, 187
The Rape of the Lock (Pope), 101, 102
Reader response, 129–137
  in action, 134–136
  apologies, 129–130
  overview, 130–134
Reader's Digest, 204
Reading
  carefully, 185
  as exploration, 91–97
  a story, 31–34
  and writing, 15–16
Reading (Smith), 135
Redford, Robert, 142–148
Rereading, and the writer, 10
A Research Guide for Undergraduate Students: English and American Literature (Baker), 202
Research writing, 195–208
  gathering information, 198–202
  getting started, 197–198
  giving credit, 206–208
  pulling the paper together, 204–206
  seeking second-hand sources, 202–204
Response voices, 73–74
Retrospective narrator, 25
Revision, and risk taking, 186
Rewriting, and the writer, 10
Rhyme, 45–46
Rhythms, 23, 43–45
  and the writer, 8–9
Risk taking, rules for, 184–186
A River Runs Through It, 97, 142–148
The Road to El Dorado, 161

Roberts, Julia, 196, 197
Rosenblatt, Louise, 131, 133
Rosencrantz and Guildenstern Are Dead (Stoppard), 141
Roy, Arundhati, 126
Rushdie, Salman, 123, 127

S
Said, Edward, 96
Saussure, Ferdinand de, 95
Schnell, Lisa, 97, 99
Scott, Helen, 97, 101, 117
Searching Writing (Macrorie), 195
Seeing, and the act of writing, 17–18
Setting, 27–28
Shakespeare, William, 14, 45, 48, 55, 61, 63, 83, 93, 96, 117, 125, 127, 141, 158, 187, 188
Shelley, Percy Bysshe, 122
Shenandoah, 172
Shepherd, Alan, 10, 21
Simian, Tom, 219
Simone, Tom, 11, 80
The Single Shot, 85–86
Six Characters in Search of an Author (Pirandello), 62
A Small Place (Kincaid), 123
Smith, Frank, 135
Song of Solomon (Morrison), 35
The Sound and the Fury (Faulkner), 7, 27, 173
Soyinka, Wole, 123
Speech, 23
Springsteen, Bruce, 140, 142
Stanford University, 120
Star, 204
Starts, 9
Star Wars, 83, 84–88
Star Wars, The First Episode, 82
Stephany, William A., 155, 183, 224
Stevens, Wallace, 47, 49
Stoppard, Tom, 141
Stopping By Home (Huddle), 50
Stops, 9
Storytelling voices, 76–78
Stowe, Harriet Beecher, 112, 113, 158
A Streetcar Named Desire, 141
Structural Anthropology (Levi-Strauss), 95
Structuralism, 95
Structuralist Poetics (Culler), 95
Structure, 49–50
Studies in Philology, 203
Style
  and fiction, 29–30
  and writing, 153
The Sun Also Rises (Hemingway), 29
Sweterlitsch, Richard, 11, 155, 195

Index

Swift, Jonathan, 65, 75, 183, 184, 185, 186, 193
Symbolism, 28–29
    types of symbols, 28
Symbols
    understanding, 9
    and visual texts, 86–88

T

Tagore, Rabindranath, 122, 127
Take-home examination, 228–229
    class notes and journals, 229
    revising and editing, 229
The Taming of the Shrew (Shakespeare), 58–59
"Tea Leaves," 31–32
Television, 64
Tennyson, Lord Alfred, 46
Their Eyes Were Watching God (Hurston), 173
To the Lighthouse (Woolf), 102, 118, 125
Theme, 30–31
    and visual texts, 86–88
    and the writer, 9
Thomas, Dylan, 50
Thoreau, Henry David, 9, 15, 16, 70, 151, 152, 212
Thoughts, and character, 23
Thurber, James, 65
Time, 204
Titles
    and MLA entry formats, 240
    and writing, 154
Tompkins, Jane, 168
Total omniscience, 26
Transitions, 9
    and writing, 153
Transworld, 157
Troilus and Criseyde (Chaucer), 189
Turley, Maureen, 67
Turner, Sarah E., 155, 157
TV Guide, 190
Twain, Mark, 114, 119, 162, 166, 193, 221, 222
Twelfth Night (Shakespeare), 45
The Types of the Folktale, 196

U

Uncle Tom's Cabin (Stowe), 112, 113, 199
Understanding How We Read (Smith), 135
Universal symbol, 28
Unreliable narrator, 25

V

Van Sant, Gus, 142
Vermont, University of, 216

Virgil, 193
Visual texts, 80–89
    analyzing, 88–89
    George Lucas's *Star Wars*, 84–88
    narrative film and literature, 82–83
    reading, 83–84
Voice, and risk taking, 185–186

W

Walcott, Derek, 123
Walden (Thoreau), 15, 16, 212
Walker, Alice, 69, 71
Walker, Nancy, 205
The Wall Street Journal, 204
Warner, Susan, 115
The Waste Land (Eliot), 51, 93, 164
Welch, Nancy, 97, 129
The Well-Wrought Urn (Brooks), 93
West, Nathanael, 161
Western Folklore, 204
What's So Funny? Humor in American Culture, 205
White, E. B., 16
Whitman, Walt, 8, 18, 38, 49, 153, 212, 227, 228
Wide, Wide, World (Warner), 115
Widener University, 204
Williams, Raymond, 95
Williams, William Carlos, 41
Wimsatt, William, 132, 137
Wolfe, Thomas, 34, 70
Woolf, Virginia, 14, 71, 73, 76, 102, 118, 125, 153, 171
Words, and the writer, 8
Wordsworth, William, 9, 219
Writing
    changing the form, 190–192
    under pressure, 220
    as a reader, 151–155
    and reading, 15–16
    and risk taking, 183–194
    and seeing, 17–18
Writing Down the Bones (Golberg), 16

X

The X-Files, 82

Y

Yale University, 96
Yeats, William Butler, 42, 45, 46

Z

Zelda: A Biography (Milford), 195

McGraw-Hill College English

Since 1901, McGraw-Hill has partnered with teachers and students to provide solutions to the challenges of the classroom. In 100 years of service, we have learned three things. We have learned to listen—in order to provide materials that you want and need. We have learned to adapt—to adjust our materials to suit each individual learning situation. But, most important of all, we have learned that there is still a lot to learn.

As we enter our second century, we renew our commitment to growing and developing as the discipline grows and develops. We will continue to listen to you, to anticipate changes in teaching style or course content, and to have new materials—class-tested and student approved—ready when you are. And we will continue to have fun—to be as enthusiastic and sincere about your classes as you are and to provide print and electronic materials that are more engaging, easier to use, and more inspiring than the ones you use now.

Yours,

Phil Butcher, publisher
Renee Deljon, sponsoring editor
Victoria Fullard, editorial coordinator
Ray Kelley, field publisher
Lisa Moore, executive editor
David Patterson, senior marketing manager
Paula Rodosevich, field publisher
Carla Samodulski, senior developmental editor
Anne Stameshkin, editorial assistant
Sarah Touborg, executive editor
Todd Vaccaro, media developer
Alexis Walker, senior developmental editor

Contributors

ANDREW BARNABY, Associate Professor of English at the University of Vermont, has written essays on Shakespeare, Marvell, Milton, Bacon, Rembrandt, and Locke. His study of the relationship between epistemological and political reform in the seventeenth century is forthcoming. He is currently at work on a study of adaptation.

MARY JANE DICKERSON is Emeritus Professor of English at the University of Vermont, where she has taught courses in American literature, nonfiction writing, and multicultural studies. She has published poetry, essays, and criticism and is the co-author of *Until I See What I Say* and *Writer's Guide: History*.

TOBY FULWILER directs the writing program at the University of Vermont, where he teaches writing and conducts writing workshops for faculty across the curriculum. His publications include *The Journal Book* (1987), *When Writing Teachers Teach Literature* (1995), and *College Writing* (2002).

KATHERINE HOFFMAN teaches writing in computer classrooms at the University of Vermont. Along with creating and maintaining half a dozen Websites, she is the Editorial Assistant for *Work in Progress,* a compilation of student writing.

MARY LOU KETE, Associate Professor of English at the University of Vermont, teaches courses in nineteenth-century American literature and feminist studies.

TONY MAGISTRALE, professor of English at the University of Vermont, teaches courses in American literature and Anglo-American gothicism. He is the recipient of two awards for best teaching at UVM. His most recent book, *Poe's Children: Connections between Tales of Terror and Detection,* was co-authored with Sidney Poger.

GHITA ORTH teaches literature and creative writing at the University of Vermont. The author of a book of poems, *The Music of What Happens* (1982), she is a co-editor of *Angles of Vision*, a co-writer of *About These Stories: Fiction for Fiction Writers and Readers,* and a contributor to *The Letter Book*.

SIDNEY POGER, Emeritus Professor of English at the University of Vermont, has taught a variety of courses in American literature, including modern poetry, detective fiction, and genre studies. He is co-author with Tony Magistrale of *Poe's Children: Connections between Tales of Terror and Detection*.

LISA SCHNELL, Assistant Professor of English at the University of Vermont, teaches undergraduae and graduate courses in Renaissance drama and poetry, the Bible as literature, and critical theory. She received an Open Society Humanities Fellowship and was recently honored as UVM's Graduate Teacher of the Year.

HELEN SCOTT, Assistant Professor of English at the University of Vermont, teaches postcolonial and Caribbean literature as well as literary theory. She has published articles in the areas of race theory and African literature and is currently writing a book about contemporary Anglophone Caribbean women writers.

ALLEN SHEPHERD, Emeritus Professor of English at the University of Vermont, has taught undergraduate and graduate courses in nineteenth- and twentieth-century American literature. He has published fiction, poetry, and nonfiction.

WILLIAM A. STEPHANY, Professor of English at the University of Vermont, teaches a variety of courses on medieval literature, drama, and culture. He is co-author, with James Howe, of *The McGraw Hill Book of Drama*.

RICHARD SWETERLITSCH teaches folklore and American literature at the University of Vermont. He publishes his research, ranging from folk legendry to proverbs in a variety of folklore journals. He has also published essays regarding writing and research techniques.

SARAH E. TURNER is currently a lecturer at the University of Vermont, where she teaches courses in race and ethnicity and also in writing. Her work explores issues of race and racism in contemporary literature and autobiography.

NANCY WELCH teaches courses in writing, theory, literacy, and women's studies. She is the author of *Getting Restless: Rethinking Revision in Writing Instruction* and co-editor of *Reinventing the Discipline: The Dissertation in Composition and Rhetoric as a Site for Change,* forthcoming from Boynton/Cook. Her short stories have appeared in *Prairie Schooner, Threepenny Review,* and elsewhere.